A Guide to the
Steam
Railways
of
Great Britain

Contents

Foreword

by John Rumens

Publicity Officer, the Association of Railway Preservation Societies

One peculiarity of the British is the intensity with which they preserve their steam heritage. There are more than one hundred steam railways and living-steam railway museums open to the public in Great Britain. Nearly all are privately owned by groups of enthusiasts, and operated on a shoestring by willing part-time volunteers. These railways can now boast of upwards of ten million visitors a year – very few of whom fail to be enthralled by magnificent scenery, stunned by the roar of a locomotive blasting its way through a tunnel, or even amused by the charming Emmett-like incompetence of some of the smaller lines.

This guide was written for the family man to get the most out of his visit – it is not a ponderous list of obscure technicalities, but an ideal combination of local information and background history on our preserved railways.

There is one curious by-product of the 'steam boom'. Traditionally the ambition of every small boy was to become an engine driver; this was rarely achieved in practice. Today, however, any person willing to work hard in his spare time on one of the preserved railways can learn to drive steam locomotives. Reader, beware! This could be the start of a new and exhilarating leisure activity!

John Rumens

Preface

This book, with its chapters contributed by a team of local specialists, has set out to give an introduction to steam railways in Britain. Each chapter covers the main steam attractions, giving a history of the line concerned, a fascinating 'trip down the line', details of the main locomotives and rolling stock, suggestions for good vantage points for photography, and other tourist attractions in the area concerned. A comprehensive gazetteer includes many extra sites and explains 'how to get there'.

All railways have their individual charms. Not every chapter in this book adopts exactly the same approach – for in the very individuality of these railways lies their lasting magic. Our aim throughout has been to make a book which can not only be enjoyed on winter evenings, but which can also be a useful companion on family excursions to discover the delights of Britain's Steam Railways.

W. Awdry
Chris Cook

Editors' Note

Some wheel arrangements are named; ones in this book include 4-4-2, Atlantic; 2-6-0, Mogul; 2-6-2, Prairie, and 4-6-2, Pacific. Power classes consist of a digit denoting the power of the engine (the higher, the more powerful) and letters denoting Passenger (P), Freight (F) or Mixed Traffic (MT). T (as in 0-6-0T) means 'tank'; PT, pannier tank; ST, saddle tank; WT, well tank (the tank slung between the sides of the frame); VB, vertical-boilered; TG, tank with geared drive.

Key to Maps

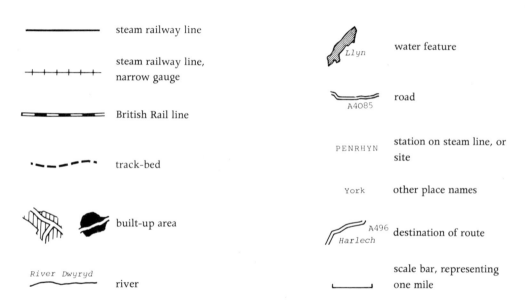

steam railway line

steam railway line, narrow gauge

British Rail line

track-bed

built-up area

River Dwyryd

river

Llyn   water feature

A4085   road

PENRHYN   station on steam line, or site

York   other place names

A496 *Harlech*   destination of route

scale bar, representing one mile

Acknowledgements

The editors and publisher wish to thank the sources listed below for their kind permission to reproduce the photographs which appear on the pages listed against them.

Photographers

John Adams: opposite 128 (top left)
Valerie Burns: 174
James Caldwell: 66
G. C. E. Carleton: 86 (bottom)
R. I. Cartwright: 133
Roger Crombleholme: 27, 105, 234
D. R. Donkin: 104
T. J. Edgington: 111, 124, 127, 142, 155, 162, 163, 188, 204
Mike Esau: 43 (top)
Brian Fisher: 47, 53, 72, 225
J. A. Gardner: 35, 106, 109, 224
R. S. Greenwood: 182, 185
P. H. Groom: 112
B. Hart: 86
G. T. Heavyside: 93, 166, 191, 228
John Hunt: 173, 177, 179, 192, 197
David Idle: 42, 91, 92, opposite 96 (top, bottom right), opposite 128

(top right, bottom), 137
G. D. King: 67 (top), 81, 82, 83, 89
Arthur Loosely: 67 (bottom)
R. Macdonald: 57
G. W. Morrison: frontispiece, 43 (bottom), opposite 129 (bottom), opposite 161 (all), 176, 178, 183, 184, 186, 187
Reg Palk: 21, 31, 223
T. A. Parkins: 147, 148
P. J. G. Ransom: 118, 119, 125, 131, 138, 143, 145, 175
R. C. Riley: opposite 96 (centre and bottom left), opposite 129 (top)
Andrew Roberts: 36, 130
Patrick Russell: 15, 19, 59, opposite 64 and 65 (all), 95, opposite 97 (top), 100, 159, opposite 160 (top), 170, 219

Graham Scott Lowe: 20, 32, 90, 103, 107, 189
Harper Shaw: 99 (bottom)
Geoff Silcock: 78, 164
B. A. Small: 75
D. H. Smith: 113
Nick Stanbra: 153
N. E. Stead 202, 203
Brian Stephenson: 39, 41, 44, 49, 50, 51, 71, 193
H. Sykes: opposite 128 (centre right), 140
A. R. Thomson: 200, 201
John Titlow: 76, 79
John Vaughan: 40
P. T. White: 102
C. M. Whitehouse: opposite 97 (bottom, both), 98 (bottom), 121, 169
P. B. Whitehouse: 13, 135
P. G. Wright: 150

Other sources
These photographs appear by courtesy of those named.

Alan Bloom: 63, 66
British Tourist Authority: opposite 160 (bottom)
Colne Valley Railway: 84
Colourviews: 98 (top), 99 (top)
Fife Railway Preservation Group: 216, 217
Great Western Society: 34
Gwili Railway Company: 149
Nene Valley Railway: 77
North of England Open Air Museum: 198
Scottish Railway Preservation Society: 209, 210, 211, 213
Steamport Southport: 167
Steamtown, Carnforth: 165

Editors and publisher would like to thank John Rumens for his continued interest in the *Guide*, and all those officers of railway preservation societies and other organizations, who have helped in providing information and photographs. The publisher would like to thank R. C. Riley, Roger Crombleholme, Patrick Russell, and particularly Andrew Roberts, for their suggestions concerning sources for pictures.

Chapters were contributed by Reg Palk (I), Bertram Vigor (II), Revd. Eric Buck (III), Edgar Jones (IV and VI), John Ransom (V), John Hume (VIII), with some editorial additions.

The text maps were drawn by Pica Design, the endpaper one by David Charles.

The editors would also like to acknowledge the considerable help given by Nicholas Jones of Pelham, particularly in collecting the photographs.

I
The South-West

Dart Valley Railway

The line and its history

A railway to Ashburton – then a thriving town – was first proposed in 1845. The junction with the main line was to have been at Newton Abbot. Brunel, engineer for the project, quoted a sum of £103,500 for a single broad-gauge line, and the company backing the project, allowing for Brunel's optimism, aimed at an authorized capital for the project of £130,000. But the scheme came to nothing. A less ambitious proposal was floated in 1864 and an Act authorizing the line from Buckfastleigh to Totnes was passed by Parliament in the same year, and an extension to Ashburton received Parliamentary approval a year later. Financial troubles caused delay, and the line was not opened till the spring of 1872, though possibly part of the line was working before this. By this time, however, Ashburton's once thriving woollen industry had dwindled, though wool traffic to and from Buckfastleigh was still considerable.

The line was owned by an independent company (The Buckfastleigh, Totnes and South Devon Railway), but it was worked by the South Devon Railway till it was absorbed by the Great Western Railway. Like other lines west of Exeter, it was converted from broad gauge to standard in the spring of 1892.

The growth of motor transport within the area, between the Wars, gave local people the option of travelling direct to Newton Abbot, instead of taking the circuitous rail route via Totnes. The railway journey was made tedious by long delays at Totnes, where the signalmen had to play a frantic 'game of chess' with the branch train from Ashburton, to ensure that it caused the least possible delay to main-line trains when running over the main line and into Totnes station. Besides being tedious, it often meant that branch passengers missed their main-line connections.

Had the promoters of the original railway been successful, and built the railway from Ashburton to Newton Abbot, the surrender of traffic from the branch railway to the roads would possibly have taken longer, but in the event, it was probably made inevitable because the G.W.R. seemed either unable or unwilling to provide a convenient timetable for the branch trains. The end came slowly; passenger traffic was withdrawn in November 1958; freight traffic lingered on until September 1962.

Preservation

All was not lost however. In September 1962 an item in the *Western Morning News* mentioned that a group of businessmen were planning to re-open the Dart Valley Railway. Eleven years before this, a small band of pioneer railway enthusiasts, led by the late Tom Rolt, had successfully formed the world's first railway preservation scheme and saved the Talyllyn Narrow-Gauge Railway in mid Wales. It is not surprising that two members of this pioneer group which had saved the Talyllyn (Patrick Whitehouse and Patrick Garland) were also prominent among the group of businessmen involved in the attempt to re-open the Dart Valley line. Being situated in a popular tourist area, and running as it does part way along the banks of the River Dart, the line had great possibilities as a tourist attraction. However, the gremlins which had been active when the railway was first proposed were obviously still in residence along the River Dart when the first attempts were made to preserve the line. Although the possible preservation of the line

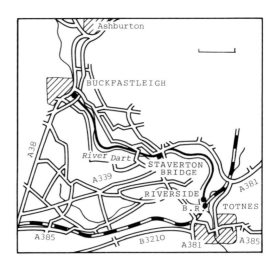

The view from Buckfastleigh signal box on the Dart Valley Railway, as it was in 1970 before the track-bed from Buckfastleigh to Ashburton was given over to the new A38 road. The locomotive is No. 1420 Bulliver.

had been proposed as early as 1962, it was not until spring 1969 that the Light Railway Order was finally granted, and the official opening was performed by Dr Richard Beeching, now Lord Beeching, in May 1969. Dr Beeching had closed it in 1962. In 1969 he said he had great pleasure in declaring it open again!

In 1962, when the Dart Valley Railway preservation project got under way, it was the first preservation scheme to abandon the normal system of appeals to the general public for funds for the line. Instead, as the promoters believed that operation of the line would be a commercially viable proposition, they decided to raise funds from normal commercial sources and formed a Company, The Dart Valley Light Railway Company. Its purpose was both to acquire the line from British Railways, and to purchase locomotives, rolling stock and other equipment needed for operating the line.

By the time the railway was officially opened to the public in spring 1969, the Company board comprised 9 Directors and a Company Secretary, and at that time employed 13 permanent paid staff (11 full-time and 2 part-time). Although the permanent staff formed the back-bone of the working team which had brought steam trains back to the Dart Valley, a working force of volunteers had nevertheless been responsible for, amongst other things, a considerable amount of permanent-way work and undergrowth clearance along the line. In autumn 1966, these volunteer workers formed an official organization known as the Dart Valley Railway Association. In addition to the usual privileges which go with membership of these organizations (free travel on the line and a journal) the Association have their own clubroom, in the

13

shape of ex-Great-Western Super Saloon Coach No. 9111, 'King George', which normally resides at Buckfastleigh. During the decade or so of the Association's existence, it has been responsible for many specialist projects, such as the replacement of signals (all signals had been removed before acquisition of the line from B.R.) and the refurbishing of stations.

The Dart Valley Railway can perhaps be described as the more rural of the two railways operated by Dart Valley Light Railway Ltd. In contrast with its sister railway, the Torbay Steam Railway, it has never carried express traffic. Since its first opening in 1872 it has been a branch line pure and simple.

Access

Buckfastleigh is the operating centre of the line and visitors are well advised to start their journeys from there. Ample car parking is provided – there are refreshment facilities and a well stocked shop. The present station approach road passes under the new dual carriageway of the A38 trunk road and joins a section of the old A38 road which now connects the town of Buckfastleigh with the roundabout at the junction with the new dual carriageway A38 road.

A journey down the line

Our chocolate-and-cream train at the platform will most likely be drawn by one of the small ex-Great-Western pannier or side tank engines, which were a common sight on Great Western branches in former days. There is usually an observation car on the train : it was once used on the Devon Belle. Passengers can travel in it by paying a small supplement to the guard.

The journey to Totnes starts rather unspectacularly, as the first place of note to be seen on the left is the local sewage works! After this, the line traverses a bridge over the river and the full charm of the scenery, with the Dart as its focal point, becomes apparent. From here on river and railway follow nearly the same course down to Totnes. The only intermediate station on the present line is at Staverton Bridge. This is a charming and typical Great Western branch station with a level crossing and ground-level signal box at its platform end. It is interesting to note that before the D.V.R. took over the line,

this signal box had been bought by a local rector for use as a garden shed. Thanks to his co-operation, the building was restored to the railway in exchange for a new garden shed ; it is now once more in its original position.

A new run-round loop has been installed beyond the platform at the Buckfastleigh end of the station by the Dart Valley company. Places worth investigation here are Staverton Bridge, one of Devon's oldest road bridges, the Staverton Mill building, and the local hostelry dating from the thirteenth century, once used by the monks of Buckfast Abbey as a rest home.

Leaving Staverton Bridge behind, we proceed down the valley towards Totnes. Our train cannot take the former branch-line route into the British Rail station at Totnes as this would involve travelling along the British Rail main line which crosses over the River Dart on a bridge before entering the station. Our train therefore comes to a halt just before the junction with British Rail at Totnes Riverside station. A grant from the Manpower Services Commission has financed the employment of building-trade workers, who have constructed a station platform, fencing, drainage, etc.

The specialist railway work, such as alterations to the track-work, signalling, station lighting, etc. has been carried out by volunteers.

Our engine now runs round the train, and the crew make preparations for the return journey, which involves harder locomotive work because the line climbs steadily up to Buckfastleigh.

Arriving back at Buckfastleigh the visitor will note that the present line now ends in buffer stops just beyond the Buckfastleigh signal cabin; the remainder of the line to Ashburton has been sacrificed to the new dual carriageway of the A38 trunk road which cut the line just beyond this point. In the early years of the preserved railway, the spacious goods shed at Ashburton was turned into the main workshop for the D.V.R., and the D.V.R.'s push-pull trains made periodic visits to this station, with its distinctive Brunel over-roof. Unfortunately the track at this end of the line has now completely disappeared. The handsome Brunel over-roof terminus building still survives however, and has been converted into a garage and service station. Now an assortment of Land

G.W.R. No. 6412 (class 64XX) leads a train of three auto-coaches on the Dart Valley line. This loco is now on the West Somerset Railway.

Rovers and Range Rovers await their turn for servicing, where for many years past the branch-line train would stand, its diminutive tank locomotive simmering quietly, waiting for the run down to Totnes. Across the road can be seen the former Railway Hotel, now aptly named The Silent Whistle.

Stock

Before we leave the site at Buckfastleigh, it would be well worth while to inspect the locomotives and rolling stock stored here. If we leave the platform through the small booking hall and turn right, following the rough roadway (which leads past the shop, the refreshment room, the maintenance workshop – once the goods shed – and behind the signal cabin), we can bear right again and, without crossing the running tracks, look over the locomotives and other vehicles which are stored either in the open, or under the partial cover of an open-sided shed.

Amongst the usual residents during the working season are the little blue 0-4-0 saddle tank locomotives built by Peckett & Sons Ltd of Bristol, one of which formerly shunted wagons at Exeter gas works. The other Peckett locomotive is the larger of the two, and is a more recent arrival, having come to the D.V.R. from Leicester in the summer of 1976.

Another small locomotive usually to be found here is No. 1369, a 0-6-0 pannier tank. She is an outside-cylinder locomotive, specially designed for work in places where the curves were too sharp for the larger inside-cylinder pannier tank engines. Only six of this type were built, all in 1934 to replace worn-out saddle tank locomotives. One interesting haunt of these locomotives was the tortuous line from the main-line station at Weymouth, along the public roads, to the harbour. For duty there, the locomotives were fitted with steam train-heating pipes and warning bells, as the working involved the hauling of the Channel Island Boat

Express through the crowded streets of the town. Another use was at the wagon works at Swindon where the loco would perform shunting duties and would have one of the one-time familiar shunter's trucks attached for this duty. (One of these trucks, No. 41873, is to be found on the line.)

Five slightly larger Swindon-built tank locomotives form the backbone of the locomotive fleet on the Dart Valley. It is most likely that you will find one of them at the head of the train if you travel on the line. Perhaps the most interesting of these are the two 0-4-2 side tank locomotives Nos. 1420 and 1450; this type of locomotive was a familiar sight on many of the quiet branch lines in the 30s and 40s and was also useful on local services on main lines.

Although at first appearance these two engines appear to be much older than tiny No. 1369, which was built in 1934, it is interesting to note that No. 1420 was built the year before No. 1369 and No. 1450 the year after! Engines of this class were in fact criticized when they originally appeared for their old-fashioned design; this appearance is however deceptive, as they had many advanced design features built into them when they were constructed. The two engines of the class which survive on the Dart Valley line now carry the names *Bulliver* and *Ashburton* on their tank sides, as well as their former Great Western number-plate.

Three of the once numerous inside-cylinder 0-6-0 pannier tank locomotives complete the group. Two of these, Nos. 6430 and 6435, were built at Swindon in 1937, and were primarily designed for working 'push-pull' trains.

The remaining engine, No. 1638, is the most modern of the five engines; although built to a Great Western design introduced by the late Mr F. W. Hawksworth (the last Chief Mechanical Engineer of the Great Western Railway), not one of these engines saw service with the Great Western. The first engine of the class appeared over a year after the nationalization of Britain's railways. No. 1638 was built at Swindon in 1951.

Before we leave locomotives, mention should be made of two much larger locomotives in residence at Buckfastleigh, both of which have been rescued from Woodham's scrapyard at Barry in South Wales, and are being gradually renovated by small groups of enthusiasts. The first of these engines arrived early in 1973, and is a British Railways Standard 2-6-4 tank locomotive No. 80064 (built at Brighton Works in 1951). The other is a comparatively new arrival to the railway, having come from Barry during the summer of 1976, an ex-Great-Western-Railway 4-6-0 mixed traffic tender locomotive, No. 4920 *Dumbleton Hall*. The engines of the Hall class were well liked by enginemen, and were the maids of all work on the Great Western main lines; whilst they were regularly to be found on vacuum-fitted fast freight trains, and the lighter passenger trains, they were quite capable of standing in for the four-cylinder Castles on much more arduous duties when the need arose, in spite of the fact that they were only two-cylindered engines.

To complete the list of motive power, mention must be made of the massive self-propelled steam crane, G.W.R. Crane No. 2, which was based at Swindon until the early 1970s, when it was acquired by the D.V.R. The crane was built by Ransomes & Rapier in 1908, and is capable of lifting 36 tons.

Moving on to coaching stock, we find an interesting selection of historic vehicles. The two former G.W.R. Super Saloons take pride of place – No. 9111, 'King George', is used by the Dart Valley Railway Association as a clubroom, and No. 9116 'Duchess of York', is used as a boardroom by the Dart Valley Light Railway Company. These vehicles are just as luxurious as Pullman Cars; although built by the G.W.R., the panelling, furnishing and fitting were carried out by a specialist firm. Another of the 'elite' vehicles on the line is the former Pullman Observation Car No. 13, one of two vehicles which were rebuilt just after World War II into observation cars for use on the Southern Railway's Devon Belle Pullman train. This vehicle is now regularly used on Dart Valley trains, and enables passengers to get an excellent view of the Dart Valley during the journey. Other rolling stock in regular use on the line are corridor coaches constructed by British Railways in the 1950s; although painted in 'chocolate-and-cream' livery, they are distinguished from the genuine Great Western coaches by the letters 'D.V.R.' on each side of the coaches instead of 'G.W.R.' insignia.

Also in regular use are the two former G.W.R. excursion coaches, built in 1937 for anticipated traffic which never fully materialized because of World War II. These vehicles can be recognized by the ornate plate-glass panels, bearing the G.W.R. monogram, which sub-divide the interior of each coach.

In early B.R. days, a number of push-pull coaches were constructed to a Hawksworth design, and they follow Great Western practice closely. The vehicles were built to replace a number of similar but aging 'trailers', as the old railwaymen called them. They have a control cab at one end, and when running with a specially adapted engine, the train can work not only the normal way, with the driver and fireman on the engine at the front of the train pulling the coach behind it, but also in the opposite direction, with the coach at the front being pushed by the engine. In this latter situation the driver sits in the control cab at the front of the coach and controls the train from there; the fireman looks after the engine at the rear. For his controls in the control cab of the trailer, the driver has a vacuum-brake control, a steam regulator handle (connected by a linkage under the coach to the regulator in the engine cab), and a large gong fitted on the end of the coach, worked by a foot treadle, which he uses to give warning of the train's approach.

Trains using these trailers were extensively used on branch lines, and for light suburban traffic, as the need to change the engine from one end of the train to the other at each end of the journey was eliminated. A train with two trailer coaches (a coach at each end and the engine in the middle) was not an uncommon sight, and was known as a 'sandwich'. The maximum size of train permitted to use this sytem was four trailer coaches (two coaches at each end and an engine in the middle); this was referred to as a 'double sandwich'.

The Dart Valley Railway originally purchased five trailer coaches, which did sterling service in the early years of the preserved line; the sight of a typical Great Western double sandwich was not uncommon. With the increase in traffic, the provision of loops, and the current thinking on safety regarding trailer-train working, trains are now again worked in the traditional manner with the engine at the front of the train. But one or other of these trailers can be seen running from time to time. One was in use on the Torbay line in 1976, and another has been loaned to the West Somerset Railway.

It is not intended to describe the whole of the rolling stock here (the exact details are in any case constantly changing), but the D.V.R. also has a former B.R. diesel shunting locomotive, and a variety of goods and engineering vehicles.

Torbay Steam Railway

The line and its history

The present railway from Paignton to King-swear follows an extremely picturesque route, and owes its existence to a compromise solution to the problem of providing rail access to Dartmouth.

The early proposals of the South Devon Railway to serve the area would have linked Exeter to Plymouth by a roundabout route through Dartmouth. Had the scheme been carried through, it is unlikely that the Torbay line would ever have been constructed. However, Isambard Kingdom Brunel, the S.D.R.'s engineer, insisted on taking the shortest practicable route, and left Dartmouth without its promised railway.

Brunel's Exeter–Plymouth main line was built to the broad gauge, and completed in the late 1840s. A branch to Torquay opened in the same period. An extension to Brixham was mooted at this time, but never materialized. Instead, a small independent company was formed, calling itself the Dartmouth and Torbay Railway Company. After much difficulty, they managed to reach Paignton in 1859, and by 1861 had got as far as Churston (then known as Brixham Road). By this time, their finances were precarious, because of the very high cost of the viaducts at Broadsands and Hookhills and the soil stabilization works at Goodrington, where the line crossed boggy land. Dartmouth, only four miles beyond Churston, never got its railway. The Company had planned to bridge the River Dart near Greenway, but local landowners strongly objected; finally, a compromise scheme was adopted which brought the line down to the east bank of the River Dart, to Kingswear, in 1864. A station was built at Dartmouth, permanently separated from the railway by the River Dart, and a ferry service was provided from the railhead at Kingswear. The railway had bypassed Brixham, so in the same year as the Kingswear branch was completed, yet another Railway Company was formed: the Torbay and Brixham. The

Company's line, which was slightly over two miles long, linked Brixham to the Torbay line (joining it at Brixham Road), and was completed late in 1867. With the opening of the line, Brixham Road station was renamed 'Churston' by which name it has been known up to the present day, in spite of the fact that the Brixham branch was closed in 1963. It is interesting to note that the Torbay and Brixham Railway retained its independent status until 1883 (seven years after the South Devon had been absorbed by the Great Western).

Apart from the conversion from the broad gauge to standard gauge in 1892, the line remained virtually unchanged until the 1920s, when considerable improvements were made to enable even the largest of the Great Western locomotives (the King class 4-6-0s) to use it. The improvements were made necessary by a great increase in holiday traffic, which enabled the line to earn good revenue throughout the 1930s. Although the line was capable of accepting King class locomotives, they were rarely seen, for Castles and Halls handled most of the through workings from the main line. The most famous through train was the Torbay Express from Paddington. Most of the local traffic was the

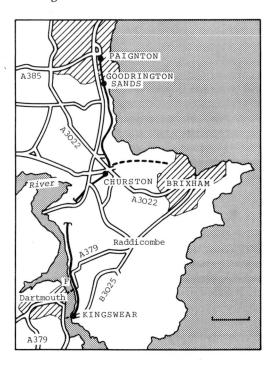

No. 6412 again, here on the Torbay Steam Railway. Note the clerestory coach in the centre.

preserve of the small Prairie (2-6-2) tanks of the 41XX and 45XX classes. Two locomotives of this type have been preserved and are regularly used on the line at present. Until the early 1960s, the Brixham branch was worked by the small 0-4-2 tank locomotives like *Bulliver* and *Ashburton*, which now operate on the Dart Valley Railway from Totnes to Buckfastleigh.

Preservation

In common with other lines, the Torbay line never regained its tourist traffic after World War II. Brixham traffic declined, and that branch was closed in 1963. Through services to Kingswear ceased in 1971, and British Rail applied to close the line from Paignton. Consent was given early in 1972, but the Dart Valley Railway Company applied to purchase the line with a view to running it as a tourist railway.

Accordingly, Devon County Council agreed to pay a subsidy which enabled British Rail to continue its operating responsibilities whilst the Dart Valley Light Railway Ltd completed their negotiations with British Rail for the purchase. These were successful and the Dart Valley company took over the running of the Torbay line in autumn 1972, after considerable track alterations had been made at Paignton so as to provide an independent line running out of Paignton, alongside the B.R. track, as far as Goodrington; British Rail carriage sidings are there, and B.R. need independent access.

Since 1972 much work had been done on the line, both on a paid and volunteer basis. Churston station is a good example of volunteer work. Fencing repairs, painting and general tidying up has all been done by people willing to give their time free of charge for the sake of seeing the line return to life. By necessity, however, some jobs on the line must be left to professional staff; for instance, since the Torbay Steam Railway's trains are under the control of

No. 5239 G.W.R. class 52XX (built 1924) at Churston. The bay with lifted track on the left was the Brixham branch platform.

the B.R. signalman working Paignton South box for a short distance west of Paignton station, it is important that the railway's train crews must be fully qualified to British Rail standards. This naturally bars an amateur, however skilled.

The line can be described as the more spectacular of the two preserved lines operated by the Dart Valley company.

Access

Paignton is possibly the most convenient point for most visitors to join the train. A multi-storey car park is within easy walking distance of the station. As the Torbay line station is immediately alongside that of British Rail, it is also the convenient starting point for people who arrive by British Rail.

The Torbay Steam Railway station entrance is tucked away on the west side of the British Rail line, and opens on to the Torbay Road.

As part of the re-organization necessary to operate the Torbay line as an independent railway, a new station has been constructed. The new and well-lit building provides booking and catering facilities and a spacious shop where railway and souvenir items are available. This building also houses the Paignton Model Railway, which is well worth a visit. The overall size of the model railway layout is 48 feet by 12 feet, and it is an excellent representation of the Great Western West Country main line during the 1930s, with typical trains in operation. The main station is a very impressive model of that at Westbury.

Returning once again to the full-size railway, a look around the station will reveal that this is the operating centre of the line and that provision is made here not only for servicing locomotives, but for maintenance and repair work as well.

A journey down the line

Our train will be of chocolate-and-cream coaches, hauled by a steam locomotive in full

20

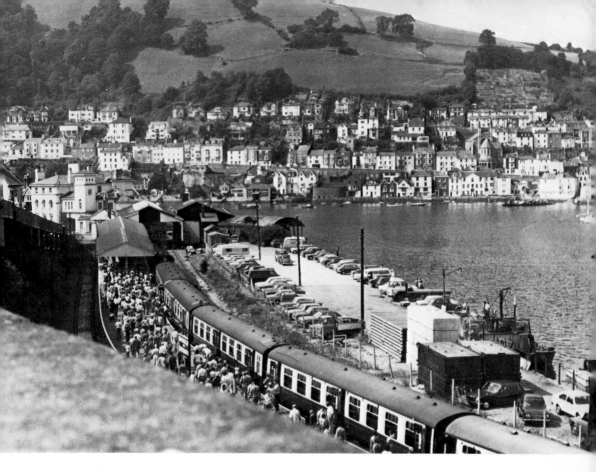

A holiday scene reminiscent of the Great Western in the 1930s. A train from Paignton arrives at Kingswear for Dartmouth.

G.W.R. livery. On leaving, we pass Paignton South signal box, over a gated level crossing, and then run alongside the British Rail carriage sidings before halting at Goodrington Sands station. As the train pulls away again, we get, on the left of the line, a sight of the open sands of Tor Bay and the sea beyond; our locomotive will now be working hard as it climbs up to Broadsands Viaduct and inland to the line's highest point at Churston. Passing under a stone railway bridge, our locomotive eases and comes to rest at Churston. Although the main station building is boarded up and the small waiting room on the other platform has been partly demolished, the old covered footbridge still remains. The bay platform for the former Brixham branch still remains between the road bridge and the main station building. After Churston station, the line runs inland, down to Greenway tunnel, beyond which it passes

through woodland, and then over Maypool viaduct. The River Dart can now be glimpsed through the trees on the right of the line. After passing a small ship-building yard, the river opens out; we can here see the Dart Marina. The next station, Britannia Crossing, is a small halt used by those who wish to use the up-river ferry across the river. The Dartmouth Naval College can be seen on the hill-side on the other side of the river, as the train finally pulls into Kingswear. The locomotive now runs round the train in readiness for the return to Paignton. There is a landing stage just beyond the end of the railway station platform. Here passengers may board the ferry to Dartmouth. This ferry, formerly railway-owned, is now operated by the local authority. It is often severely congested and prospective passengers are warned to allow a spare half-hour or so when travelling across from Dartmouth to make their connection with the Torbay Railway trains at Kingswear.

Stock
The Torbay line is usually worked by the larger

21

steam locomotives belonging to the Dart Valley company; the two former Great Western small Prairie 2-6-2 tank locomotives (Nos. 4555 and 4588) are the mainstay of the service. No. 4555 was the last locomotive to work the Dart Valley line from Totnes to Ashburton under British Railways, and she returned to the Dart Valley line in autumn 1965. The other Prairie (No. 4588) can be distinguished easily from her counterpart because her water tanks slope down in front. The tank tops on the other locomotive (No. 4555) are straight.

No. 4555 was saved by purchase direct from British Rail, but No. 4588 was sold to Messrs. Woodhams, scrap merchants of Barry; she remained there for some eight years before the Dart Valley Railway rescued her.

The only named locomotive used regularly on the Torbay line is the 4-6-0 tender locomotive No. 7828, *Lydham Manor*. After four years in Barry scrapyard, she was rescued, with enthusiastic help from the Dart Valley Association, and can now be seen, fully restored to her former Great Western livery, working the heaviest of the seasonal summer traffic.

When the Dart Valley company took over the Torbay line, more passenger coaches were needed to cope with summer tourist traffic on this line. As a result, the then-small fleet of readily available former British Rail Mark I coaches was quickly expanded to meet the needs of the Torbay traffic. These vehicles, although painted in chocolate-and-cream livery are distinguished from their Great-Western-built counterparts by the letters 'D.V.R.' on their sides, instead of the usual Great Western insignia. A typical peak-season train on the Torbay line will be made up almost entirely of these vehicles, with the addition of one of the Hawksworth auto-coaches on the Kingswear end of the train. The line also handles through-excursion trains from British Rail. The track was relaid into the bay platform at Kingswear during 1976, to enable B.R. excursion stock to be stabled there whilst regular timetable services carry on unhindered.

The latest addition to the carriage fleet are three non-gangwayed second class coaches which worked until the end of 1977 on King's Cross outer suburban services. They were repainted in D.V.R. chocolate and cream during 1978.

The West Somerset Railway

The line and its history

Brunel's broad-gauge Bristol–Exeter main line reached Taunton in 1842. The next railway proposal for the area was for a small mineral line to link iron workings high in the Brendon Hills with the little sea port of Watchet. This was the West Somerset Mineral Railway, and its last three-quarter-mile run up into the Brendons was laid on a massive 1-in-4 incline. Work started in 1856, and the first section was opened, from Watchet to Roadwater, the following year. The incline, which was worked by a stationary steam engine hauling wagons up and down by means of a long cable, was first brought into use in 1858. The lengthy extension on the upper section, to Gupworthy, was eventually completed in 1864. The railway, unlike most in the area, was laid to standard 4 ft 8½ in. gauge. The choice of this gauge for this line brought about a minor 'war of the gauges' in the Watchet area, when another company, the West Somerset Railway (with Brunel as engineer), constructed a broad-gauge branch which left the main line at Norton Fitzwarren and terminated at Watchet. This broad-gauge line, with an extension to the East Pier at

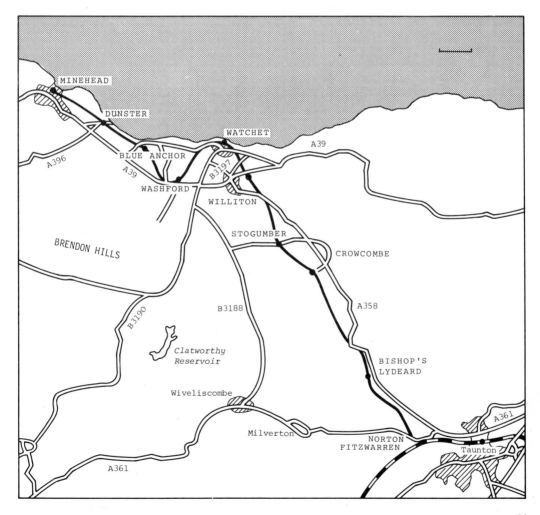

Watchet, was opened in spring 1862. The broad-gauge promoters had tried without success to obtain running powers over the narrow-gauge Mineral Railway track-bed by converting the track to mixed gauge. As the two companies would not co-operate, the little port of Watchet had two piers and two completely separate railways, the narrow-gauge line using the West Pier, and the broad-gauge the East Pier. The broad-gauge line was extended from Watchet to Minehead in 1874, under the auspices of the Minehead Railway Company. The broad-gauge West Somerset line and the extension (the Minehead Railway) were both worked by the Bristol and Exeter Railway until all were absorbed by the Great Western.

The narrow-gauge mineral line closed in 1898, but renewed interest in iron ore led to its re-opening in 1907. Its revival proved to be short-lived, however, and the line was again closed in 1910. The track was left, however, and two years later an Australian inventor used a section to demonstrate his system of automatic train control. During World War I the rails were commandeered for scrap; the operating company was finally wound up in the mid 1920s.

The broad-gauge West Somerset line from Taunton to Minehead was converted to standard gauge in 1882. It was taken over in due course by the Great Western Railway, and apart from the 1930s when some improvements were carried out on the line by the G.W.R. under the auspices of a Government unemployment relief scheme, time passed uneventfully on the line until 1948 when the branch became part of British Railways.

The opening of Butlin's Holiday Camp at Minehead in 1962 brought a welcome injection of traffic, but B.R. issued a closure notice for passenger services to apply from 6 January 1969. Objections and an enquiry delayed the closure until 4 January 1971. The last two trains to run on the line were two Specials organized by the Great Western Society Ltd and Minehead Round Table. These ran on 2 January 1971 (the last actual day of service).

Tank engines have always worked the line. The once-numerous 0-6-0 pannier tanks were well in evidence latterly, together with the small Prairie (2-6-2) side tank locomotives. Large Prairies of the 41XX and 61XX classes were also used. Although introduced by Churchward as early as 1903, these swift and powerful tank locomotives were still being built at Swindon in the 1940s (some, in fact, were built after nationalization). Tender locomotives were used from time to time; double-framed 4-4-0s of the Bulldog class sometimes found their way to Minehead, as well as Collett's 0-6-0s of the 2251 class.

Towards the end of British Rail operation, the line was reduced as an economy measure, to single track throughout, apart from the section between Norton Fitzwarren and Bishops Lydeard, and the short length from Dunster to the Minehead terminus. Another economy was the introduction of conductor-guards in October 1968.

Preservation

Shortly after the closure a new organization was formed, calling itself the West Somerset Railway Company. The object of the new Company was to purchase and re-open the line, and negotiations with B.R. were begun. Two years later, the Somerset County Council became involved, and agreed to buy the line and lease it to the West Somerset Railway Company.

Formal agreement was finally reached between B.R. and the County Council in the summer of 1973, but due to objections the granting of a Light Railway Order to enable the line to be re-opened was delayed. In fact the Order was eventually made, late in 1974, by the Department of the Environment, to British Rail. All that remained to complete the formalities to enable the line to open was the granting of a 'Light Railway Transfer Order' to the Company. By autumn 1975 approval had been given to the granting of the transfer order, and the scene was set for the line to open early in 1976.

The official re-opening of the first stage of the revived railway took place on 28 March 1976, when after a short ceremony on Minehead platform, witnessed by a large crowd of onlookers, Lord Montagu of Beaulieu, resplendent in a top hat, waved the green flag to give the 'right away' to the first of the new Company's trains to carry fare-paying passengers. The train comprised ex-British-Rail Mark I coaches still in B.R. blue-and-grey livery, drawn by the Bagnall 0-6-0 saddle tank locomotive *Victor*, gaily bedecked in bunting. The train left Minehead station to an accompaniment of music from the Watchet British Legion Band, and a volley of exploding detonators.

The new service, which initially ran from Minehead through Dunster and terminated at Blue Anchor (a journey of just over 3 miles), continued to operate through the summer of 1976. The railway was fortunate in receiving a grant of £49,000 from the Manpower Services Commission which covered the cost of employing 45 men for a period of 6 months. This additional labour made a not inconsiderable contribution to refurbishing along the line, and the Company was able to re-open a further stretch of line, from Blue Anchor to Williton, at the start of the Late Summer Holiday of 1976, on Saturday 28 August. In spite of a rather wild start to the day, with waves breaking over the Minehead promenade within fifty yards or so of the station platforms, the storms held off until well after the 'first train to Williton' had completed its return trip. For the second time that year, the bunting appeared at Minehead station and a further touch of ceremony was added by an elderly town crier, in scarlet uniform and white gaiters and black tricorn hat, ringing his handbell and inviting prospective travellers to: 'Take a trip on the Steam Train of the West Somerset Railway running from Minehead to Blue Anchor, Watchet Harbour and Williton.' *Victor* then drew out of the platform with the train of former B.R. coaches (by now repainted in the company's maroon-and-cream livery).

Access
The most convenient point for the present-day visitor to join the train is Minehead, as the summer steam service operates from this end of the line as far as Williton. Minehead station is conveniently situated next to the promenade, and a small but handy car park is provided in the station forecourt. The stone-built station buildings, although modernized by the G.W.R. in the early 1930s, still retain a strong Victorian appearance. The facilities here include the booking office, a light-refreshments room, and a souvenir shop. For those visitors requiring a cooked meal, a large café is on the sea-front near the station. Between this café and Butlin's Camp

is a fascinating model village complete with church, shops, airport and – of course – a working $3\frac{1}{2}$ in. gauge model railway. Also to be found on the same site is a passenger-carrying miniature railway which has a red-liveried model of the British Rail Western class diesel-hydraulic locomotive as its motive power. At the half-way point of its circuit the miniature railway train passes alongside the West Somerset line. There is also an attractive miniature golf course.

A journey down the line
For the full-size railway, we obtain our tickets from the tiny ticket window in the Victorian booking hall, and pass through on to the station platform. The Victorian era is still with us, in the form of a beautifully preserved drinking fountain of ornate design set in the station wall. Our train will probably consist of ex-British-Rail coaches in the maroon-and-cream livery of the W.S.R.; our locomotive may be an ex-Great-Western tank loco, or perhaps one of the two Bagnall-built 0-6-0 tank locomotives once used at Austin's Longbridge factory.

As the train pulls out of the platform we pass the miniature railway on our left and beyond this again on our left is the massive Butlin's complex which has spread itself along the coastline between the promenade and the railway. Soon we are in open country passing over marshlands on a straight stretch of line laid with double tracks. The first stop on the journey is Dunster; by then the track is reduced to single line. The handsome stone-built goods shed stands marooned, its track removed, but still sports a loading gauge. Dunster village is about ten minutes' walk from the station. For visitors with a taste for historic buildings, Dunster has much to offer, with its exquisite Yarn Market forming the focal point in a picturesque Somerset street scene. Also worth mention is Dunster Castle, built in 1070 on the site of a Saxon fortress and now the property of the National Trust. The Castle is open to visitors only on certain weekdays; prospective visitors are advised to check before making the journey.

As the train pulls away from Dunster, we pass over Dunster beach crossing (level crossing gates here have been replaced by modern warning bells and flashing lights). The countryside is still very flat: the line sweeps gradually around the back of Blue Anchor Bay, over the old gated level crossing (still controlled from a traditional signal box) and into Blue Anchor station. The station has two platforms and a passing loop, and was of course the temporary terminus during 1976. The holiday caravans and adjacent beach help to give the place a strong seaside atmosphere.

Leaving Blue Anchor, the train enters a shallow cutting; the line curves sharply away from the coast, and enters low farmland, with the Brendon Hills in the background to the right. The line then enters a deep cutting, and beyond this runs alongside the busy A39 road to enter Washford station. The track here is again single-line, with the addition of one short siding. The twelfth-century Cleeve Abbey is within easy reach.

After Washford, the line curves back towards the coast, and we are soon passing the pictures-que village of Old Cleeve on the left and the B.B.C. transmitter on the right. After a cutting, the line runs through open country for a short distance. The scene then suddenly changes, and we pass the busy Wansborough Paper Mills, then under a road bridge and into Watchet station. The train pulls out of Watchet past a busy dock area which will be crowded with goods ranging from timber to new tractors. Beyond the docks, the line climbs and curves sharply to the right and passes a beach with an assortment of holiday caravans and a few chalets. From here the line runs inland, to Williton, which is the terminus for the steam-hauled summer tourist trains. We will have to alight here on the up platform and cross over to the down platform, whilst the loco runs round its train and shunts it to the other platform ready for the return run to Minehead.

It is planned that the remainder of the route to Taunton from Williton, through Stogumber, Crowcombe, Bishops Lydeard and Norton Fitzwarren, will be served by diesel multiple unit trains. It is not intended to extend the summer steam service over this part of the line.

Due to difficulties concerning the running of the Company's trains into Taunton (British Rail) Station it is doubtful if the envisaged Taunton to Minehead commuter service will materialize for some while yet. It is likely, however, that the $8\frac{1}{2}$ miles of line between Stogumber and Norton Fitzwarren will be brought up to standard shortly to enable through running of B.R. excursion trains.

How the line is run

The organization behind a fully operational private railway is quite complex, and it is worth discussing it in some detail. The new West Somerset Railway Company was incorporated on 5 May 1971. The Board comprises 7 Directors and a Company Secretary. The Company went public in spring 1976; the £65,000 share capital (in 10p shares) was quickly over-subscribed. The Railway employs a General Manager (Mr D. J. L. Butcher, who was British Rail Area Manager at Westbury); his wife played an important part in the refurbishing of the Minehead station buildings for the first season.

In addition to the present West Somerset Railway Company, whose object was the re-opening and is the running of the line, two other allied organizations have been created to complement the work of the Company.

The West Somerset Railway Association was formed in 1971 to provide volunteer support, chiefly in the restoration, operating and main-tenance of stock, permanent way and buildings. The Association has its headquarters at Bishops Lydeard, and when renovated, the station buildings there will become the Association's office and information centre. Engineering and repair facilities will be established in the nearby goods shed.

The Association's main sales outlet for railway books and souvenirs has been estab-lished in the station building on the down platform at Blue Anchor.

The Stock Fund is an organization closely related to the Association. Its purpose is to act as a holding company, acquiring locomotives and stock with Association funds, and then leasing them to the Railway Company. The most significant item acquired so far is the ex-G.W.R. 0-6-0 pannier tank locomotive No. 6412, which was formerly owned by the Dart Valley Rail-way. This locomotive shared the steam work-ings with Bagnall 0-6-0 *Victor* during 1976.

Stock

Apart from the 0-6-0 pannier tank, Stock Fund acquisitions include some ex-British-Rail Mark I

Minehead Station on the West Somerset Railway, with the diesel multiple unit set intended to return to its old Taunton–Minehead run in due course.

coaches, a steam crane, and three ex-G.W.R. 2-6-2 tank locos known in Great Western circles as 'small Prairies'. These locomotives (obtained from the Barry scrapyards), Nos. 4561, 5521 and 5542, still require a considerable amount of restoration work to bring them into running order. One of them was completely stripped down to the frames in Minehead station during the summer of 1976, and a collecting box was on hand for visitors to make donations towards the locomotive's restoration.

Whilst on the subject of locomotives mention should be made that the two Bagnall 0-6-0 saddle tank engines, *Victor* and *Vulcan*, are both on loan from an Association member. *Victor* was in excellent working order at the commencement of steam working in spring 1976 and, as previously mentioned, hauled the two opening trains.

Turning now to diesel power, two twin-car Park Royal diesel multiple unit trains were acquired from British Rail, both sets having been purchased from the Taunton–Minehead commuter service. One set was in service in May 1976 on the Minehead–Blue Anchor run; it was

also running on the Minehead–Williton run on the day of the Williton opening in August 1976. A 1937 Ruston Hornsby $7\frac{1}{2}$-ton diesel loco was donated to the Stock Fund by Unigate Foods Ltd of Chard. During 1976 this was housed in the goods shed at Bishops Lydeard.

Other rolling stock includes an assortment of goods vehicles and a six-wheel parcels van. Three ex-Great-Western toplight camping coaches have been saved from the breakers and help contribute to the Great Western atmosphere. Another Swindon-built vehicle is a Hawksworth auto-coach on loan from the Dart Valley Railway.

The line also acts as hosts to two rather interesting locomotives: the Somerset and Dorset Joint Railway tender locomotive (B.R. No. 53808) which belongs to the Somerset and Dorset Railway Museum Trust, and the diesel-hydraulic Hymek locomotive belonging to the Diesel and Electric Group.

The Bicton Woodland Railway

The line and its history

Bicton Gardens and the adjoining Bicton House, (originally referred to as 'The Manor Bukinton') came into existence in early mediaeval times, when King Henry I granted the estate to John Janitor in recognition for his services to the crown in maintaining the Castle Gate and gaol at Exeter Castle.

By distinct contrast, the Bicton Woodland Railway has a very short history, the line being first mooted around 1961. On the death of the then Lord Clinton in 1957, the title passed to his great grandson, the present owner of Bicton Gardens. In 1957 Bicton House (and the Home Farm which adjoins it) were sold to the Devon County Council to be used as an Agricultural Institute, leaving the present gardens and wood still in the estate ownership.

In 1961 the present owner decided to open the gardens to the public, but the Bicton House had been sold four years earlier; it was felt that if the public were to be attracted to the gardens in reasonable numbers, at least one further attraction should be added, to make up for the loss in tourist attraction caused by the non-availability of the House for public viewing.

It was decided in the autumn of 1961 that a miniature passenger-carrying railway (similar to the Romney, Hythe and Dymchurch in Kent) would meet the requirement, and enquiry to a London company who supplied narrow-gauge railway equipment to civil engineering contractors produced results. The firm knew of an 18 in. gauge steam locomotive lying in a Northamptonshire yard, which they thought might suit.

This locomotive had, until shortly before, worked on the Woolwich Arsenal Railway. The locomotive was inspected late in November 1961; it appeared quite suitable, and it was decided to purchase her, subject to her passing the necessary tests. The boiler was found to be in remarkably good condition, being probably less than five years old. A Bedfordshire firm put the locomotive into working order, and atten-

tion was now turned to building the track. After a detailed survey, the track components were purchased – except for the sleepers. These were cut at the estate's own sawmills, from timber grown on the estate. In order to save time and expense in cutting rails, the track joints were staggered.

By early April 1962, the little steam locomotive was ready for acceptance trials. Work done on her included the replacement of the 'spark-arrester' chimney necessary for her former duties at the Royal Arsenal with one of a more conventional pattern. She was tested in steam whilst still in Northamptonshire, and after acceptance was transported to Bicton immediately. She was unloaded onto two lengths of channel iron. Actual track-laying started early in May 1962 in Bicton Gardens station. By the middle of the month enough track was laid to justify placing the steam locomotive on the track. A length of temporary track was laid from the engine to the railhead and, with the aid of a winch-equipped Land Rover, the railing operation was quickly accomplished. A few days later the locomotive was steamed for the first time at Bicton and, after the curing of a few minor problems, she proved an excellent aid to the laying of the permanent way. The one major unsolved problem still outstanding in spring 1962 was that of providing the line with suitable rolling stock. Seven goods vehicles were purchased from the Royal Arsenal in spring 1962; six covered bogie wagons (previously used for transporting explosives), and an open bogie goods truck. But since the trucks had been used for explosives, the Arsenal regulations decreed that the timber bodies of the six covered vehicles must be burned before the vehicles were sold. This meant that six body-less wagon frames and one open wagon arrived at Bicton in June 1962. The open wagon proved valuable for permanent-way construction. It is retained on the line in its original form.

A covered coach from a 24 in. gauge Air Ministry line in Staffordshire was acquired the following month and was re-gauged to 18 in. Unfortunately, the chassis was unreliable, and so the body was soon transferred to an ex-Arsenal underframe. Further passenger vehicles were built on the ex-Arsenal frames by the estate staff.

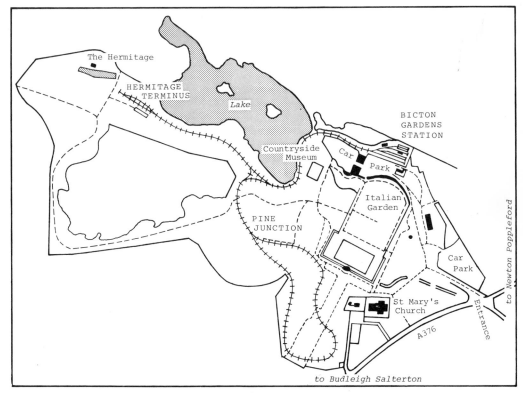

The Hermitage

HERMITAGE
TERMINUS

Lake

BICTON
GARDENS
STATION

Countryside
Museum

Car
Park

Italian
Garden

PINE
JUNCTION

Car
Park

St Mary's
Church

A376

Entrance

to Newton Poppleford

to Budleigh Salterton

Bicton's 'main line' was completed in August 1962 when the ends of the two tracks from Pine Junction were joined on the down line. (The point is almost directly in line with the obelisk when viewed from the centre of the Italian gardens.) A small ceremony was held, Lord Clinton driving in the last spike to close the circuit. Although a 'golden spike' was not available, a small commemorative plate was affixed to the adjoining sleeper to record the event.

A finishing touch was soon added when some ex-London-and-South-Western-Railway lattice-type signal posts were acquired from British Rail. These were shortened to fit into their new setting, but retain the full-size signal arms.

Early the following year, a small siding was constructed at Pine Junction to house a buffet car. The buffet car, in which teas were served during high season, comprised a body built by the estate staff on one of the ex-Woolwich-Arsenal underframes.

1963 also saw the acquisition of the railway's first diesel locomotive. This small engine, weighing a mere 3 tons, had worked in a War Department storage depot in Leicestershire during World War II.

Early in 1966, a further diesel locomotive was acquired. This locomotive is powerful enough to handle the heaviest trains on the line. She is a relatively modern machine and, like Bicton's steam loco, had been retired from service in Woolwich Arsenal.

In order to provide much-needed additional siding accommodation at Bicton Gardens station, it was decided to lift the buffet car siding at Pine Junction and transfer the point and trackwork to the Gardens station. At this time the buffet car was converted into a passenger coach (bringing the total passenger-carrying vehicles to six, three open and three covered coaches), all of which are on ex-Woolwich underframes.

The increase in traffic during the early summer of 1966 emphasized the need for yet another passenger vehicle, and when the surplus ex-Air-Ministry underframe and bogies had been successfully modified and fitted with an estate-built open body, the new vehicle entered service in July 1966.

At Bicton Gardens station, the original locomotive shed (built for two locomotives in 1962) was extended to accommodate a third in 1966, and an island platform was added at the station in the same year. This was to make working with two trains possible at busy times.

After this chain of developments in 1966, the 'dreaded competition' from alternative transport arrived – in the shape of two small and ancient open-sided buses, which transported their passengers from the main car park, across the railway crossing, and along the roadway around the outskirts of the estate to the delightful little nineteenth-century summer retreat known as the Hermitage. It is pleasing to record however that the iron road fought back, and in spring 1976 Lady Clinton planted a tree to commemorate the opening of the third-of-a-mile extension to the railway, which leaves the main line at a junction between the lake and the roadway crossing, and terminates a short walk away from the Hermitage. With the bringing into use of this short branch line, the vintage bus service has been discontinued.

Access

The visitor can reach Bicton Gardens via the A376 road between Newton Poppleford and Budleigh Salterton. The entrance to the gardens is slightly to the north of St Mary's Church. Ample parking is provided for cars and coaches, and the car park adjoins the railway. For visitors coming by bus, the Devon General operates, during the summer months, a half-hourly service passing the gates.

Entering the Bicton Gardens station area, the character of the line soon becomes apparent. The station area is extremely tidy, and the combination of this and the spotless royal blue locomotives with their bright red underframes tends to remind the more railway-oriented visitor of the standard-gauge Longmoor Military Railway in its later days.

When only one train is operating, it may alternate between trips on the main line and trips on the branch to the Hermitage; it is as well to make sure which route the train is taking before you board.

The main line

Leaving the terminus, our train passes the main car park on the left. Beyond this, the line curves sharply to the left, following the shore of the lake (now on the right). In the distance beyond the lake is Bicton House; on the left down the embankment can be seen the Countryside Museum. Taking the left-hand route at the junction (the original route), we enter woodland, and are soon passing over the level crossing previously used by the vintage bus service to the Hermitage. The line still curves to the left. As we enter Pine Junction, we take the left-hand line, which winds around through woodland until we suddenly enter a clearing and are confronted with the beautiful Italian gardens, the Temple forming a background to the scene. At this point we pass over the sleeper where the last spike was driven in to complete the main line. The line then goes back into woodland, and curves sharply around in a semi-circle, out in the clearing again briefly, and then climbs up to enter Pine Junction again. From there, the return journey is made over the same route, back to Bicton Gardens.

Other attractions

Before we take our second railway trip, on the branch line to the Hermitage, we will take a look around the various non-railway attractions which Bicton has to offer. These include a well-stocked souvenir shop, and a garden shop stocking numerous varieties of plants. The shops adjoin Bicton Gardens station, and from here the Italian and American gardens are within easy reach. Ice cream, cold drinks, etc. are available from a small kiosk adjoining the Palm House, and for those who require a meal, afternoon teas are served in the rather stately atmosphere of the Temple which overlooks the Italian Gardens. For those with an interest in farming, engineering or early transport, a visit to the Countryside Museum near the main car parks is worthwhile. The rather plain appearance of the outside of the building skilfully hides the mass of contrasting colour which greets the visitor on entering. The most prominent display in the main hall is a comprehensive collection of farm tractors, stationary engines, and farm machinery; at the back of the hall is a collection of steam-powered items

including a large stationary engine, a traction engine, and a 1926 steam roller. In the side hall, there is a display of horse-drawn carts and wagons; the pride of this collection is a massive miller's wagon of the 1860s. There are many other smaller displays in the Museum.

The Hermitage branch line

The train for the branch line to the Hermitage, as before, leaves the terminus past the car park and travels alongside the lake to the junction. Here, however, the train takes the right-hand route,

Bicton Woodland Railway. 0-4-0 Woolwich waits at Hermitage terminus, ready for the return journey to Bicton Gardens station.

and still keeping within a short distance of the lakeside, climbs to enter a shallow cutting; after passing through another much deeper cutting the train is some twenty feet or so above the lake. Just beyond the end of the lake, it enters the terminus which is a very simple affair with a run-round loop and only a single platform.

The East Somerset Railway

The East Somerset Railway is based at Cranmore station near Shepton Mallet, and consists of several lengths of track, an engine shed built in the 1970s to Victorian designs, a signal box with an art gallery, a shop and refreshments. The Railway is essentially the inspiration of the railway artist David Shepherd, and many of his works are on sale. Among the locomotives which have been restored is the Southern Railway Schools class 4-4-0, No. 928, *Stowe*, built in 1938. There is also a B.R. Standard 9F, designed for heavy freight, the 2-10-0, No. 92203, which has since been named *Black Prince*. There is a B.R. 4MT class, 4-6-0, No. 75029, which has been named *The Green Knight*. There are a number of coaches, all built under British Rail. They include a BSO bogie carriage No. 9241 (1955), an L.N.E.R.-designed second-class sleeper, No. 1767 (1951), and one L.M.S. first-class saloon coach, No. 3322, built in 1929. The last is at present being rebuilt as a luxury first-class carriage for use on the railway at Cranmore. There is also an experimental all-fibreglass coach No. 1000, the first and last of its kind. There is also a variety of goods rolling stock from various companies.

Riddles class 9F 2-10-0 Black Prince *was built as recently as 1959. Purchased by David Shepherd only eight years later, it was one of the first arrivals at Cranmore. Behind is the 2-road engine shed built in 1976 to traditional G.W.R. design.*

The E.S.R. purchased about a mile of track in 1978, running to Merryfield Lane, Doulting, the next village west of Cranmore. Application has been made for a Light Railway Order so that a public service can be run.

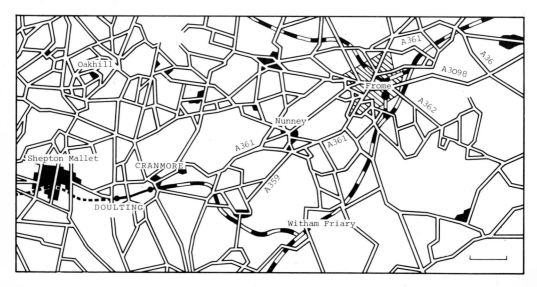

The Great Western Society, Didcot

Although railway enthusiasts tend to think in terms of famous lines, trains or stations, one of the most important centres for the restoration and preservation of steam locomotives has no direct connection with any of these. It is an old maintenance depot at Didcot Junction. Didcot, with its medium-sized station, yards and triangular configuration of tracks, has developed under the auspices of the Great Western Society to become one of the most successful steam enterprises in the country. While the Society lacks a long stretch of line to run its trains at speed, they have succeeded in amassing a wide variety of Great Western locomotives, coaches, rolling stock and memorabilia. In addition, they have gathered together a magnificent range of repair facilities, including cranes, lifting gear, and machine tools. The depot also features the numerous sheds, a coaling stage, water tower and (more recently) a turntable. The site is easily approached from the British Rail station to which it is linked by an underground passage under the main line running to Bristol and Paddington.

Historically, the junction owes its importance to the desire to link the Welsh Borders with the main line constructed by Brunel between London and the South-West. The important market centres of Worcester and Hereford, and the growing industrial might of Birmingham, called out for a rail link with Paddington. The obvious place from which to make the extension was Didcot. The line was constructed, running north to take in the outskirts of Oxford, and then Banbury, where it split, going to Worcestershire, and also continuing north into the Black Country. The connection to Oxford proved a particularly popular one. The engine storage and maintenance yard is at the point where this line joined the main line to the West.

The origin of the Great Western Society lies with the 48XX Class Preservation Society founded in 1961. Its aim then, was modest enough: to preserve this engine with its auto-coach (see page 17 for details of an auto-coach).

With small numbers, the task was a difficult one, and it was not until 1964 that the Society was able to purchase the now well-known tank engine, No. 1466. In the following year the Society, which had meantime changed its name to the present form, set up a fund to preserve a larger locomotive. In 1966, No. 6998, *Burton Agnes Hall*, was acquired. Regional branches were opened in areas once served by the old Great Western, and the scope and scale of the Society's operations was expanded. Shortly afterwards the Bristol Group were responsible for the purchase of *Cookham Manor*, another 4-6-0 loco. In 1967 the Society moved in to Didcot, when British Rail decided that the depot was no longer of value, the transition to diesel being almost complete. Since this important acquisition – until then the Society had contented themselves with short runs on the branch line from Cholsey to Wallingford – the programme of preservation, restoration and main line running has prospered. The depot now features an impressive display of engines and rolling stock.

Among the finely restored engines of distinction at Didcot is No. 5900, *Hinderton Hall*, one of the more recently preserved locomotives. Designed by Collett, the Hall class was a general purpose two-cylinder engine. It was used for mixed passenger and goods trains working over longish distances; Halls were the maids of all

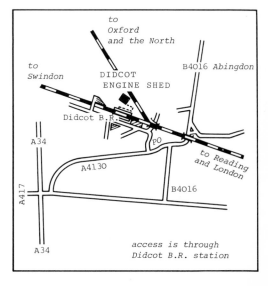

to
Oxford
and the North

to
Swindon

DIDCOT
ENGINE SHED

B4016 *Abingdon*

Didcot B.R.

A34

PO

A4130

to Reading
and London

A417

B4016

A34

access is through
Didcot B.R. station

work on the Great Western. *Hinderton Hall* was built in 1930, and has now been thoroughly overhauled, turned out in Swindon green livery. The other 4-6-0 engines which have been completed are *Burton Agnes Hall* and *Cookham Manor*. The former is a 'modified Hall'. More recent than 5900, built in 1949, this engine was the product of the revisionary work of Hawksworth, the Chief Mechanical Engineer who had succeeded Collett. *Burton Agnes Hall* (No. 6998) was purchased on the completion of her service with British Rail, and was said to be the last Great Western loco to haul a passenger train on B.R. Fully restored, No. 6998 is now painted in post-war Great Western livery. The engine is easily distinguished from the other 4-6-0s at Didcot by its tender, which has straight sides, as distinct from the more stylish flanged tenders of the pre-war period. *Burton Agnes Hall* has been used for many of the recent steam runs made by

A line-up of Great Western locomotives at Didcot for an open day.

the Society on B.R. lines.

No. 7808, *Cookham Manor*, was built in 1938. The Manor class is the smallest of this 4-6-0 class. The small driving wheels were incorporated largely to provide a loco to work on the Cambrian Coast line. They were however, powerful engines, with high pressure boilers. At Didcot, but still in the process of restoration, are two of the best-known Collett design, No. 5029, *Nunney Castle*, and No. 5051, *Drysllwyn Castle*. These were two of the famous engines used to haul the major express trains running to the holiday resorts of Devon and Cornwall and to South Wales. The last of these two was renamed *Earl Bathurst* after the Second World War because certain peers had objected to their titles being used on then antiquated locomotives. The names were switched by the G.W.R. in order to keep their custom. It is true that the Society does not possess one of the most powerful of all Great Western engines, the Kings, at Didcot, but they do have permission to operate No. 6000, *King George V*, which is maintained by Bulmers and kept at Hereford.

In addition to these bigger locos, the Great Western Society has a number of suburban and goods engines from various periods of the Company's history. Apart from No. 1466, their first acquisition, there is No. 6697, one of the classic 0-6-2 tank engine designs. Produced for work in South Wales, they were ideal for hauling short-distance goods and passenger trains. Larger, but of similar appearance, is No. 6106, a suburban tank designed to work out of Paddington with commuter trains to Reading. This engine, built in 1931, is a 2-6-2, and may be distinguished by the words 'Great Western' painted in yellow and red on the sides of the water tanks, and by the outside cylinders. Also well remembered on the Great Western are the pannier tank engines which were used for shunting duties and light trains. The Society has two of these at present under restoration, Nos. 3650 and 3738. They were part of one of the most numerous classes of engines on the system, numbering some eight hundred.

One of the oldest engines preserved at Didcot is the Churchward-designed No. 5322, a 2-6-0 tender engine. This class, Mogul, was introduced as early as 1910. This particular loco built in 1917 actually saw service in France during World War I. They were used for mixed traffic. This particular engine is distinguished by its old-fashioned cab reminiscent of Victorian days. It leaves the crew scarcely protected, having no glass side windows. The engine remains in her green livery, and is exceptionally attractive. In addition, there are a number of small industrial locomotives at Didcot. Of these, probably the most interesting is *Shannon*, believed to be the oldest working standard-gauge locomotive. She was built in 1858 for Captain Peel, son of the prime minister, who had his own private railway and who had commanded a ship of that name while in the Royal Navy.

No Great Western depot would be complete without a vision of the famous chocolate-and-cream coaches. Didcot offers the visitor a wide choice of these liveried designs. Coach designs vary much more than people imagine. Carriages

1936-built No. 1466 (class 48XX) runs with auto-trailer No. 231 (of 1951) on the demonstration line at Didcot.

are classified into suburban, excursion, buffet, ocean saloon, and auto-carriage, not to mention the variations produced on these. The Society has tried to build up a picture of how carriages changed and differed. There are carriages (requiring extensive restoration) from the Victorian era, and one 'Dreadnought' coach, 70 feet long, from the first decade of the twentieth century. The Society has two of the famous ocean saloons, 'Queen Mary' and 'Princess Elizabeth'; these were exceptionally luxurious, and more expensive to travel in than first class. Of later design is No. 9002; its class is unusual in that each bogie has six rather than four wheels. These too were beautifully fitted carriages. This particular coach was designed with a lounge,

Didcot has excellent engineering facilities. Here, the boiler of No. 5051 Earl Bathurst *(formerly Drysllwyn Castle) undergoes a steam test in the lifting shop.*

conference room and kitchen.

The Society also has a number of freight vehicles, including the distinctive 'Royal Daylight' petrol tanker, a milk-churn van, a cattle wagon, coal wagons and a curious weed-killer truck. There are also a few vans used by permanent way staff in their work of maintaining the line.

At Didcot it is possible to obtain a comprehensive picture of most facets of the operation of the Great Western Railway.

II

London and the Home Counties

Bluebell Railway

The Bluebell Railway has the distinction of having been the first standard-gauge railway to re-open after closure by British Railways (though the Middleton Railway – see p. 190 – was the first preserved standard-gauge line of all); the official re-opening ceremony was conducted on Sunday 7 August 1960.

The line and its history
The track, which is single, and approximately five miles long, links Sheffield Park station at the southernmost end with Horsted Keynes station to the north after a climb of some two hundred feet. It was formerly a part of the old Lewes and East Grinstead railway, proposed in 1876 and opened on 1 August 1883. Like so many rural systems, the project was never a money spinner, passing as it did through countryside which was devoted mainly to agriculture, sparsely populated, and with most villages rather remote from the stations bearing their names. Furthermore, the train services appeared to be geared to milk and mineral traffic rather than the needs of passengers, who experienced long waits whilst loading was in progress. The stations really came to life in the days of social functions at nearby stately homes, of which Sheffield Park probably attracted the largest contingents. Among Lord Sheffield's visitors were the Australian touring cricketers, whose first match in this country was always played on the pitch at the Park. (Cricket lovers may connect this with the Sheffield Shield, awarded in inter-state competition in Australia, for which Lord Sheffield donated the trophy.) A period of great activity at the stations came during World War I when much of the countryside came under control of the War Office for troop training. The unmechanized army threw a heavy load onto the railways.

Trains on the Bluebell line continued to jog along into the early years of nationalization. An amazing assortment of locomotives contributed to the scene, from 'Terriers' to Brighton Atlantics (4-4-2s) and Moguls (2-6-0s), some of

Bulleid's West Country and Battle of Britain classes, and even ex-S.E. & C.R. and ex-L. & S.W.R. engines. All these were then joined by engines of British Railways design, including one of the early diesels, Bo-Bo No. 10800. All this was too good to last. Following two enquiries, British Railways closed the line from East Grinstead through Horsted Keynes to Culver Junction (where it converged with the Tunbridge Wells to Lewes line), from 28 May 1955.

However, an astute local lady pointed out that under a clause in its original Act, the line could not legally be closed in this way; British Railways were obliged to re-introduce a minimum service. They made the timetable as inconvenient as possible, with four trains each way daily from Monday to Saturday. This commenced in August 1956; the programme fell within the scope of an eight-hour shift for train crews. Once B.R. had adjusted their legal position they withdrew this pathetic train service, on 16 March 1958. British Railways did

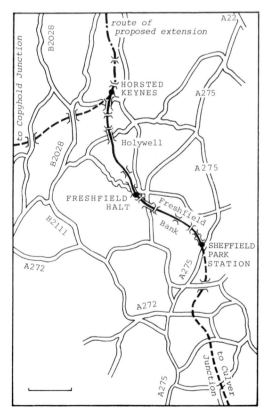

however retain the electrified route from Haywards Heath through Ardingly to Horsted Keynes, this being expedient from a traffic rather than revenue point of view.

Preservation

In 1959, three young students called a meeting of interested people, to discuss the possibility of operating the line on a private basis. As a result the authorities at Waterloo were approached. Eventually it became possible to lease the section of line between Sheffield Park station and a point south of Horsted Keynes station (without access to the latter), and a price was quoted for eventual purchase. A second meeting held at Haywards Heath resulted in the founding of The Bluebell Railway Preservation Society on 14 June 1959. The founders could hardly have visualized that in little over a decade the annual passenger journeys over the preserved line would be in the order of a quarter of a million!

At first British Railways refused to allow Bluebell trains into Horsted Keynes station; the Society had to build Bluebell Halt, clear of the junction but within easy walking distance.

Former S.E. & C.R. tank No. 323, Bluebell, shunts L.B. & S.C.R. Directors' saloon No. 60 (built in 1910 and 1913 respectively), in Horsted Keynes station.

There was no run-round loop, so trains had to be run with an engine at each end. After a while British Railways relented somewhat, and allowed Bluebell trains to use one platform at Horsted Keynes; they rather negated this concession by insisting that a British Railways pilotman should join or leave the Bluebell engine at the halt and inevitably this tiresome service was not provided free of charge. A bitter blow followed in 1963 when the Haywards Heath–Horsted Keynes branch was closed. Lifting of the tracks isolated the preserved line. All future deliveries of locomotives and rolling stock had perforce to rely upon road haulage, over somewhat winding routes. Thanks to the one-hundred-per-cent co-operation of the Sussex Police, many giant loads over the years have been safely delivered without undue dislocation of road traffic – indeed, most motorists appear to be intrigued rather than antagonized.

Freshfield Bank, a gradient of 1 in 75, always provides fine smoke. Here, G.W.R. 4-4-0 Earl of Berkeley heads a four-coach passenger train from Sheffield Park to Horsted Keynes.

Access

The station at Sheffield Park has been restored to its former L.B. & S.C.R. colour scheme, and houses, in addition to administrative offices, a very interesting museum, and a solidly built bookshop offering a wide variety of Bluebell and other railway interest publications. Refreshments are available near the same platform. The headquarters of the Locomotive Department are at Sheffield Park and here may be seen those locomotives not actually in steam, some undergoing repair and some restoration.

At the northern end of the line Horsted Keynes station is unusually spacious, with five platforms. The predominant atmosphere here is one of Southern Railway days, with decor in accordance with that company's colour scheme. Again refreshments are available from the original refreshment room on the island platform (2 and 3), but the premises like those at Sheffield Park are now unlicensed. As one approaches Horsted Keynes by train, the large carriage shed is passed on the east side of the track; this is the headquarters of the Carriage

and Wagon Department. Adjoining the station is a large picnic area in a delightfully rural setting with the station facilities conveniently to hand.

A round trip on the railway can be made in just under three-quarters of an hour, but this leaves little time for inspecting the many attractive exhibits after the first leg of the journey. You do not, however, have to return immediately, for the choice of train is your own.

For those wishing to visit the railway in their own cars, Sheffield Park station lies just off the A275 East Grinstead to Lewes road, approximately midway between those towns.

Horsted Keynes station, situated in the middle of nowhere and over a mile from the village of that name, is approached by secondary roads, the most direct of which is that from West Hoathly to Horsted Keynes, thence along a

L. & S. W. R. 4-4-2, built in 1885, No. 488, was designed for suburban passenger work, but ended her British Rail days on the tortuous Lyme Regis branch in 1960.

road running westwards at Great Oddynes turning. There is also another approach, this time from the west, using a turning off the B2028 Turners Hill–Lindfield road at a point south of Ardingly and which includes, shortly before reaching the station, an extremely restricted bridge over which Bluebell trains pass. Should you have need to ask the way, the correct pronunciation of Keynes is 'Canes', whilst Ardingly is locally 'Arding-lie'.

A long-term Bluebell project involves the possible re-instatement of the 6¼-mile connection between Horsted Keynes and East Grinstead, linking up at the latter with the Southern Region's route from London via East Croydon and Oxted. This would include the Imberhorne Viaduct at East Grinstead and the 730-yard-long West Hoathly tunnel. There are,

however, many problems to be overcome, such as the sale by British Railways of some of the original route to nearby landowners, and the filling-in of a cutting towards East Grinstead. Much diplomacy and patience will have to be exercised if the scheme is to be brought to fruition.

Stock
The Bluebell Railway today offers a wide selection of locomotives, passenger coaches and goods wagons. Of the locomotives, the most numerous of one class are three ex-S.E. & C.R. P class tanks, Nos. 27, 323, and 1178. Next come two ex-L.B. & S.C.R. 'Terrier' tanks, Nos. 55, *Stepney* (Bluebell's first engine) and No. 72 *Fenchurch*. (The latter was built in 1872 and was among the preserved locomotives in steam at the Shildon 'Rail 150' parade in 1975.) These five small engines provide a striking contrast with four tender engines; Nos. 21C123, *Blackmore Vale*, of West Country class; a British Railways 4-6-0, No. 75027; an ex-Great-Western 4-4-0 Dukedog class, No. 3217, *Earl of Berkeley*; and

41

Wainwright C class No. 592, built in 1901, here heads one of the goods trains which the Bluebell Railway runs each month for photography and authenticity.

finally an ex-S.E. & C.R. C class 0-6-0, No. 592. Between these extremes are several medium-sized engines: an ex-L.B. & S.C.R. E4 class 0-6-2T, No. 473, *Birch Grove*; an ex-L. & S.W.R. Adams radial 4-4-2T, No. 488, an ex-S.E. & C.R. H class 0-4-4-T, No. 263, a 0-6-0T, No. 2650 from the old North London Railway; and an American 0-6-0T (used by S.R. after World War II at Southampton Docks). Two tiny locomotives deserve mention; an ex-L. & S.W.R. Docks tank, No. 96 (which for many years could be seen shunting wagons round the sharp curves at Winchester City station); and finally *Baxter*, which spent the greater part of its life in the quarries at Betchworth in Surrey. Both of these last two engines are 0-4-0 tanks. The entire range of locomotives embraces some 105 years of progress in design and construction.

Passenger rolling stock, too, covers a long period of development. Pre-grouping railways are well represented, yet one may travel if one wishes in British-Railways-built compartment coaches. The 'in-between' period of the Southern Railway is represented by the products of Maunsell and Bulleid. (The latter, in the writer's opinion, are the acme of comfort and layout.) Three further vehicles are worthy of special mention, these being the old L.B. & S.C.R. Directors' saloon, carried on six-wheel bogies; a rather similar vehicle originating from the old Great Northern Railway; and a London and North Western observation car once used on the scenic lines of North Wales.

The first-named vehicles are used only on special occasions when their limited seating capacity is not a drawback. The observation car however, is used frequently, passengers in it being charged a small supplementary fare. It has a useful seating capacity of seventy-two. Other passenger vehicles will be seen, reserved for departmental use. Curiously, it was until 1974 possible to make the Bluebell trip seated in bogie coach No. 3339 from the Caledonian Railway, but this vehicle has now returned to Scotland. This was not, however, the only Caledonian product to visit Sussex: on 15 September 1963 the famous 'Caley Single' No. 123 came to the Bluebell on a special train from Victoria. In her blue livery, with whitewashed coal, she was a

ABOVE: *Inside the cab of No. 592.*

RIGHT: *West Country class 21C123,* Blackmore Vale, *here leaving Sheffield Park, was built in 1946 to Bulleid's design, and joined the Bluebell in 1971 after withdrawal from B.R. Southern Region in 1967.*

wonderful sight; she attracted large crowds throughout the day.

A journey down the line

The Bluebell traveller will see rural England at its best as the train threads its way through farmland interspersed with woods and copses displaying masses of bluebells, primroses and other wild flowers. Wild life of all varieties can be seen, especially from the first train of the day in the summer. The noise of the approaching train sends birds of many species into the air.

Shortly after leaving Sheffield Park station, you may see a white post on the east of the track, inscribed 'Greenwich Meridian': the Bluebell must be the only preserved line to serve two hemispheres. Next is the bridge spanning the River Ouse; little more than a brook in summer, it rises to turbulent levels after autumn rains. In the 1830s, the river was the scene of great

USA tank No. 30064 approaches Horsted Keynes on a November evening. The tank was withdrawn from Eastleigh shed in 1967, having worked to the end of steam on the Southern Region. It appeared in the film Young Winston.

activity when some eleven million Dutch-made bricks were ferried up-river from Newhaven to the thirty-seven-arch viaduct a few miles upstream from Sheffield Park on the Brighton main line. Little remains of this giant task – disused locks here and there, a building named 'Wharf Cottage' by the A275 near Sheffield Bridge, and an inn named 'The Sloop' overlooking the once-navigable river.

The area around
The surrounding countryside has much to offer in the way of stately homes, gardens, and other attractions open to the public during the summer. Of these the most convenient are the National Trust gardens at Sheffield Park (the mansion is privately owned) and Wings Haven Bird Sanctuary and Hospital (where birds are restored to health after accident or illness). In the grounds of Beech Hurst Park on the A272 road at Haywards Heath, the Sussex Miniature Locomotive Society operates, on summer weekends and Bank Holidays from 2 to 5.30 p.m., a service of trains on tracks of $3\frac{1}{2}$ in. and 5 in. gauge, over a circuit of half a mile. Trains carry passengers and are hauled by a wide variety of steam locomotives modelled on their main-line counterparts, plus some of 'freelance' design. Rather further afield, at Hove, is the Brighton and Hove Engineerium, housed in the old Goldstone Pumping station. There is an admission fee here, but among the many exhibits is an extremely rare working beam engine recreating the earliest days of steam power.

Romney, Hythe and Dymchurch Light Railway

The line and its history

The Kent Coast is justifiably popular among holiday makers, one much-favoured area being that in the south-east of the County. Here one finds a railway of world-wide repute known as the Romney, Hythe and Dymchurch Light Railway. It is in no sense a preserved line, having provided local people and holiday makers with a summer service since its opening in 1927 (although closed to the public during World War II). The main terminus is at Hythe, from which, travelling in a westerly direction, trains run alongside the Royal Military Canal (a defence relic from the Napoleonic Wars). The line then traverses a portion of Romney Marsh, before arriving at Dymchurch, a place famous for its association with Russell Thorndyke's novels about Dr Syn. St Mary's Bay follows, after which one arrives at the busy station of New Romney, headquarters of the line and $8\frac{1}{4}$ miles from the starting point. The railway, following the wide sweep of St Mary's Bay, continues through more holiday centres, now running southwards, and arrives at Dungeness ($13\frac{3}{4}$ miles) with its great shingle banks and lighthouses. Dungeness, however, is not a true terminus, for before reaching the station the railway divides and describes a giant loop round which trains run in a clockwise direction. The station is approximately in the centre of the loop, and affords an intriguing sight of the approaching and departing trains.

One might think the line just a coastal route which has escaped the axe, but it is laid to a gauge of fifteen inches (approximately one quarter of the standard gauge), and in the summer, it carries passengers by the thousand.

In the early nineteen-twenties, two racing drivers were making headlines – Captain J. E. P. Howey, and Count Zbrowski, by birth a Pole. Both men were steam enthusiasts as well as racing drivers, and this combination led to a close friendship. Together they planned a 15 in. gauge railway, to use steam as motive power, and situated in a locality with commercial possibilities. Unfortunately, before their plans matured the Count was killed in a car crash at Monza. Although Captain Howey was thus left to pursue the scheme on his own, he did continue, and the Romney, Hythe and Dymchurch Light Railway was built. The first section of the railway was opened in June 1927, from Hythe to New Romney; the extension to Dungeness followed in two stages in 1928–9. The Southern Railway supported the new line, for it provided a link between two of their ailing branches, that from Sandling Junction to Hythe and that from Appledore to Dungeness and New Romney. Unfortunately the coming of the family car blunted any possible increase in passengers on these branches; both have been closed.

Stock

Captain Howey appointed for his Engineer the late Mr Henry Greenly, who had vast experience in miniature railway design. For motive power, Greenly designed Pacific-type engines which were Gresley's fine A1 class scaled down, in the case of rail gauge to approximately quarter-scale, and, since there were no loading-gauge problems, to one-third full-size for the superstructures. This enabled him to use large boilers, and he blended the two scales so cleverly that there is no difference whatever to the average observer. Ten steam locomotives were built between 1925 and 1931, eight of which were of the 4-6-2 wheel arrangement and the remainder 4-8-2s. Until 1927, all the locomotives were built by Davey Paxman of Colchester: they supplied six Pacifics and the two 4-8-2s. The two further Pacifics were delivered in 1931 from the Yorkshire Engine Co. Ltd, both being based on Canadian Pacific practice, in striking contrast to the Gresley-outline Pacifics and original 4-8-2s. In early days the locomotives and trains were equipped with the Westinghouse automatic air brake, but the detailed precision required for maintenance in such a small scale prompted the substitution of the automatic vacuum brake, which is now standard on the railway. Passenger rolling stock comprised four- and eight-wheel coaches, and wagons were put into service too, in anticipation of a certain amount of goods traffic.

The official opening took place on Saturday 16

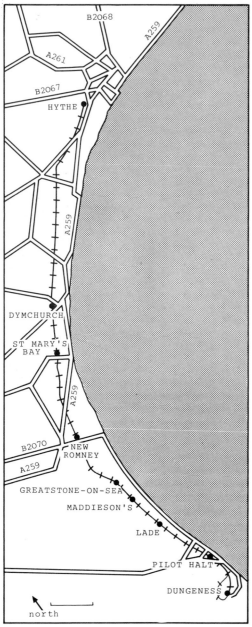

the engines and was granted a footplate ride, accompanied by Captain Howey and Nigel (later Sir Nigel) Gresley; the journey began at a bridge, since named 'Duke of York's Bridge'.

After the official opening, the railway provided an all-the-year-round service. The winter service however, was not a success, for local residents, aware of conditions when the winds blew across the Channel direct from a frozen Continent, wisely remained indoors. But trains in the holiday season were packed, as the area began to develop. The line prospered until the outbreak of World War II. With the fall of France in 1940, the R.H. & D.R. found itself in a prohibited area, and for the remainder of the War its trains became part of the War effort; an armoured train was built and run. The railway's greatest achievement came before the Allied landings in Normandy in 1944. It had been decided to supply the invasion forces with petrol from England by means of an undersea pipe line, safe from enemy action. The feed source of 'PLUTO' (Pipe Line Under The Ocean) was at Lade, between New Romney and Dungeness. The R.H. & D.R. was used to convey the piping and all necessary equipment to the site, after its transfer from the Southern Railway. As can well be imagined, the rolling stock and track took a terrible pounding. After the War, two years were needed to restore the line to running order. This restoration was very costly and Captain Howey decided to reinstate only a single line towards Dungeness from New Romney, instead of the original double track. The reopening was performed by the two world-famous comedians Stan Laurel and Oliver Hardy.

Captain Howey died in 1963; his life-long interest passed into the control of others; nevertheless the line carries on as ever, its trains still hauled by those magnificently designed and built locomotives dating from the late 1920s.

The area around

Whilst in the area, do not miss a marshland tour by car. Here is an expanse of pasturage where sheep may safely graze and small villages cluster around giant parish churches. In the graveyard at St Mary-in-the-Marsh is buried E. Nesbit, authoress of *The Railway Children* (filmed first nearly 20 years ago by the B.B.C. on the S.R.

July 1927, but almost a year before this, whilst the line was still under construction, a member of the Royal Family showed interest in what was going on. In those days a children's holiday centre at Jesson was sponsored by the then Duke of York (later King George VI). It was known as the Duke of York's Camp. His Royal Highness expressed a wish to travel on one of

At the Dungeness terminus, the driver prepares Hurricane *for the return to Hythe. Behind are the old Dungeness lighthouse, and 'A' and 'B' nuclear power stations.*

Horsham–Guildford branch, and latterly for the large screen on the preserved Keighley and Worth Valley Railway).

A marshland church worthy of note is St Augustine's at Brookland, on the main A259 road. Its unique feature is that it has a spire resembling three candle extinguishers one above the other, standing not on the traditional tower, but at ground level by the church. The writer has heard that after all material had been delivered, it was realized that the marshy foundations would not bear the weight of both tower and spire.

Just inland, at the Dungeness end of the line, is the little town of Lydd, from which was derived the name of the explosive Lyddite. The parish church of All Saints, devastated by bombing in 1940 and rebuilt 1951–8, deserves a visit; it is quite breathtaking and it fully justifies its reputation as 'The Cathedral of the Marsh'.

The Kent and East Sussex Railway

The line and its history

The Kent and East Sussex Railway owes its origin to the late Colonel H. F. Stephens, a pioneer of light railway projects in this country, and dates from 1900. It was then known as the Rother Valley Light Railway. It linked Robertsbridge, on the main South Eastern and Chatham Railway London–Hastings line, with the market town of Tenterden – or at least within one-and-a-half miles of the latter! As its name implies, the railway traversed the valley of the River Rother (sometimes referred to as the Eastern Rother in order to avoid confusion with the Western Rother at the opposite end of Sussex), and its length was some twelve miles. Often called 'The Farmers' Line' it ran through open country devoted almost entirely to agriculture, with the accent on fruit and hops. The railway was extended in 1902, first to Tenterden Town after a stiff climb out of the valley, and then in 1904–5, through Biddenden, to Headcorn, a station on the S.E. & C.R.'s main London–Dover route. The total length of the railway was now twenty-one-and-a-half miles, and plans were made for further extensions.

Lack of capital, however, and very heavy engineering problems, prevented these being put in hand and Colonel Stephens contented himself with the Robertsbridge to Headcorn line, renaming it the Kent and East Sussex Light Railway; the original Tenterden station was renamed Rolvenden. The boundary between the two counties occurs where the railway crosses the River Rother just to the east of Northiam station.

A remarkable collection of locomotives was acquired to run the line. These included some outside-cylinder tank engines; 'Terrier' 0-6-0 tank engines from the L.B. & S.C.R.; a couple of 0-6-0 tender engines of the Ilfracombe goods class of the L. & S.W.R.; and, last but not least, a sturdy 0-8-0 tank engine weighing no less than $43\frac{1}{2}$ tons. This unique engine, named *Hecate*, saw but little service. Much too heavy for the lightly laid track, she was acquired by the Southern Railway in 1932, being utilized for stock marshalling at Clapham Junction, a duty for which she was well suited.

Passenger rolling stock, too, was very varied, including bogie, six-wheeled and four-wheeled coaches from various pre-grouping companies, mainly the L. & S.W.R. Among the four-wheeled examples was the royal saloon built for the South Western Railway in 1848. With the increase in road competition three different versions of rail car were tried – one steam-driven and two with internal combustion engines, but they achieved little success. A miscellaneous collection of goods wagons completed the picture.

The K. & E.S.R. escaped grouping in 1923 and preserved its identity right up to nationalization, apart from a period during World War II when it was requisitioned. At that time the Southern Railway loaned several locomotives to keep trains moving. Upon nationalization, the line was merged into the Southern Region, but its passenger services were withdrawn in 1954. Goods traffic continued on the Robertsbridge–Tenterden section until complete closure in 1961. For the last few years the goods traffic was operated by a 0-6-0 Drewry diesel locomotive, which on occasion hauled special passenger trains. It is interesting to note that during this period a steam engine was kept in reserve at St Leonards nearby.

Preservation

Immediately after closure, enthusiasts proposed plans for operating the line as a tourist attrac-

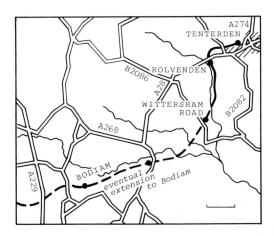

G.W.R. diesel railcar No. 20, built in 1940, provides a Sunday morning service on the Kent and East Sussex line.

tion, using volunteer labour. They persevered in the face of endless obstruction from B.R. and the Ministry of Transport. A severe set-back occurred when the then Minister of Transport refused sanction to re-open the section between Robertsbridge and Bodiam because of its main-road level crossings. This reduced the line to the Tenterden–Bodiam length, some ten miles, and isolated it from all B.R. contact. The pre-servationists pressed on however. They re-claimed station buildings, track, bridges and signalling equipment, ready for the day when the bark of 'Terrier' tanks would again echo over the countryside. This work could be done only at weekends, for all the volunteer staff were otherwise occupied during the week. Reward for their efforts came in 1974, when the line from Tenterden to Rolvenden was passed for traffic; and passengers could be carried for the first time since 1954. All this had been done by volunteer labour as had been intended, but

in 1976 the K. & E.S. was able to take advantage of the Government's Job Creation programme. The scheme worked well and within months rather than years, the line has been extended to Wittersham Road. It is not yet over the border into Sussex, but there is a five-mile run from Tenterden. The next phase of restoration will take the railway over the county boundary into East Sussex, and the Railway's title will be fully justified.

Stock

Over the years there has been a steady influx of locomotives and rolling stock, and its wide variety would surely have made Colonel Stephens sigh with envy. Appropriately, the locomotive stock includes two ex-L.B. & S.C.R. 'Terrier' tanks. One has quite a history, for it is the one which Colonel Stephens bought to work his original Rother Valley line in 1901. It was then No. 3 on the Company's books, and named *Bodiam*. Built at Brighton Works in 1872, it carried the name *Poplar* until it came to the Rother Valley. Apart from some prolonged periods of inactivity, it performed its daily tasks

49

This L.B. & S.C.R. 'Terrier' (Stroudley A1 class) was built in 1876. In the tradition of the L.B. & S.C.R., it was named to match the locality in which it worked, and so, built as Whitechapel, *it became* Fishbourne *when moved to the Isle of Wight in 1930, and was nameless from 1937, when used for shunting duties. In 1963, it was sold to Sutton Borough Council, and named* Sutton. *Here, it crosses the A28 towards Wittersham Road, piloting the Norwegian No. 19, which is running tender-first, and hence is only just visible.*

right up to nationalization, when B.R. robbed it of its name and renumbered it 32670, thus restoring it to its original slot in the 'Terrier' list. Upon the withdrawal of the Tenterden passenger service in 1954, B.R. transferred it to Hampshire, where it worked the Hayling Island branch until the closure of that in 1963. It was then purchased privately. The new owner placed it on permanent loan to the K. & E.S.R.; it now proudly bears again its number '3' and of course its name, *Bodiam*. *Bodiam*'s shed mates include the other 'Terrier', No. 10, *Sutton*; a

S.E. & C.R. P class 0-6-0 tank, which bears the name *Pride of Sussex* (bestowed on it by its previous owners, who traded in that county), and some saddle tanks and one side tank complete the list of small engines. The larger engines include an American tank named *Maunsell*, sister engine *Wainwright*, three Hunslet Austerity 0-6-0 tanks, and a Norwegian State Railways 2-6-0 tender engine. Whilst it is interesting to see so wide a variety of locomotives, one is tempted to ask what will happen when spare parts are needed – particularly for the Norwegian engine, on which everything is doubtless to metric measurements. In addition to steam, diesels are also used as a form of motive power – they even have an ex-Great-Western railcar.

Passenger rolling stock is equally varied, with Pullman cars, Maunsell coaches, ex-S.E. & C.R. 'birdcages', an L. & S.W.R. bogie coach, and a unique four-wheel brake-end coach of London and North Western Railway origin. The goods stock side has not been neglected, and much renovation work has been done. Apart from a Shell tank wagon, all

Norwegian 2-6-0 No. 19 rounds Orpin's curve just outside Tenterden. Built in 1919, it provides the motive power for many of the K. & E.S.R.'s scheduled services.

vehicles appear to bear K. & E.S.R. lettering, which tends to obscure their true pedigree.

The K. & E.S.R., like the Bluebell line, is one of those lines where one can hear the once-familiar sound of the Westinghouse donkey pumps of the air brakes on the ex-L.B. & S.C.R. and Norwegian State locomotives, and most people would agree that the melodious note of steam whistles is preferable to the banshee braying of the two-tone horns carried on today's trains and locomotives.

Access and the area around

How does one get to the K. & E.S.R.; what other attractions are there in the area? Access is by road, with Tenterden and Rolvenden served by the A28 between Hastings and Ashford. This in turn is intersected at Northiam (which the railway has yet to reach) by the A268 Rye–Flimwell road, the latter diverging at Flimwell from the A21 London–Hastings road. From Maidstone and the Medway towns, use the A274 to Biddenden, turning eastwards there and finally converging with the A28 north of Tenterden. And if you have been to, or wish to go on to the Romney, Hythe and Dymchurch Railway, your road is the B2080 Tenterden–New Romney. Furthermore, a visit to the K. & E.S.R. will bring you to a historic corner of England. Bodiam Castle is an almost perfect example of a moated stronghold, dating back to 1386. Battle Abbey near Hastings is a little further afield. Other places of interest within easy reach are the Hastings Old Town (with its Castle), St Clement's Caves, and Winchelsea, and Rye, which will both well repay a visit. As you drive around you will notice features peculiar to this part of the Kent/Sussex borders, such as a wealth of weather-boarded houses, and those buildings with a cone-shaped tiled roof surmounted by a white rotating cowl. These are oast houses, once used for drying hops by a method now almost, if not quite, obsolete. The solidly built oast houses have survived.

The Mid-Hants 'Watercress' Railway

The line and its history

The Mid-Hants 'Watercress' line operated between Winchester and Alton for nearly 108 years before it was closed by British Railways in 1973. Why 'Watercress'? The line runs through part of the Itchen valley, a river whose water favours the growth of excellent cress.

The railway was built by a private company, as the Alton, Alresford and Winchester Railway. Generally speaking it followed an east–west course. It left the main London–Southampton line at Winchester Junction, some two miles north of Winchester station, and after a 17-mile run, made an end-on junction at Alton with the L. & S.W.R. branch at that place. The countryside is undulating, entailing stiff gradients in places, especially between Medstead and Alton. The route was often referred to as 'Over the Alps'. The L. & S.W.R. bought out the private company in 1884, and used the line as an alternative route to Southampton in addition to their existing service via Basingstoke and Worting Junction. However, when the Southern Railway electrified the Woking–Farnham–Alton line in 1937, through services were withdrawn and a purely local service between Southampton Terminus and Alton, via Eastleigh and Winchester, took their place. The line became a preserve for the ex-

L. & S.W.R. 0-4-4 tanks, class M7, usually with two, sometimes with three coaches. The two-coach trains were for the most part pull-and-push units; this simplified movements at Alton, now the terminus for a half-hourly electric train service. When diesel-electric multiple units ('Hampshire units') took over from steam in November 1957, a more frequent even-interval service – still between Southampton Terminus and Alton – was introduced, and passenger traffic increased in consequence. Steam traction did not entirely disappear, for the line provided a useful alternative route when the main London to Southampton was obstructed by derailments or engineering work, (the latter particularly at weekends). Owing to the heavy gradients, many of these diverted trains required double heading and an hour or so spent by the Watercress line could prove very rewarding to the engine spotter.

British Railways' proposal to close it in 1968 met with severe opposition both from rail users and Rural District Councils. At length, after three or more public enquiries, the Ministry of Transport confirmed their previous closure decision. The line ceased operating in February 1973.

Preservation

An effort to continue train services resulted in the formation of two companies, The Winchester and Alton Railway Ltd, and the Mid-Hants Railway Preservation Society Ltd, of which the former, in 1975, endeavoured to raise the necessary funds by a public share issue amount-

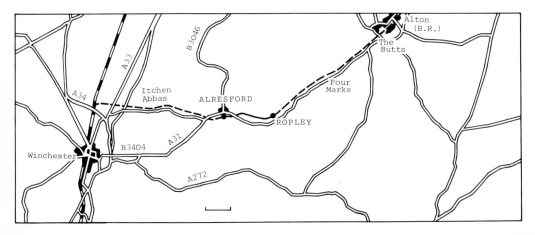

Tablet exchange at Alresford on the Mid-Hants. The S.R. class N, No. 31874, now named Anzar Line *after the company who helped financially in its restoration, was built largely of parts made at Woolwich Arsenal as part of a scheme to relieve post World War I unemployment, and actually assembled, as a mixed-traffic loco, at Ashford.*

ing to over £600,000. The result, after the forty statutory days, was most discouraging; the hoped-for through train service had to be curtailed into the section of line between Alresford and Alton, towards which the necessary capital was assured. By this time British Rail had lifted the track between Alton and Ropley, but had been persuaded not to lift that between Ropley and Alresford, a distance of 2¾ miles. This is the Preservation Society's initial running track. Should this short section prosper, it is hoped to relay the 7¼ miles between Ropley and Alton. Unless the economic situation changes very much for the better, the odds seem rather against so ambitious a project, attractive though it might sound. Much will depend upon support given by the public to the Alresford–Ropley venture, where, with both stations only just off the main A31 Alton–Winchester road, any question of inaccessibility should not arise.

Stock

An interesting collection of ex-Southern-

Railway locomotives can be seen, among them being N class 2-6-0, No. 31874; a Urie-designed 4-6-0 of the S15 class, No. 30506 (actually built at Eastleigh in L. & S.W.R. days); and a U class 2-6-0, No. 31806. Apart from these three powerful tender engines, there are two saddle tank locomotives, one a 0-6-0 of Hudswell Clarke origin, and the other a Bagnall 0-4-0. A number of passenger coaches arrived on site a few days before the tracks were lifted by British Rail east of Ropley; all future deliveries will of necessity have to be made by road transport. Meanwhile the work of restoration continues. The first train to Ropley ran on 12 June 1977, and brisk business has been done at weekends throughout the first seasons.

The area around

Only eight miles away is the cathedral city of Winchester, once capital of Wessex. The present Cathedral dates back to Norman days and superseded a much earlier Saxon building. The city too has much of interest to offer. There is now only one railway station, that on the old L. & S. W. R. London–Southampton main line, although until recent years the Didcot, Newbury and Southampton Railway served the town at an entirely separate station eventually named Winchester Chesil. From 1957 onwards, for a few years, a celebrated engine was seen on this line: the G.W.R.'s *City of Truro* was brought out of retirement, and overhauled for use on enthusiasts' specials. In between times she did light duties on the G.W.R. line to Southampton. But her re-activated life lasted only a few years – she is now in Swindon Museum.

Should you prefer wild animals to cathedral cities, there is, on the Winchester–Portsmouth A333 road, at Colden Common, about half way between Winchester and Bishops Waltham, the Marwell Zoological Park. The surrounding countryside has rolling hills attractive villages and small towns, and the Meon Valley (through which a railway once ran from Alton to Fareham but now, alas, is no more). The economy axe has fallen very heavily upon railways of Hampshire, and its eastern neighbour Sussex; but thanks to preservationists, all is not lost.

The Isle of Wight Steam Railway

The line and its history

The Isle of Wight was formerly covered with a fairly comprehensive railway network. The centre of the system was Newport, and from the west the Freshwater, Yarmouth and Newport Railway ran almost directly to the island's capital. Running almost due north–south, splitting the Isle in half, was the Isle of Wight Central Railway. There were two connecting branches from this line to another north–south railway in the east. This was the Isle of Wight Railway, still in operation, although in a reduced form. It ran from Ryde Pier Head, south to Ventnor. It is rather sad that an island which was once so rich in steam railways is now reduced to a short electric line and one preserved steam society. The Isle of Wight Steam Locomotive Society operates a restricted section of track north from Haven Street Station, towards Wooton. This is part of the former Isle of Wight Central Railway, the northernmost link between the Cowes–Ventnor line and the east coast line. It ran from Newport to Smallbrook Junction and today is derelict except for the restored section.

Unfortunately the island's railways proved to be unpopular amongst the local inhabitants. They were really designed for holidaymakers, and their prices and facilities were attuned to their requirements. Fares were high in the winter season when there were no trippers to fill the trains, and there were few third-class carriages. Until 1914 trains were composed of first- and second-class stock only. As soon as the motor car started to steal away passengers in the post-war period, the railways began to suffer. The Isle of Wight was among the steam railways to suffer closures. Some had argued that the island had an over-generous supply of lines anyway. In 1952 the Merstone–Ventnor section was shut down. Then in the following September, the Freshwater-Newport line was closed, the only line in the west. The Newport–Sandown branch managed to survive until February 1956. There was a storm of protest over this spate of closures and the Transport Commission was forced to pledge that five years' notice would be given in future if any more closures were being considered. This promise was repudiated in 1964. It was argued that the publication of the Beeching Report effectively annulled the earlier agreement. Ryde–Cowes passenger trains (including the Haven Street section) ceased to run from 21 February 1966, Shanklin–Ventnor closed in the following April, and freight services ended in the May. The only remaining line, Ryde Pier to Shanklin, was temporarily closed for electrification, and re-opened in March 1967 using ex-London Transport tube stock.

Stock

For forty years or so, L. & S.W.R. 0-4-4 tank No. 24, *Calbourne* (class 02), served the Island's railways. She was one of the first purchases when the moves to preserve something of the I.O.W.'s unique railway heritage were made. Overhauled in 1976–7, she headed all the passenger trains run in the 1977 season. Before that, the mainstay of the 'tourist' service was a Hawthorn Leslie 0-4-0 saddle tank, No. 37, *Invincible*, originally built for the Woolwich Arsenal during World War I. She had to be fitted with Westinghouse brake equipment to make her suitable for passenger work. She has outside cylinders, and is in a mid-green livery, lined in yellow and black.

Recently restored is a 'Terrier', an A1X class 0-6-0, No. 11, *Newport*. Originally L.B. & S.C.R. No. 40, *Brighton*, she was sold to the I.W.C.R. in 1902. Withdrawn from B.R. in 1963, she returned to the I.O.W. Steam Railway in 1973 after a time at a Butlin's camp, and is now restored to I.W.C. livery: white-and-red-lined black, with 'I W C' in gold. The 'Terriers' were designed by William Stroudley for use on the L.B. & S.C.R., and introduced in 1872. Though relatively small and simple, they were exceptionally powerful for their size, with a tractive effort of 10,695 lb. They were used for light shunting and short passenger trains. Those which operated on the Southern were named after the districts they served. (*Stepney* and *Fenchurch* are now on the Bluebell line; *Bodiam* and *Sutton* on the Kent and East Sussex.)

There is also an industrial 0-6-0, *Ajax*, and a Ruston Hornsby diesel.

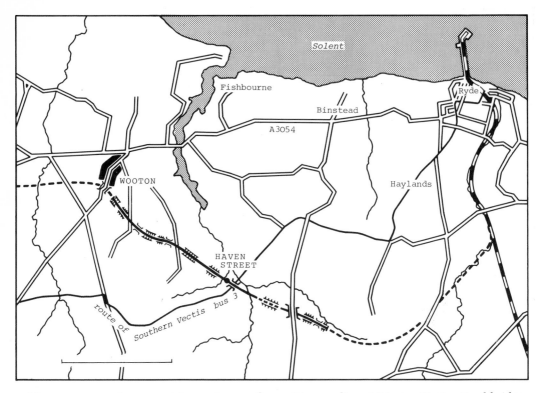

There are several appropriate carriages, of L.B. & S.C.R., L.C.D.R., S.E. & C.R. or I.W.R. origin. The three in regular use for the passenger service are non-corridor compartments, and fit in perfectly with the general atmosphere. They have been repainted in Southern green and had yellow '3's painted on the carriage doors. Inside, they still have the moquette-covered benches and small framed advertisements and maps. Leather straps with perforations are used to open the windows, and there are running boards to assist entry. When sitting in one of these behind a 'Terrier' chugging through the pleasant countryside it is easy to imagine that one is back fifty or so years.

A journey down the line

Though the journey from Haven Street to Wooton is not particularly long, it is certainly picturesque. Haven Street station was rebuilt by the Southern Railway in 1926, a passing place on the Ryde–Newport line. Leaving this station, the line passes between fields bordered with trees and thick hedges. The fields give way to woods, and the line passes through a thickly wooded cutting, ending at Wooton Station Road bridge. The train has to stop here, some two miles from Haven Street. The original Wooton Station, on the other side of the bridge, was closed, and the buildings demolished, in 1953. Although it was hoped to re-open on the original site, an extensive land slip has made that impossible. A completely new Wooton Station is therefore being built, designed with care to I.O.W. railway traditions.

New sidings and inspection pits are being built at Haven Street, and a small shed and workshop is planned. At first, when the train reached Wooton, it had to back to Haven Street. Run-round facilities at Wooton are now complete, however.

Haven Street Station has a small museum nearby, which has a collection of station signs, signals, rail chairs, timetables, tickets, badges and photographs. The station, an island platform, has a water tower intact, and the original semaphore signals have survived.

Access

Southern Vectis bus 3, from Newport, stops

At the Isle of Wight Railway headquarters at Haven Street, L. & S.W.R. 0-4-4 Calbourne *takes on fuel.*

outside Haven Street station. On steam days, tickets including a ride on the Railway are available from many S.R. stations, as 'Away-days'. Operation is on Sundays and Bank Holidays from May to September, with some mid-week trains in peak season.

The area around
Newport, the island's commercial capital, is not far from Haven Street, situated on the River Medina.

Carisbrooke was of course the island's former capital. It was both a market and administrative centre. As a result the Isle's major castle was built here. The main buildings are set on a plateau 150 feet above sea level. The turrets and walls date from the Norman to the Jacobean period demonstrating a continuing pre-occupation with military security. The keep is Norman. The Well House is a restored sixteenth-century building, though the deep well was actually sunk in 1150. Water is still raised today in buckets wound up by donkeys. There is a fine museum depicting varied aspects of the island's history.

Slightly to the north and east of the railway is the village of Binstead. Here is Quarr Abbey, originally built by Cistercian monks in 1132. The monks were then forced out and it later became a defensive blockhouse, and then a farm. The ruins may now be compared with the new abbey maintained by the Benedictines who live half a mile distant. There is also a shell museum in the village.

The Sittingbourne and Kemsley Light Railway

The line and its history

Not all preserved steam railways in England are operated over former British Rail lines with standard-gauge locomotives. Many industrial concerns which required their raw materials brought some distance from depot or dock laid down their own railway system. Often these were of standard-gauge using small 0-6-0 tank engines to haul short trains to and from the works. Where the scale of the enterprise did not require such powerful engines, narrow-gauge railways were constructed. This was the case with the Sittingbourne paper mill. In 1906 a 2 ft 6 in. gauge railway was laid between the mill and a wharf at Milton Creek. The mill belonged to Edward Lloyd and Co. It was an expanding company and it was soon realized that the existing dock facilities were inadequate. Accordingly it was decided to build a dock on the River Swale which could accommodate ocean-going ships. Work started in 1913 but was interrupted the following year by the outbreak of World War I. The new dock was not completed until 1919. After the War the demand for newsprint rose steadily, so it was decided to construct a new and larger paper mill at Kemsley, half way along the line between Sittingbourne and Ridham. This was opened in 1924. A number of new locomotives were purchased to cope with the increased traffic using the railway. Fresh rolling stock was also acquired and extensive sidings laid down to accommodate the expansion in business. The railway continued to operate twenty-four hours a day throughout World War II. Never were the mills closed down because of any failure to get supplies through to the works. In 1948 Edward Lloyd was taken over by the large Bowater Group to form an additional part of their papermaking complex. More engines were purchased and the line well maintained. The most noticable acquisition in post-war years was the new Bagnall articulated 0-4-4-0 tank engine named *Monarch*. The line was working at its peak in the late 1950s, when there were no

less than 13 locomotives at work on the railway. The line was not only used to carry pulp and newsprint, but also to carry workmen to the mills, and so performed a passenger as well as a freight function.

In 1965 Bowaters called in a time-and-motion study group to assess the railway's efficiency. By this time railways generally were being closed down and steam engines were being withdrawn. Public opinion was against the line. The study concluded that the firm would be better off closing the line and employing a fleet of lorries. Bowater's reluctantly accepted this economic argument, but felt that part of the line should be preserved in recognition of its valuable service and interesting history. Consequently the firm contacted the Locomotive Club of Great Britain in 1969. They handed over the section of the line, a mile or so long, between Kemsley Down and Sittingbourne stations. They also donated three 0-4-2 saddle tanks, *Leader, Premier* and *Mellor*, and three 0-6-2 tank engines named *Alpha, Triumph* and *Superb*.

A journey down the line

The journey itself is quite varied. Starting at Sittingbourne the line moves north to cross

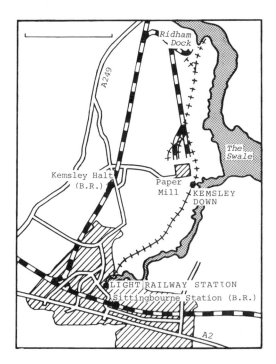

Bagnall 0-6-2 No. 2624 Superb *crosses the Milton Creek viaduct on the Sittingbourne and Kemsley Railway.*

Milton Creek. The surroundings here are not particularly attractive. The tracks are carried by a quarter-mile viaduct through an area of light industry and much debris. Milton Creek itself is not a clear stretch of water, but has been polluted by effluent from the paper mill.

The scenery improves once the Creek has been crossed. Marshy fields give way to a small orchard and Milton Regis church is visible. There are refreshments at both stations, as well as souvenir shops. A grassed picnic area has been established at Kemsley, together with swings for children. Parties are welcomed, though advance warning is preferred. Sittingbourne station can be reached from the British Rail town station in Milton Road. There are regular trains to here from Charing Cross, Waterloo, London Bridge and Victoria.

Stock
There is a wide variety of rolling stock preserved on the railway. At first the line was worked by teams of horses, but it was decided to change to steam, and three 0-4-2 saddle tanks were purchased, from Kerr-Stuart. These were manufactured in 1905 and introduced on the line three years later. Two of these have been preserved. They are No. 886, named *Premier*, and No. 926 *Leader*. These locomotives sufficed until 1920 when the first 0-6-2, *Superior*, was purchased, another Kerr-Stuart engine. Five more of this class were bought between 1932 and 1940, four brand new and manufactured by Bagnall, and one second-hand Manning Wardle built in 1915. These four have been retained and are being restored. They are No. 2216 *Unique*, No. 2472 *Alpha*, No. 2519 *Triumph*, and No. 2624 *Superb*. All the engines have outside frames, and special spark-arresting chimneys, a vital requirement in a paper mill. The 0-6-2 tank engines have prominent sand boxes fitted on

top of their boilers, which, with their wide-topped chimneys, make them look very American.

In addition, the Light Railway Company has acquired a number of types of narrow-gauge locomotives from elsewhere. There is a Hunslet diesel inherited from Bowaters. In October 1972 this loco was named *Victor* by the actor Richard Hearne. There is a Ruston and Hornsby diesel, No. 434403, which has been named *Edward Lloyd* after the first owner of the railway. It was built in 1961 and formerly worked on the Whipsnade Zoo Railway from whom it was purchased in 1972. There are two other, older, steam engines. Indeed the earliest loco is a Peckett 0-4-0 saddle tank. This is No. 614, *Bear*, built in 1896. There is also the anonymous No. 4, a Hawthorne Leslie 0-4-0 saddle tank (1926).

There are a variety of passenger coaches on the line. They included five former workmen's vehicles (one for staff use), an open coach constructed by the railway in 1971, and two open standees for use at peak periods. A semi-open coach with a welded tubular steel framework has also been built by the Company for passengers. Residual from the railway's freight days are the fifty wagons, mostly fitted with bogies. There is a variety of tippers, hoppers, coal and rubbish boxes, wooden- and steel-bodied flats. Some are in general use, while a selection have been restored in their original condition for permanent display.

There is a regular, timetabled service on Saturdays and Sundays from the end of March to mid-October, and extra trains on Easter and Summer Bank Holidays. The journey itself takes about fifteen minutes and there are trains about every half-hour. Full details appear in the British Rail timetable.

The area around
Unfortunately Sittingbourne is not a town with a rich history. The British Rail station on the former London Chatham and Dover Railway is possibly one of the most interesting features of the town. The buildings were erected as early as 1858 and in common with the company's other prestigious stations, the roofs were designed with elegant, delicately curved brackets supported by iron columns. It is a fairly simple brick structure which appears to have been enlarged in the 1870s. The line continued on eastwards either to Dover or Margate and was a popular holiday route for Londoners.

III
East Anglia

The Bressingham Live Steam Museum

Alan Bloom is a name known and respected not only in the world of preserved steam but also in the world of hardy plants.

At Bressingham, a small village on the boundary between Norfolk and Suffolk, by the River Waveney, is the embodiment of his vision of a living steam museum. Bressingham Hall offered him scope for both his farming and a horticultural nursery, and space to indulge his passion for steam. Since his purchase of the Hall in 1946, he has established what is now certainly a mecca for those fired by the same passion.

The small beginning was 'Bertha', a traction-engine made by the famous Burrell's of Thetford. From that start, the Live Steam Museum has grown, which is unique not only in having steam engines of all kinds, but also in its setting, within beautiful gardens, a busy farm and a thriving and interesting nursery.

Traction engines and steam wagons continued to arrive at Bressingham throughout the 50s, many in a state of abject deterioration through neglect, but all, in due course, to be lovingly and accurately restored. Steam-engine rallies were arranged there from 1963 on, and in this short space of time the collection of traction engines, steam-rollers, steam-wagons and portable engines was stretching the resources of the owner in time and cash to the limit. All had been purchased from Alan Bloom's own pocket. There are now fourteen engines that once used the roads, and the like of which played a vital part in East Anglian agriculture. Very recently a new exhibition hall has been built for them and there they may be enjoyed in their bright paint and shining brass-work.

The first visitors to Bressingham came to see the gardens which Mr and Mrs Bloom laid out on an acre of meadow in front of the Hall. To satisfy their love of plants, they allowed plants to grow naturally: island beds were carved out in the extensive lawns, and in them beautiful and often exotically rare plants displayed themselves.

It was in 1958 that, after a few special openings at the request of charitable organizations and for horticultural societies, the gardens were first opened to the public.

A visitor to the gardens in 1961, peering under the 'tilt' which sheltered 'Bertha' from the elements, asked if she could not be brought to life again. This probably really triggered off the chain of happenings which was to make the Bloom collection of steam engines in variety freely available for an enthusiastic public.

Bressingham Hall is now the nerve-centre of 480 acres of land and the estate is an entity. The intertwining of its various activities must be recorded. The farm, the nursery, the gardens, the Live Steam Museum, and the practical railways are all there on the same site. Each limb has its own particular function and its own unique attraction but all belong to the same body – hence the more than passing references to farm and nursery.

The arrival of railways

Steam railways now enter the scene. Rail locomotion, now the largest and most compellingly interesting part of the whole enterprise at Bressingham, began in a small way. A $9\frac{1}{2}$ in. gauge locomotive, freely modelled on the L.M.S. 4-6-2 Princess class, and built specially for passenger hauling, was purchased in 1964, along with five hundred yards of track and some

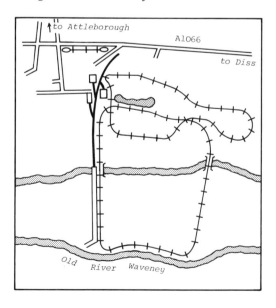

bogie trucks for passengers. Purists will look with a tinge of regret, perhaps, on its under-size wheels, but it is their reduced dimensions which provide a hauling capacity beyond what its size would suggest. In 1965 was born the 'Garden Railway', a 750-yard length of track on the northern boundary of the garden frontage, with turning loops at each end. Here it was discovered that visitors were eager to pay for their ride and this little railway was soon to have the appearance of a mini-commuter line as children, pressed by equally enthusiastic parents, surged forward to savour the thrill of steam propulsion.

The startling success of the Garden Railway encouraged further expansion. The more distant nursery fields (a riot of colour in the summer) and parts of the farm should not be completely out of bounds to visitors (although in a busy commercial enterprise they could not be allowed unlimited access). Alan Bloom's capacity to transform a hard necessity into a pleasant virtue is seen in his conclusion that a railway through the nursery fields, where winter access, because of the nature of the soil, was always hazardous, would serve business needs as well as provide an additional attraction for the visitors who were, after 1965, to make Bressingham a place of pilgrimage.

A journey to North Wales by Alan Bloom and his helper Roger Garnham was the prelude to the first two-foot-gauge railway through the nurseries. At the Penrhyn Slate Quarries, near the North Wales coast, steam had succumbed to diesel traction. Much of the steam equipment had already been sold but two engines, despite their sorry condition, looked capable of restoration at Bressingham. They, together with some track, a few slate-carrying trucks, and some venerable 'toast-rack' coaches provided for the slate workers, ended up at Bressingham. One of the locomotives still bore a name *George Sholto*; the other was not only nameless but also faceless, no more than a rust-ravaged chassis, but fortunately still equipped with its intriguing Walschaerts valve-gear, which holds many people spellbound with its graceful movement.

In 1966 the 'Nursery Line' of half a mile was at work. It ran along the northern edge of a two-acre lake, before doubling back alongside plunge beds where six hundred thousand pot-grown plants and alpines were laid out. It

Alan Bloom on the footplate of Bronllwyd, *one of the engines rescued from the Penrhyn Slate Quarries which now provide the motive power on the 2 ft gauge Nursery Line at Bressingham.*

operated from a station very near the entrance to the actual gardens, and became an immediate attraction. Extensions to the line had to be made, and it now provides a ride of over two miles, passing the large Museum building and the end of the lake down to the fen fields. Turning east, with woods and ditches on one side, it reaches a sandy area pleasantly dotted with oaks and birches, before turning westwards again and, having passed several fields of colourful flowers and myriads of pot plants, completes the circuit. The open 'toast-rack' coaches, while a bit primitive in appearance, are authentic for the gauge, and not only give passengers a clear view of the terrain, but also give them a closer appreciation of the feel and atmosphere of a locomotive at work. The writer has been invited by Mr Bloom to be at the regulator of a locomotive on this line and can vouch for the real thrill of the foot-plate. Four locomotives now share the work there and include *Bronllwyd*, the once-sorry chassis at Penrhyn; *Gwynedd*, also once at Penrhyn and built by the well-known Hunslet Engineering Company of Leeds; and *Eigiau* and *Brunhilde*, both of German origin. The Nursery Line is still as popular as ever and further interest is excited by the discovery, to the surprise of many passengers, that their driver is not only the driver, but also the founder of the whole enterprise. In his overalls, wielding his shovel, he undoubtedly gathers a whole store of visitors' reactions to Bressingham.

Just one narrow-gauge line traversing the farm land soon revealed its inadequacy to meet the demand for rides. So in the winter of 1968–9, another line was laid. The 'Woodland Line' took visitors due south from the station behind the museum, through an attractive avenue of mature trees down into the Waveney valley itself, and over the Bressingham Drain (a relief channel for the inadequate river). The work entailed in pioneering this route through swampy woods, involving bridge-building, drain-digging and track-laying, was daunting, done as it was in winter; it was completed, however, in time to enable the first trip over this line to be made on 17 May 1969. The southern part of this line took passengers on to higher ground where rhododendrons flourished in the spring, among the boxwood and the overhanging oaks and pines.

Four narrow-gauge railways were in operation between 1970 and 1972, the last one making use of the lake a short distance from the Museum. Till 1955 the lake was a small pond, but diggings with tractor-scoop then and later, to provide soil for the raising up of hollows in the adjoining fields and giving body to the soil, had increased it to an area of two acres. Water lilies and other aquatic plants soon established themselves, and with other flora colonizing the edges it had scenic qualities ripe for exploitation. In 1970 a $10\frac{1}{4}$ in. gauge track made a half-mile circuit round the lake, but the 'Lakeside' never

became a going concern, due largely to the constraints imposed by the sharp curves. So this railway ceased operation in 1972.

To cope with the ever-growing traffic, a railway of at least 15 in. gauge was needed. At about this time, two locomotives of this gauge in Germany were for sale. A dash to Cologne resulted in the arrival, just before Christmas 1972, of two very attractive 4-6-2 locomotives, and 19 well-appointed coaches. Built by the famous Krupps of Essen in 1937, for use in an exhibition park at Dusseldorf, they were then destined for a similar park by the Rhine at Cologne. But they were never used there, and Cologne's loss of *Rosenkavalier* and *Männertreu* became Bressingham's gain. In building the new 15 in. gauge railway, it soon became clear that a much more attractive line could be made by using only one side of the lake. To do so, however, would involve duplicating the existing Woodland Line. By the opening of the 1973 season, more than a mile of new track had been laid, crossing the Nursery Line on the level, and Bressingham Drain by a new bridge. The Woodland Line has now become the 'Waveney Line', $2\frac{1}{4}$ miles long and following much of the former line's course. While one two-foot-gauge line has had to go, Mr Bloom does not rule out that there may be another one in the future.

Standard-gauge locomotives

The standard-gauge railway locomotive section was the last to be established. It must be said that the standard-gauge engines there dwarf all other exhibits in majesty and beauty.

The over-hasty replacement of steam by diesel traction on British Railways presented enthusiasts with the opportunity of saving for preservation some of the glorious relics of the Age of Steam from the breakers and cutter's torch. It was open to anyone to acquire a

OPPOSITE, TOP: *G.W.R. pannier tank No. 6412 runs into Kingswear on the Torbay Steam Railway, before it was sold to the West Somerset Railway. The Royal Naval College, Dartmouth, dominates the hill.*

BOTTOM: *Also on the Torbay line, G.W.R. 2-6-2 side tank No. 4588 emerges from Greenway tunnel (p. 18).*

withdrawn locomotive if he could meet the scrap price (measured in thousands of pounds) together with the transport costs (which might well be more than the locomotive). Railway engines which had thrilled him were still fixed images in the vision of Alan Bloom and the more the vision was pondered the more insistent became its realization.

In 1968, the first standard-gauge locomotive, *William Francis*, the last of its kind in Great Britain, arrived. This locomotive was built on an articulated chassis with four cylinders powering two sets of driving wheels, and was redundant to the Coal Board. Another steam enthusiast, Mr J. R. Price, with the co-operation of the Association of Railway Preservation Societies, purchased it and had it removed from Baddesley Colliery to Bressingham. Its condition was poor, after a long period of neglect. The challenge of restoring it to its original form was a massive one, but the 1970 season saw it running along a track some two hundred yards long.

1951 had been a notable year on the Eastern Region of British Railways. The first B.R.-designed engines, Britannias, were assigned there. Something of a minor revolution in British locomotive design, they were, in 1952, on the line between Ipswich and Norwich which had never been the scene of very high speeds, responsible for the third fastest run in Great Britain. In 1961, Alan Bloom was accorded the privilege of a foot-plate ride from Diss to London on No. 70034, *Thomas Hardy*, of that class. Was this the seed of a later growth at Bressingham?

Under the Transport Act of 1968, certain steam locomotives were to be scheduled for preservation. The capacity of York and Clapham Museums would be insufficient for them — Clapham was due to close in any case. Of the Britannia class, the first of them, No. 70000, *Britannia*, was understandably the one marked

OPPOSITE, TOP: *Crossing the river on the Dart Valley line, G.W.R. tank 0-4-2 No. 1420 has the Devon Belle observation car leading the train (p. 12).*

BOTTOM: *The last Minehead–Williton train of the day turns inland from Watchet on the West Somerset Railway, headed by Bagnall 0-6-0 Victor, built in 1951 (p. 23).*

for preservation. Steam haulage on British Rail was to cease by the end of 1968, and another of the class No. 70013, *Oliver Cromwell*, recently overhauled at Crewe, was to be used on 'specials' until the final rites of sale for scrap. But *Oliver Cromwell* was finally allocated to the Bressingham Museum. In the autumn of 1968, by rail from Carlisle to Diss and thence by low-loader on road, it returned to within ear-shot of the sounds of its former great exploits. Meanwhile a museum building covering 12,500 square feet had been erected, a pre-condition of B.R. allocating engines to Bressingham.

In another building some twelve miles away at Attleborough, another episode in the saga of railway preservation had begun. In the old goods shed there, known to only a handful of people all sworn to secrecy, stood *Thundersley*, a 4-4-2 tank engine which had earned its keep on the London, Tilbury and Southend Railway. It was scheduled for preservation. The secret storage was necessary because railway relics, and especially any removable parts of locomotives, like name-plates, whistles and brass or copper accessories, had by then become big business, and 'asset-stripping' was growing apace. The Hellifield shed in West Yorkshire, its previous storage place, was insecure, and a move for *Thundersley* from there had become urgent. The museum building at Bressingham was not yet ready to take it. The Norfolk Railway Society found that the Attleborough goods shed could be made available. With a signalman on duty in the box opposite, its safety there seemed assured. Moreover, members of the Society, under the skilled direction and enthusiasm of Mr David (Bill) Harvey, ex-Shedmaster at Norwich, would undertake her restoration. In March 1968, the resplendent *Thundersley* emerged from her hiding-place to move to Bressingham, the first B.R. locomotive there on permanent loan (*Oliver Cromwell* was first in steam there on 22 September 1968).

The Live Steam Museum was now firmly established. British Rail, satisfied and pleased with the facilities, were to make other locomotives available and another was soon to join the three then there. Fittingly enough a 2-6-4 tank engine built by the L.M.S. in 1934 to replace the *Thundersley* class was allocated to Bressingham. Two industrial locomotives 'Beck-

Männertreu, a 15 in. gauge Krupps 4-6-2, heads a Waveney Valley Line train.

ton No. 25' and 'Beckton No. 1', had spent their life in London's gas-making town Beckton, on the Essex side of the Thames.

Butlin's Holiday Camps' proprietors had not been slow to appreciate the magnetic pull of a steam locomotive. Two of the most famous engines on the Midland Region (born in the L.M.S. era) had been allocated to holiday camps: the first was No. 6100, *Royal Scot*, built in 1927 by one of the most famous locomotive-building concerns in the country, the North British Locomotive Company of Glasgow, to inaugurate the big-engine policy of the former L.M.S. In the salt-laden air of Skegness, she had deteriorated sadly. In 1971 this historic locomotive came into care at Bressingham, where she was restored at terrific cost and steamed. The second was the last pre-1939 development in loco-motive engineering, the *Duchess of Sutherland*, built in 1938; a massive locomotive of 4-6-2 wheel arrangement, she had hauled the express trains on the West Coast route to Scotland in the

late thirties, among them the Coronation Scot; she was one of the most powerful class of that time. In 1971 as well, the *Duchess* was hauled 'dead' from Ayr to Diss, to be followed by one of the widely-loved 'Brighton Terrier' 0-6-0 tank engines, *Martello*, and a former stable-mate of *Royal Scot* at Skegness, a 0-4-0 which had seen service at Southampton docks.

More engines were to follow: *Solomon*, a small shunting engine, was removed from a plinth at Dagenham, where it had served at Messrs Samuel Williams Wharf Ltd; and *Mill-field*, a crane-engine from Sunderland (another presentation by Mr J. M. Price). Another ex-Great-Eastern engine was to come home, when the last steam locomotive to be stationed in East Anglia, a 0-6-0 of the powerful J17 class, one of the national collection, arrived to stand along-side the larger passenger engines.

With thirteen standard-gauge engines in his charge at Bressingham, Alan Bloom might well have been pardoned for declaring his hands to be full. They were indeed, but in 1975 two 'foreigners' were to find happy exile on Norfolk soil. Both these engines can only be described as

ABOVE: Royal Scot *was built in 1927 for the L.M.S., was withdrawn in 1962 and went to Butlin's at Skegness, whence she was transferred to Bressingham in 1971.* Royal Scot *was one of seventy locos in the Royal Scot class.*

RIGHT: Oliver Cromwell, *Riddles class 7MT, a 4-6-2, No. 70013, was built in 1951. After pulling the last B.R. steam train over the Manchester-Carlisle section, it was then withdrawn from Carnforth shed, where this photograph was taken, on 11 August 1968. It was sent to Bressingham, on loan from the British Railways Board, immediately on withdrawal.*

gigantic, and, in external appearance, they are strangers to the British railway scene. Because they were conspicuously fine examples of later developments outside Britain, and in danger of being lost to posterity, they were purchased by Mr Bloom.

One is a German engine, of the 2-10-0 Kreiglok class, which class numbered nine thousand. Built in 1944, it was sent for service in occupied Norway; overhauled in 1953, it was stored away in a tunnel to be remembered only some twenty years later. No. 5856 represents the most numerous class of European locomotives. It well illustrates German thoroughness and attention to detail.

The second is one of thirteen hundred built under the Marshall Plan to aid war-torn Europe: French railways had been devastated in the war, and the Lima works in Ohio combined elements of French and American practice to produce these heavy, 156-ton, successful locomotives. Both these locomotives are in running order and in the main need painting only.

The length of standard-gauge track is now over five hundred yards and passengers have been able to ride for that distance on a locomotive.

Long efforts to establish the Steam Museum as a charitable trust came to fruition in 1973 and Alan Bloom is very happy that it will continue to give pleasure and provide interest for future generations.

Other attractions

Bressingham provides much for the lovers of steam. It offers more.

There are the steam roundabouts retrieved from Scotland in 1967; 'Flora's Gallopers', powered by the authentic engine, works overtime in the summer months.

In the new exhibition hall, a host of interesting relics, ranging from guards' lamps to a steam-driven fire-fighting pump of 1890 (used locally by the Norwich firm of Jeremiah Colman), catch the eye. Plans are in hand to extend this hall to accommodate further exhibits and provide an internal gallery and a shop selling railway souvenirs and books.

There are the gardens, several refreshment points and a tea room, no restrictions on those wishing to picnic, and numerous vantage points for the photographer.

Enormous costs are incurred in maintaining the Live Steam Museum; the restoration of *Duchess of Sutherland* cost £17,000; one steaming of a large engine on an open day costs £80. A permanent staff of eight and a part-time one of two are needed. But admission charges are very reasonable.

The North Norfolk Railway

It is fortunate that of the $183\frac{1}{4}$ miles of the former Midland and Great Northern Joint Railway, the three miles that now see passenger trains running again are without doubt the most scenically attractive of the whole system. The three miles are to be found on the North Norfolk coast, in a designated 'Area of Outstanding Natural Beauty'. They link the attractive seaside town of Sheringham with Weybourne: the village is some two miles west of Sheringham, but the station lies at the foot of a ridge about one mile inland. Weybourne Station is planned to be a terminus only temporarily, as the North Norfolk Railway Company, which operates the line, hopes to extend the line, by about a mile, over the beautiful Kelling Heath.

The closure; the beginnings of the Preservation Society
In early 1959, the axe was laid to the very trunk of the vast M. & G.N.J.R. system; passenger traffic over most of the long west–east axis from Little Bytham in Lincolnshire to Great Yarmouth on the east Norfolk coast was withdrawn. The railway enthusiasts of the late fifties resolved that the railway should not be allowed to become extinct. The M. & G.N.J.R. was an odd intruder into Great Eastern territory but it inspired a great respect and affection among those who lived near it or used it for cross-country journeys, to visit Norfolk and Suffolk seaside resorts, to go to Norwich, or perhaps journey to school in its distinctive yellowish-brown coaches. 28 February 1959 saw withdrawal of passenger services over all but about twenty miles; some eighty miles of the system were to be closed completely.

The last train on the day of closure left Yarmouth South Town at 10.48 p.m. for Melton Constable, the nerve-centre of the system which once had its own locomotive-building works. A band of loyal enthusiasts travelled on it; also, they left on the station typed notices: 'Save the M. & G.N. Join the Preservation Society'. These typed messages were to start something. Ideas

exchanged on the train changed a concept into a reality – a Preservation Society to re-open part of the line in Norfolk.

Among those present at the birth of the Society were David Rees of Ilford, Founder of the Society, and Bernard Amies of Worstead. Bernard Amies, from his farm-house home, had watched the distinctive mustard-yellow M. & G.N. locomotives climbing (with protest) the Honing bank. When steam trains stopped, he was determined to 'get the puffers running again somewhere'. He has remained faithful to this ambition for over twenty eventful years.

Over-optimistic plans
The first Newsletter of the Society, issued in April 1960, suggested grandiose plans for re-opening the Aylsham (North)–Yarmouth Beach, and Melton Constable–Norwich (City) sections, and even sections to the west of the system, including King's Lynn–Fakenham, Sutton Bridge–Bourne, and Peterborough–Sutton Bridge; in all, the suggested routes totalled 119 miles. None of these was really viable. Parts of the line between Aylsham and Yarmouth were to become re-aligned roads, and the Beach Station at Yarmouth was to become a terminal for buses instead of trains. No local authority support would be forthcoming for this plan.

The Melton Constable–Norwich (City) line had a lot in its favour. The countryside round Melton Constable is attractive, and the small town, built, like a small-scale Crewe or Swindon, as a railway town, was the hub of the system of radiating lines. Moreover, as the M. & G.N. works, it had sheds and other facilities for sorting and maintaining locomotives and rolling stock. But it was fortunate that the difficulties in the way of this plan were too formidable to overcome: hindsight was to show that accessibility and outstanding scenic or other special interests are essential to the success of a preserved railway.

The first stock
In 1961 the society began locomotive pre-servation: it planned to buy two locomotives. One was the last remaining B12, a 4-6-0 class of express engine which had done yeoman service on the G.E.R. system for over forty years; No. 61572 was soon to be withdrawn. The other was

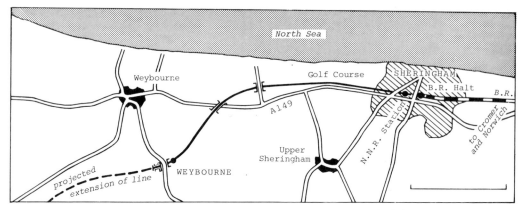

No. 65469, a J15 class 0-6-0 tender engine. British Rail quoted prices of £1500 for the B12 and £850 for the J15. An appeal fund was promptly launched.

Track projects

The second Annual General Meeting of the Society, in November 1961, showed that the frustrations in acquiring a section of line had put the whole future of the project in jeopardy. Some members had become sick with waiting and only 31 attended the meeting out of a membership of 178. However, the prospect of locomotive purchase looked bright: subscriptions of £314 and a loan of £500 had come in.

It was proposed to set up the 'Central Norfolk Railway Company' with a share capital of £17,000, the sum estimated as being the minimum required to relay track and operate a railway for just over two miles southwards from Melton Constable to Hindolveston. While this was conceived as the fore-runner of a more extensive project, with long-range sights still set on Norwich City station, the operation of this short stretch would surely convince British Railways that M. & G.N.R.P.S. members could run a railway. For the reason that they were not yet operating a railway British Rail made it a condition that the name of the company should be changed to Central Norfolk Enterprises Ltd. A short time, however, was to show that insufficient capital would be attracted to this venture. But at least by 1964 the Society took possession of two locomotives from B.R., Nos. 61572 and 65462, the second being a substitute J15, replacing No. 65469, which had been found

to have a badly cracked frame.

Further negotiations with British Rail were fruitless: the Society could gain no option on a length of line. Its fortunes were now at their nadir. 'M. & G.N.' had always been jokingly supposed to stand for 'Muddle and Get Nowhere'. This seemed to be true of the Preservation Society.

Five years, in railway preservation, is a long time. Not only does it become more difficult and costly to acquire the material of railway operations as time goes on, but hope continually deferred is in danger of dying. It was not till 1964 that further developments produced realistic proposals. The last passenger train was run between Melton Constable and Sheringham. This section was most attractive, especially at the northern extremity between Holt and Sheringham, where the line ran over heathlands, between the hills carved by the ice ages, to the attractive holiday town (which owed its development as a resort to the coming of the Midland and Great Northern in 1887).

Acquiring the eleven-mile length now became the aim. But B.R. valued it at £85,000, and early in 1965 a scrap-dealer started lifting the track. B.R. was persuaded, however, to leave the three miles between Weybourne and Sheringham *in situ*, and to give the re-openers a chance to raise a much lower amount. In August 1965, Central Norfolk Enterprises, aided by loans, paid £17,000 for the track.

The railway is established

Now that the railway had a physical base, with a station headquarters at Weybourne, the project, six years in the waiting, had reached the

G.E.R. No. 564, a 0-6-0 J15, on its first day in service with the North Norfolk Railway (23 October 1977), with the North Sea and Sheringham Golf Course in the background. The last four coaches of its train are an L.N.E.R. Gresley 'quad-art' set: four bodies articulated to run on five bogies. They were originally used on North London suburban lines.

jumping-off point. The enthusiasts now set to work. Weybourne Station became full of life at weekends and members scoured the country-side for all kinds of railway equipment. Two modern diesel-engined railbuses were pur-chased, with a view to future stand-by use; members of the locomotive department were busy on the two steam locomotives, then housed at sheds at March in Cambridgeshire; a M. & G.N.R. gangers' trolley, buffer-stops and an ex-G.E.R. bogie coach were bought, the coach a joint purchase by the home Society, the G.E.R. Group, and the London Railway Preservation Society. These were followed by a 'quad' set (four coaches articulated on five bogies instead of eight) designed by Gresley.

In January 1967, the old M. & G.N. station at Sheringham was abandoned by British Rail, and a new halt built to the east of the level crossing. The Society accepted terms for a lease on the old station until it should be sold; the disused station then became the headquarters. In June, the two steam locomotives, two diesel railbuses, the G.E.R. coach and the 'quad' set arrived at Sheringham to the accompaniment of much television and press publicity.

Equipment of all kinds continued to arrive at Sheringham; No. 65462 (the J15) was steamed at Easter 1968 for testing purposes, and Mr Geoffrey Sircom loaned a splendid L. & N.W.R. Directors' saloon. A third locomotive, an industrial 0-6-0 saddle tank (made by Peckett's of Bristol, it had worked with the National Coal Board) joined the two G.E.R. engines. A Colman's Mustard goods van, another Directors'

The quad set again, headed by Peckett 0-6-0 saddle tank No. 5. The five bogies can be clearly seen.

saloon (Lancashire and Yorkshire Railway) and an open second-class B.R. coach arrived on the scene.

The preserved section is part of the former Eastern and Midlands Railway from Melton Constable to Cromer Beach. This line was authorized by Parliament in 1880 and opened to Holt in October 1884, being extended to Cromer by a further Act in June 1887. The E. & M. was subsequently taken over by the Midland and Great Northern Joint Company on 1 July 1893. In 1923 it became part of the L.N.E.R.

The first railway to Cromer had been projected by the East Norfolk with assistance from the Great Eastern, the extension from North Walsham, more or less due south of Cromer, being completed in March 1877. It fell under complete G.E.R. control in 1881. The purpose of the E. & M. branch to Cromer was to provide a direct link to this popular holiday resort from the North and Midlands, a link which was not reliant on the Great Eastern. In contrast with most other British regions, East Anglia was virtually controlled by one monopolistic railway, the G.E.R. However, most of its lines radiated from London with connecting branches in between. There was room, therefore, for a railway to be constructed on an east–west axis across the northern quarter of the region. The branch from Melton Constable to Cromer was simply a further extension of the Midland and Great Northern's rival route from the Midlands, that via Spalding, in the Fens, to South Lynn, Fakenham, North Walsham and Yarmouth. There was also a branch from Melton Constable south-east to Norwich City.

Continued growth

1969 was the year that saw the beginning of assured success: Sir John Betjeman accepted the Presidency of the Society and the North Norfolk Railway Company Ltd was set up to raise money by offering shares, and to negotiate for a Light Railway Order to enable the running of trains for the public.

The Company prospectus showed the need for a share capital of £11,000 at once, and for one whose stated prospects were of never paying a dividend, the response was astonishing. £14,000 was raised in the statutory forty days.

To bring the railway up to the operating and safety standards needed for a Light Railway Order meant unremitting hard work and a steady inflow of cash. Both were now forthcoming as never before. Membership of the M. & G.N. Society leapt ahead, as only members were able to have steam rides on open days.

The more settled period attracted more locomotives, largely saddle tanks, and more rolling stock was bought, partly from the proceeds of the sale of books and souvenirs, and the profits from rail tours. More and more exhibits arrived for the museum; the station at Sheringham was re-painted in M. & G.N. tan-and-stone; a shop was set up in the station; part of the L. & N.W.R. Directors' Saloon became a refreshment room.

A run-round loop was provided at Weybourne, sidings laid, and the re-erection of the Norwich (City) engine-shed begun; at Sheringham, more roads were laid, a water tank erected, an inspection-pit dug, and locomotives, wagons and coaches repaired and re-painted. Temporary track from B.R.'s halt, across Station Road into Sheringham station, was laid overnight to enable two Southern Region Pullman cars of the famous Brighton Belle to come on loan from Ind Coope, to be restored at their new home at Sheringham.

A rigorous and approved series of training courses for drivers, firemen, guards and others started and the rapid progress the railway was now making culminated in the granting of a Light Railway Order to British Rail in 1973. This was transferred to the North Norfolk Railway in April 1976. Thereafter a service for the public was inaugurated.

What to see, and a journey down the line
Visitors should start at Sheringham station, where they will find the museum, and a shop offering a wide range of railway and holiday books, cards and souvenirs. Where railway directors once sipped their brandy, visitors may now sip their tea and relax comfortably. At one end of the platform is a grassed area with small tables and sunshades, a favourite spot for watching trains leave for Weybourne.

From Sheringham, the line rises on a fairly severe gradient. Beyond the summit lies a succession of glorious views for two miles or more. Leaving behind the western outskirts of the town, the golf course comes into view on the right. Then a V-shaped depression on the course reveals a triangle of sea. To the left, the land rises to rounded and wooded hills. As the line turns away from the sea, the view is over a typical Norfolk agricultural landscape of fields and meadows. Weybourne Station is the present end of the line, but the prospects of the line climbing another mile or so to the highest point of Kelling Heath are encouraging. The area round Weybourne Station is pleasant undulating country and the station itself offers refreshments and books.

The Nene Valley Railway

The Reverend Richard Paten, also a Chartered Engineer, was a curate in the cathedral city of Peterborough in the late sixties. When, in 1968, he purchased for preservation a British Railways class 5 mixed-traffic locomotive, No. 73050, he could have had no idea that it was to lead to a five-and-a-half-mile steam railway running through a large pleasure park.

No. 73050, then nameless, came straight out of service from Patricroft Shed to Peterborough. The original idea was that it should be preserved on a plinth outside the Technical College there, as a reminder of the city's railway and engineering heritage. But so good was its condition that Mr Paten and four or five fellow enthusiasts decided to undertake what little restoration was needed – mainly painting – to preserve it as a working exhibit. A local engineering firm, Baker Perkins, offered a siding where the work could be done.

Now in possession of a fine locomotive that could run under its own steam, Mr Paten – and his colleagues, now growing in number – felt strongly that the loco must be more than a static display. The sympathetic manager of the British Sugar Corporation factory at Peterborough welcomed the engine to their sidings, where it was soon steamed and giving footplate rides. It was to provide more than pleasure at the factory, for when a boiler there was out of commission, No. 73050 deputized as a stationary boiler most successfully. The owner was invited to leave it there. The Peterborough Locomotive Society had been born.

In 1971 a second locomotive came into the hands of the Society, a little 0-6-0 saddle tank engine *Jack's Green*. It had worked in the nearby Nassington iron-ore quarries, whence it travelled under its own steam.

With the dispersal of locomotives from the Clapham Museum pending, the Society, with the support of local authorities, conceived the idea of having a railway museum at the old Peterborough East Station, with a working steam section on the former L. & N.W.R. line then *in situ* as far as Oundle. While the scheme was not acceptable to the government, it did raise the possibility of a steam centre at Peterborough. About this time, the Peterborough Development Corporation was planning Nene Park, a pleasure area some five miles in length and straddling the River Nene from Orton westwards to Castor. Could the old L. & N.W.R. metals through the area be the basis of a

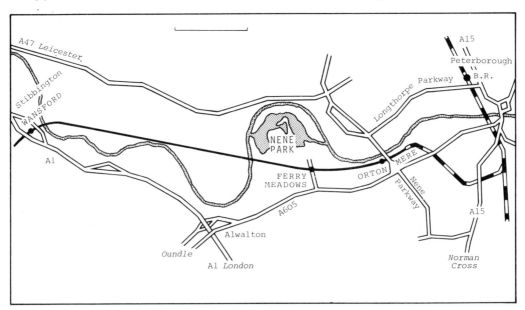

No. 73050, now named City of Peterborough, *the B.R. 5MT 4-6-0 which started it all on the Nene Valley Railway, passes beneath the A1.*

pleasure railway through the park? A feasibility study was undertaken by the Society and it was concluded that it could be done.

In 1972 the plan was presented to the Development Corporation, just as B.R. were preparing to abandon the line. The Corporation looked favourably on another amenity in their proposed pleasure park, and in 1973 purchased the single track from Longueville Junction to Yarwell Junction, paying £66,000 for some six miles of track, which was then leased to what had now become the Peterborough Railway Society Limited, a registered charity.

Meanwhile, locomotives continued to arrive. The firm of Derek Crouch offered another 0-6-0 saddle tank, formerly used on the Wissington Light Railway in south-west Norfolk, which served a beet sugar factory. Named *Derek Crouch*, it is now with the Society on permanent loan. In 1973 arrived two more 0-6-0 engines (one of which was later to be named *Thomas* by the Reverend W. Awdry), and a coach was purchased from the profits of open days and

from members' gifts and subscriptions. This was to provide rides behind No. 73050, now aptly named *City of Peterborough* (its nominal ownership had now passed to the City Council, who in turn leased it to the Society on a 99-year lease).

Wansford became the operating centre for the Society in 1974, and locomotives and stock were transferred there. The station there offered great possibilities, with space for additional sidings, an engine shed and car parking. Unfortunately, the station building, built of local stone and architecturally of enough interest to be 'listed', is in private hands. Across the road from the station is Wansford signal box, the largest preserved fully-equipped box in the country.

The Society ran its first steam trains under B.R. supervision with the approval of the Railway Inspectorate, until, at the end of 1974, B.R. were happy to allow the Society to run its trains unsupervised. The first trains ran for about one mile, westwards through the 616-yard Wansford Tunnel, to Yarwell. The tunnel has some interesting features, among them being the incorporation in the eastern portal of some two-foot-square granite sleeper blocks from the early days of railways.

Now that the Society had earned the full

confidence of British Rail, the Development Corporation and the local authorities, and was firmly established at Wansford, its suitability as a home for preserved locomotives was noticed by other owners. A great advantage of Wansford is its easy physical connection with B.R. metals, and other locomotives, mainly small industrial types, continued to arrive. In 1973, Suffolk farmer Richard Hurlock asked the Society if a home could be found there for a Swedish tank locomotive, a 2-6-4, No. 1928: the difficulty here was the dimensions of the locomotive, which is too large for the British loading gauge. A survey of the line revealed that little work would be needed to accommodate larger continental engines, and the idea of being able to operate continental trains offered new attractions; the Railway Inspectorate was approached for advice on the matter. The Society decided to adopt the Berne loading gauge along the Nene Valley Railway, although running over-size stock does present problems, like setting platform faces further back for clearance, which means an unacceptable gap between platform and footboards on British stock, and involves fitting wider boards. Signals too have to be set back, and the six-foot way between the tracks has to be widened by some two feet.

In 1975 Richard Hurlock offered two more

Danish class F, 0-6-0 No. 656 stands in Platform 3 at Wansford, with a Nene Valley permanent way train which includes a Smith Rodley 5-ton steam crane of 1934.

OPPOSITE: *The N.V.R. runs a commercial freight service for an insulation company, moving stock from Stirling to a depot in the former station yard at Wansford. The Swedish oil-burning engine, 2-6-4 No. 1928 (built 1953) pulls the through train on the last leg of the journey.*

continental locomotives on permanent loan: one came from Danish Railways, 0-6-0 No. 656; the other was another Swedish loco, 2-6-2 tank engine No. 1178, built in 1914. The closure of Ashford Steam Centre in Kent meant that a magnificent French locomotive would be homeless. This was a Nord engine (Northern Railway of France), one of the 3500 class of 4-6-0s which set new standards of locomotive performance in Europe between the wars. No. 3628, now at Wansford, is in impeccable condition; whilst its appearance may be unusual to British eyes, with many of the mechanisms, pipes and apparatus exposed, it is perhaps exposure of its works which makes it all the more interesting. Built in 1911, it had 54 years in main-line service and is the only working example of its class left. Among the famous trains it headed is the Rome

During 1978, the Essex Locomotive Society's S.R. 4-6-0 No. 841 Greene King *was based at Wansford on the Nene Valley Railway. Here, it crosses the Nene on a 'Santa Special'.*

Express. It belongs to the Nord Locomotive Preservation Group, who can now see it hauling continental coaching stock along the Nene Valley Railway. It has been used in filming the B.B.C. series 'Secret Army'.

The Southern Electric Group owned six third-rail electric multiple coaches, and asked if these could be moved from Ashford to Wansford. These vehicles are air-braked, whereas all British preserved steam locomotives are vacuum-braked. At Wansford there were air-braked continental locomotives needing air-braked stock. The arrival of the ex-Southern vehicles meant that trains could now be made up behind the continental locomotives. The six coaches are in the old Southern olive green.

Battle of Britain class No. 34081, *92 Squadron*, has recently been saved from the rust of Barry scrapyard.

Peter Brotherhoods of Peterborough have undertaken the mechanical overhaul of *Jack's Green*, and the apprentices at Baker Perkins overhauled, as part of their training, a petrol-driven Wickham trolley. A small four-wheeled diesel locomotive bought from British Oil and Cake Mills in 1972 was rebuilt by Perkins Engines, and they installed one of their own engines. Named *Frank* after one of the Perkins family, it carries a plaque naming five other firms associated in restoring it.

Other firms have helped the project in their own special way. A.R.C. have provided blocks for platform building; Dowmac, concrete sleepers; Ready-Mix, concrete. An interest-free loan from the Peterborough City Council enabled the Society to buy an old cattle-market building which is being turned into a serviceable engine shed at Wansford. The Northamptonshire County Council have made a gift of Barnwell Station Office, and Ross Foods are assisting in its restoration. It is to serve as a sales centre at the station. A water tower is being built, and Perkins Engines have found the site of the engine shed a very useful testbed for their diesel engines. The Manpower Services Commission sees the railway as a viable enterprise, and made a grant available in 1976 enabling

After working another 'Santa Special', French Nord 4-6-0 No. 3.628 stands in Wansford station with a train of Danish and Norwegian coaches. 5.30 p.m. on a December evening.

the Society to employ thirteen men.

Preserved railways are pleasure railways, but already the Peterborough Society's railway has served commercial interests. A boat-building firm, Seasteel, based at Nassington Quarries, has provided freight traffic, and one of the engines has been the motive power for the track-lifting trains between Peterborough and Yarwell.

Steam trains operate on Sundays and Bank Holidays between Wansford and Orwell Mere. Family tickets for train rides are issued. On steam days, refreshments, souvenirs and books are available. On other days, the station at Wansford is open to visitors, who are welcome. Photographers may click at will in the station, but are asked to be sensible when engines are in steam. In the Nene Park itself are numerous vantage points.

The Park around

The future of the Nene Valley Railway is indissolubly linked with that of the Nene Park. This is the result of the Development Corporation's insistence on assuring an expanding population of a wide range of leisure facilities. The Park runs for some five miles either side of the Nene, between Orton in the east and Castor in the west. It is bounded by the A47 road to the north and the A605 to the south. The railway cuts a straight line through this attractive stretch of pastoral countryside, crossing the river twice. A golf course and boating lakes are built or planned. Nature trails are laid, and cycle ways built. Where the Nene and the A47 come close together at Milton, there is a pack-horse bridge of interest.

The Nene Valley Railway is a major attraction of the Park. Between Wansford and Orton are three other stations, one serving the main entrance (Ferry Meadows), one to the east (Overton) and one to the west (Castor). The Building Industry Training Board has built two intermediate platforms. The Park opened officially in 1978, when the railway too opened officially – although it had been operating since June 1977.

The Stour Valley Railway

Preservation

The Stour Valley Railway began as a pre-servation society on 24 December 1968, when a number of enthusiasts decided that a part of the great Great Eastern Railway must be preserved. The first objective, somewhat ambitious in hindsight, was to save a part, or even the whole, of the line from Sudbury to Shelford on the main Cambridge–Liverpool Street line. Passenger services had been withdrawn beyond Sudbury. The part finally selected was between Sudbury and Long Melford, just over three miles, but British Rail sold the track before sufficient funds could be attracted to the scheme to enable the Society to purchase it.

A sound financial base is a *sine qua non* of railway preservation, so in February 1970 a private company, the Branch Line Preservation Society, was formed. Its intentions were specific: to raise funds and negotiate with British Rail the purchase of a part of the Stour Valley Branch. As the Marks Tey–Sudbury branch was, unhappily, a candidate for closure, the company felt that funds might be more readily attracted to a project which would save a stretch of line presently being worked, so that not only track-bed but also track could be acquired.

On the Stour Valley branch, stations had been reduced to unstaffed halts. Chappel and Wakes Colne, perched on the northern slope of the Colne Valley, and with a spacious goods yard, goods shed and signal box, would serve well as headquarters for the Society and home for locomotives and rolling stock. The need for some three to five miles of track was still in the forefront of the Society's plans and two stretches of line of that length were kept in view: northwards from Chappel to Bures and southwards from Chappel to Marks Tey.

In December 1970, the Society moved to Chappel and Wakes Colne station. The station building, signal box and goods shed bore the customary marks of neglect and the stealthy visits of vandals. The goods yard was a scene of depressing and daunting dereliction. Part of it

had become a convenient dumping ground for ash from Colchester locomotive yard and weeds and bushes had colonized it. All the track had been lifted, and lay piled up in heaps ready for removal by scrap merchants. Among the debris in the yard was found the broken remains of the lever frame from the signal box, now no more than a shell. Prompt action by two members some time earlier had saved the track. The contractors and British Rail co-operated in giving the Company time in which to purchase the waiting piles of track. Gifts and loans came in quickly to make this possible.

The hard work of relaying track and points then began. More track was brought in, too: a private siding from Margaretting near Chelmsford, and the Acton sidings of Cerebos Salt, given to the Society by the Company. In about three months, a third of a mile of track had been relaid in the goods yard.

Initial stock

The railway first provided rides for members on 13 March 1971, the train being drawn by a 0-6-0 saddle tank *Gunby* of the War Department

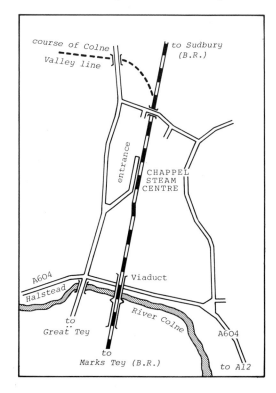

The Stour Valley Railway operates at present only within the former yard of Chappel and Wakes Colne B.R. station, the site being known as the Chappel Steam Centre. The 'main' line is only a quarter of a mile or so, and, accepting this limitation, the Centre concentrates on details of railway operation, permanent way, etc. Visitors have unusually free access to everything within the site, and Chappel can provide opportunities to see details which cannot be closely studied on more 'conventional' preserved railways. An example is the lever frame in this picture of No. 54, a 0-6-0 saddle tank built in 1941, shunting. The track on the right is the B.R. Sudbury–Marks Tey line.

Austerity class. She had come from an iron-ore quarry to Chappel about a month previously. Another 0-6-0 saddle tank, *Jupiter*, had arrived three days after *Gunby*.

The next year saw the arrival of three more locomotives, first, a small 0-6-0 saddle tank *Belvoir* (now finely restored), then a side tank, No. 7597, which had been bought by the '7597 Fund' (later to become the Railway Vehicle Preservations Group). In September 1972, the Essex Locomotive Society provided Chappel and Wakes Colne with its real pride and joy, an ex-Southern-Railway 4-6-0 S15 class, No. 841, which had been a very adaptable work-horse at the head of passenger and express goods trains. After a long and expensive programme of restoration which involved the fabrication of many new parts, in recognition of the great help accorded by the local brewery, Greene King, this fine locomotive was named *Greene King*. Its restoration was carried out to such a high standard that she was selected to be one of the engines appearing in the Cavalcade of Steam at Shildon on 31 August 1975, when the 150th anniversary of steam railways in Britain was celebrated. Three more locomotives in 1973 brought the total at Chappel to eight.

In the next year, the first locomotive to be owned by the Society arrived. This was No. 80151, a 2-6-4 tank of B.R. design. It was rescued just in time from the graveyard of locomotives at Barry. Like No. 841, she has had some essential parts removed and rust has eaten into her steel plate, but she is capable of being restored to full working condition. There is also

the last Great Eastern loco to be built at Stratford Works, 0-6-2 tank, No. 999.

Jupiter, a 0-6-0 saddle tank built in 1950, collects the staff (the token of the right to pass over a line) from the Chappel North box.

Other equipment

There is great temptation to concentrate on the locomotives in a railway preservation enterprise. But the running of locomotives needs not only track and points, but signalling equipment, coaches for passengers, and many other far-from-glamorous but nevertheless essential items. A new signal box has been erected at the northern limit of the Society's track and fitted with equipment from as far afield as East Lincolnshire. Signals, points and crossing gates are fully interlocking to conform to normal railway practice. Engine movements are under the discipline of the staff-and-token system, which means that no driver may move his engine unless the signalman has handed him the necessary staff or token. The signal box by the B.R. tracks, which became redundant with the de-staffing of the station, has also been reinstated as a working box, and it is hoped that this may be moved on to the land leased by the Society. The frame, found in several pieces in the goods yard, has been repaired and replaced. The goods shed is now a well-equipped workshop.

Rolling stock

A very interesting collection of rolling stock has been assembled at the station. A veritable railway antique is a six-wheel coach, No. 373, of the old Manchester, Sheffield and Lincolnshire Railway, built in 1899. Another six-wheeler, even older, was built in 1890 by the Great Eastern Railway. Numbered 550, it is owned by the Great Eastern Railway Group and is due to be restored to its 1915 state. Of more ancient lineage still is a four-wheeled first-class coach of the Great Eastern which was built in 1877 at a cost of £281. Restoration is proceeding on this vehicle.

The Railway Vehicle Preservation Group has two vehicles of outstanding interest at Chappel. One is an ex-L.N.E.R. Post Office tender No. E70268 built in 1951 to carry mail; the other is a coach for first- and third-class passengers built at York in 1924 for the then-new Flying Scotsman. It is 61 ft long.

The Southern Railway features again in a Pullman motor-brake third-class coach built in 1931 for the Southern Belle. It is on temporary

One advantage of having a site adjacent to B.R. metals is the ease of moving stock to and from the site. But it has to be done outside B.R. running hours, of course. No. 841 in the B.R. platform of Chappel at 2.30 a.m., on 12 September 1976, prior to working a railtour from Ipswich. It went to the Nene Valley Railway shortly afterwards.

loan from Courage, the brewers.

Other vehicles of interest are a four-wheel Grafton Steam Crane, on loan from the Felixstowe Dock and Railway Co. Ltd, which is of great use for lifting sleepers, track, and saddle tanks from locomotives, and one (E765W) of two wagons only of a special kind built at Stratford Works in 1951, on six wheels, used for transporting horses (between the two horse compartments is one for the groom). There is a strong Great Eastern element in the rolling stock.

What to see on a visit

While a longer trip behind a steam locomotive must await the acquisition of more track (consequent perhaps on the possible closure by B.R. of the Mark's Tey–Sudbury branch, or, in the event of that line remaining open, on re-establishment on a new site, there is very much there to draw the visitor. Entry to the railway is through the Booking Office which now serves also as a well-stocked shop with a fine display of books, cards and other railway souvenirs. Other rooms serve as refreshment rooms. Photographs may be taken within the area leased by the Society only. This is a safety measure as B.R. trains still run through the station and their line has to be crossed to reach the Society's running tracks. The station building is very attractive architecturally, quite different from the usual Great Eastern station, constructed in brick of unusual shades and with unique decorative touches on the exterior.

Access to the Stour Valley Railway is easy. Just off the A604 at Chappel a B.R. sign points the way to the station.

Less than a quarter mile from the station is the imposing Chappel viaduct spanning the Colne Valley. It is a listed structure. It was the longest viaduct on the Great Eastern Railway, 1,066 ft long, 75 ft high at the maximum, and supported on 32 graceful arches. Those visiting the railway should also see this great monument to railway civil engineering of the last century.

The Colne Valley Railway

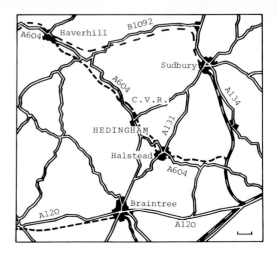

This preservation venture has but a short history. Early in 1972, Dick Hymas purchased a 0-6-0 saddle tank No. 190, an Austerity class built for the War Department. Gordon Warren, another local enthusiast, joined Hymas at the head of a small group and then decided to try to re-open about one mile of the railway to provide a home for 190 and other engines. A private company, the Colne Valley Railway Co. Ltd, was formed to launch the scheme. There was so much local interest, that a supporting body for the general public was soon in being – the Colne Valley Railway Preservation Society.

The Colne Valley Railway is being built on the track-bed of the old line. Work began ten years after the track had been lifted. Castle Hedingham station was moved two miles. Track-laying in progress in July 1975 on the newly-cleared bed. The beginnings of the new platform are on the left.

Long negotiations with British Rail came to a conclusion when the Company purchased a one-mile length of track-bed at Castle Hedingham, close to the A604 road and the River Colne. Late in 1973, they gained access to the area, from which the track had been lifted ten years previously. Three months clearing the track-bed caused workers to wonder if a nature reserve might have been a more suitable project!

Austerity class 0-6-0 W.D. No. 190, with 0-4-0 Barrington, pulled the first train on 31 May 1978.

Just enough track – about 60 ft – was laid, including an inspection pit, to take one locomotive comfortably. In September 1973, No. 190 was transferred to the place prepared for her.

No buildings, not even a platelayer's hut, stood on the mile of track-bed. A search began for authentic Colne Valley Railway buildings. Fortunately, three of the original station buildings remained, and one, at Castle and Sible Hedingham, had been recently sold to Rippers Ltd. The station was more or less structurally sound and solidly built. On being approached and learning of the intentions for the station, Messrs Rippers generously gave it to the Society. Members set to work on reducing the building to its component parts, In six weeks they were moved the two miles. The station was re-built to look exactly as it had at Castle Hedingham. A two-hundred-foot platform was built around it, and on the opposite side a similar platform, which accommodates another station building containing offices, a shop, a cafe, and the museum.

So track-laying proceeded, yard-by-yard on £5 sleepers, slowly but steadily towards Yeldham.

With more track laid there was room for more locomotives; W.D. No. 190 was joined by others, all industrials, some in group ownership. Among them is a beautifully restored Avonside 0-4-0 saddle-tank locomotive named *Barrington*, expertly painted and lined out in L.M.S. maroon, owned by the Avonside Steam Preservation Group.

Essex County Council offered the Society the old crossing-keeper's ground-frame hut at White Colne; this too was dismantled, taken to the new railway, and reconstructed as it was before. An engine shed became a priority, and the Great Yeldham goods shed was acquired.

The foundations of a re-born stretch of the Colne Valley and Halstead railway are truly laid.

The rebuilt Castle Hedingham station as it is now, exactly as it had been before being moved.

Over the one mile it is a close replica of the original. The five engines, and the rolling-stock (including a B.R. second-class saloon, an ex-L.M.S. brake van and a signal-post wagon dating back to 1911) can be see from the A604 road between Great Yeldham and Castle Hedingham. A spacious lay-by provides both a stopping place and easy access to the railway. Pictures may be taken anywhere along the line.

IV
The Midlands

The Severn Valley Railway

The line and its history

The Severn Valley Railway formerly ran from Shrewsbury in Shropshire to Hartlebury in Worcestershire. The route selected by the original promoters included historic towns such as Ironbridge, Bewdley and Stourport. A railway linking Worcester with Shrewsbury was proposed by the Oxford, Worcester and Wolverhampton Railway in the 1850s, and the railway obtained its Act in August 1853. Work began in 1858, and apart from earth slips caused by heavy rain in the summer of 1860 there were no great engineering difficulties. The line was completed in the autumn of 1861, but the opening was delayed in view of previous earthslips, to allow the track-bed to consolidate. The line was finally opened with great rejoicing in January 1862. By 1863, the Severn Valley, though then absorbed by the new West Midland Railway, was operating as part of the G.W.R., but its formal amalgamation was not until 1872.

The Severn Valley Railway remained part of the G.W.R. till nationalization. During World War II, it was of great importance as a supply route for air bases at Bridgnorth and Hartlebury, but it was never part of any main route, and with few towns of any size near, it was not an economic line in post-War conditions. In 1962, following the Beeching report, the line was scheduled for closure.

After the passing of the 1962 Transport Act, the passenger service ended on 7 September 1963, and freight traffic ceased on 30 November. South of Aveley, the line remained open for local coal traffic, but the track north of Buildwas was lifted in 1965, and later as far south as Bridgnorth.

Preservation

In February 1966 the Severn Valley Railway Society, formed the previous year to preserve the line for steam traction, purchased the line between Bridgnorth and Hampton Loade for £25,000; this line was re-opened in the summer of 1970. This was but a small section of the original line, and money was raised to extend the tracks southwards to join the Western Region main line from Worcester Foregate to Birmingham. Once the track-bed had been purchased from B.R., volunteers set about re-laying the line and restoring the station buildings. The Society now operates a regular, timetabled service from the northern terminus at Bridgnorth, south to Eardington, Hampton Loade, Highley, Arley, Northwood and Bewdley. There are trains every 40 minutes along the complete length of the line. It is proposed to extend the railway to the last stop at Foley Park, and then link up with British Rail from here. The total length of the line is $12\frac{1}{2}$ miles from Bridgnorth to Bewdley; Foley Park is a further 2 miles on.

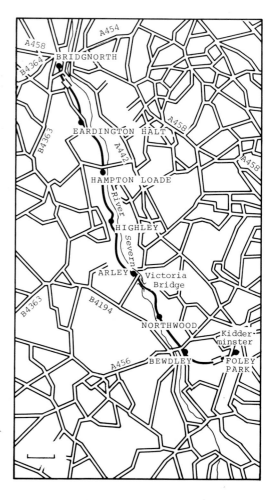

Bridgnorth on the Severn Valley Railway. Stanier 8F 2-8-0 No. 8233, in original L.M.S. livery, has hauled ten-coach trains, including a special from Bridgnorth to Chester. Here, running tender-first, it crosses G.W.R. 4-6-0 Hinton Manor.

Stock

Many locomotives and rolling stock preserved on the line today are a living reminder of what the railway was like in the past. One of the best known engines is No. 8233, a 8F class designed by Sir William Stanier, 2-8-0. She was built in 1940 by the North British Locomotive Co. at Glasgow to operate in France on war work, but with the collapse of France she was delivered to the L.M.S. In 1941 she was requisitioned to serve in Persia, and it was not till 1952, after a further spell on the Egyptian State Railways,

that she returned to England, to work on the Longmoor Military Railway. Before the end of steam on British Railways she returned to the Glasgow district, and was finally acquired by the 8F Locomotive Society. She came to Bridgnorth in January 1969, and has given reliable service ever since. She was one of the locomotives selected to take part in the Rail 150 cavalcade at Shildon in August 1975.

Though basically Great Western in design, No. 8233 was an L.M.S. engine, and prior to preservation never worked on the Severn Valley line. Collett 0-6-0 No. 3205 is more typical of the locomotives which worked it. Built at Swindon in 1946, she was originally shedded at Gloucester to work local passenger and freight services in the Ross, Hereford, Cheltenham and Swindon area. She was trans-

Since 1974, the S.V.R. has been running passenger services from Bridgnorth through to Bewdley. Hunslet 0-6-0 No. 193, now named Shropshire *sets out with the noon service to Arley on Boxing Day 1975.*

ferred to Worcester in 1956, and actually worked on the Severn Valley line until her withdrawal from service. She was then bought by the 2251 Preservation Group, and restored at Buckfastleigh in 1965–6. She was subsequently towed to the Severn Valley, and hauled the first public passenger train on the opening day in May 1970.

No. 45110 *R.A.F. Biggin Hill* is one of the largest locomotives preserved at Bridgnorth. This 4-6-0 class 5 L.M.S. engine was designed by Sir William Stanier, and built at the Vulcan Foundry in 1935. Shedded at Holyhead, she worked fast passenger and freight trains to Chester, Birmingham, Manchester, Liverpool and London. She was purchased for preservation at Ashford, Kent, but was moved to the Severn Valley for complete restoration when the Ashford centre closed.

An oddity among the locomotive stock is the 0-6-0 tank engine No. 686, *Lady Armaghdale.* Built by the Hunslet Engine Co. at Leeds in 1898 for the Manchester Ship Canal Railway, she has an unusually short wheelbase, designed to cope with the many short-radius curves which abound on that particular railway. First sold to

I.C.I. at Blackley, she was abandoned in 1968, and brought to Bridgnorth in the following year. She is now used for shunting duties.

In addition, the Severn Valley also possesses a collection of Ivatt-designed L.M.S. steam engines. These include No. 46443, a 2-6-0 tender locomotive. H. G. Ivatt was the last Chief Mechanical Engineer of the L.M.S. before nationalization, and this class of engine continued to be built after British Railways had come into existence; No. 46443 was laid down in 1950. After delivery she was based on Derby and worked trains in the Central Midlands. Another Ivatt-designed 2-6-0 here is No. 43106, again built under B.R. She worked on the Eastern Region, and was finally transferred to Preston before purchase by the Severn Valley Company.

For G.W.R. enthusiasts, one of the most familiar-looking locomotives on the line will be

On the S.V.R., L.M.S. Ivatt class 2MT No. 46521 (sister to No. 46443 seen in the colour plate) in correct B.R. livery (it was built by B.R. in 1953 to the L.M.S. design). The inscription on the bridge reads: 'Victoria Bridge', and then, from left to right across the arch: 'Messrs. Brabbey & Co., Contractors' '1861. John Fowler, Engineer.' 'Cast and erected by the Coalbrookdale Company.' The bridge featured in the 1979 version of The Thirty-Nine Steps.

the 0-6-0 pannier tank No. 1501. Built at Swindon in 1949, she is distinguished from the earlier G.W.R. models by having outside cylinders. This more modern design was by the Great Western's last Chief Mechanical Engineer, F. W. Hawksworth. These engines were built for shunting and moving coaches to and from stations for express trains. No. 1501 was based at Old Oak Common, and worked stock to and from Paddington.

Last but not least there is No. 70000, *Britannia*. She provides an example of B.R. locomotive design, and completes the picture of steam engines in Britain. She was the first major standard locomotive to be built by the newly nationalized B.R. Completed at Crewe in 1951, she was designed to pull the heaviest passenger trains, and operated variously from Crewe, Brighton, and Stratford. She was selected to haul King George VI's funeral train in 1952. In 1970 she was bought from British Rail by enthusiasts to save her from being scrapped. They leased her to the Severn Valley Company, and she is shedded at Bridgnorth.

The area around
Although the Severn Valley railway runs through attractive countryside, it is also associated with a whole variety of industrial remains. The town of Ironbridge, for example, set on the steep limestone slopes above the River Severn, received its name because it was the site of the world's first iron bridge, built in 1778. It was designed and cast by the famous ironmaster Abraham Darby, at his foundry in nearby Coalbrookdale. Its single cast-iron span is of 100 feet. Today, the bridge, weakened by 200 years of traffic, is limited to foot passengers alone.

At Coalbrookdale itself is the Museum of Ironfounding. Here Abraham Darby pioneered

2-10-0 Gordon, No. 600, leaves Knowlsands Tunnel just south of Bridgnorth, en route for Bewdley, on 20 September 1975. Built in 1943 for the Ministry of Supply, Gordon *worked on the Longmoor Military Railway, whose livery it carries.*

the use of coke as a fuel for iron smelting in place of charcoal. The museum exhibits early iron castings, and a selection of some early cast-iron rails. There are also some early locomotives and stationary steam engines, together with a collection of machinery used in the manufacture of iron goods.

Further south is the well-known canal town of Stourport. The story runs that James Brindley, looking for an outlet to the Severn for his Trent and Mersey Canal, selected the then thriving town of Bewdley. The residents felt that the new-fangled canal would lower the tone of their town, and opposed his plans. Accordingly Brindley moved to Stourport, where a series of docks, wharves, and warehouses was built. Much business followed, and Stourport thrived while Bewdley declined. Today much of Stourport's Georgian charm remains, including the warehouses built by the canal company.

Nearby is Tickenhill Manor, originally a medieval building given to Roger Mortimer by Edward IV. The Manor is faced with Georgian brickwork, but the interior shows glimpses of the earlier house. The Great Hall for example, has much Tudor work and the beams date from the thirteenth century.

Bridgnorth is not known merely for its railway. It is an old town with building dating from the twelfth century. There are some remains of the castle keep, destroyed by Cromwell's forces in 1646. The castle grounds are now an attractive park. The church of St Mary Magdalene was designed by the civil engineer Thomas Telford in the early nineteenth century in the then fashionable Italianate style.

At Shrewsbury is Rowley's House, containing the City Museum, which has a variety of exhibits dating from Roman times to the nineteenth century. There is also a military museum at the Sir John Moore Barracks which features the County Regiment, The Shropshire Light Infantry.

B.R. built, L.M.S. design. Ivatt class 4MT, 2-6-0
No. 43106, runs into Hampton Loade.

Great Central Railway (Main Line Steam Trust)

Of all the railway preservation projects, one of the most ambitious has been the return to steam on the former Great Central. The Main Line Steam Trust (as the preservation group was originally called) set out to fulfill the dream of many steam enthusiasts: not merely to recreate the lost age of steam on relatively short branch lines, but to acquire a section of a former main line, and restore it to steam running. The line chosen for its activities was the former Great Central route, from Loughborough south towards Leicester. That line had finally been abandoned and closed by British Rail on 5 May 1969. It had been decided to retain the former Midland Railway's route to Loughborough, via Leicester to St Pancras, and reduce Marylebone to the status of a commuter terminus. The base of operations was the $3\frac{3}{4}$-acre site at Loughborough Central Station, which was leased to the Trust. In 1977 the Trust bought the track from Loughborough to Rothley for nearly £250,000.

There was a double irony that the Great Central should have been chosen, for the G.C.R. was the last main line to be built in Britain, with much scepticism from those who thought it unnecessary. It had only been opened to passenger traffic in March 1899, providing a direct route from Marylebone to Rugby, Leicester, Nottingham, Sheffield, Yorkshire and Lancashire. It was aptly named, for a plan of the Company's lines in 1922 resembles the letter *T*. There was the main line running almost due north from London. It had virtually no branches or east–west offshoots until it reached the North Midlands. There, routes broke off due west to Liverpool and Manchester, and due east to Lincoln, Grimsby and Cleethorpes. The railway continued north as far as Doncaster and Wakefield. The Great Central was to continue as a main-line trunk route, with a well-deserved reputation for fast, comfortable and frequent express trains, for over sixty years. In its halcyon days under British Railways, the line boasted such named expresses as the Master Cutler and the South Yorkshireman. In 1923 the Great Central had, of course, been absorbed into the L.N.E.R.

A journey down the line
As the train leaves Loughborough's Great Central Station, it is tempting to put the clock back two decades – to the happier days of the mid-1950s when a beautifully turned out A3 *Prince Palatine,* or *Solario* perhaps, might have been pulling away from here on an express to London Marylebone, calling only at Leicester and Rugby. But those golden days are gone and the train will now only travel as far as Rothley, via Quorn and Woodhouse. Rothley is just to the north of Leicester. The journey is some $5\frac{1}{2}$ miles.

But it is still an enchanting journey through the beautiful Leicestershire countryside. In the old days, very fast running was the general rule between Loughborough and Leicester. The railway was built for high speeds – no gradient

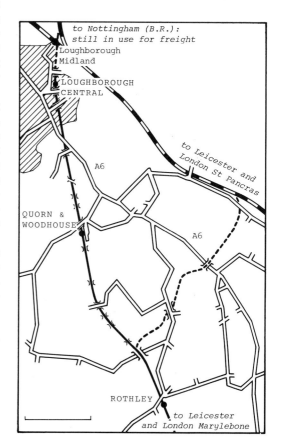

An L.M.S. 5MT 4-6-0, now named 3rd Volunteer Battalion, The Worcestershire and Sherwood Foresters Regiment, *No. 5231 was built in 1936 and withdrawn from Carnforth shed in 1968. It is clear that the M.L.S.T. track is a true main line, built with gentle gradients and curves. Sadly, since this photograph was taken, the line has been reduced to single track – since £125,000 would have been needed to purchase the second.*

was more testing than a gentle 1 in 176, and the alignment and curvature allowed speeds of up to 80 m.p.h. Alas, the present speed restrictions permit only a fraction of that as the train travels the two miles from Loughborough to Quorn and Woodhouse through gently rolling countryside.

Quorn is an ideal spot to explore the Leicestershire hunting country. The village of Woodhouse lies only 1 mile away, while the famous local landmark, Charnwood Beacon (818 ft) is a further 2 miles on. Quorn station is a simple island arrangement, with the tracks running either side of a single platform with umbrella awnings. It is a typical example of a Great Central rural station. Like so many of its kind, Quorn was closed when the Beeching Axe was wielded in the early 1960s.

Leaving Quorn, the train chunters gently on, with the local beauty spot of Chuddon Wood on the left and the wild Charnwood Forest region away in the distance on the right. This is the territory of Lady Jane Grey, the tragic queen whose short reign finished at the scaffold. There opens up a tremendous view, a beautiful patchwork of arable farmland, scattered copses, and then the more heavily wooded countryside as the train approaches Swithland Reservoir (one of the reservoirs which provides Leicester with its water). From the viaducts which take the railway across Swithland, some of the loveliest views of all are to be seen. Far to the right lies Swithland Hall, the ancestral seat of the Earl of Lanesborough, the G.C.R.'s President. For the ornithologist the fringes of the reservoir provide a natural home for a re-markably variety of birds.

As the first houses on the left come into view, the train is nearing Rothley Station, reaching the last hundred yards of its journey. Rothley Station is an industrial site not to be missed. It has been carefully restored so that it is almost as it was when opened in 1899 - even down to the gas lighting. A refreshment room is provided, and to remind the visitor of its Victorian origins, the waiting room is decorated with a portrait of Queen Victoria. Rothley Station is also an ideal base for an excursion - the village of Rothley lies one mile away, and Swithland Reservoir can be more closely explored from here. One of Leicester's most popular picnic spots - and a place well worth a visit - is the highly attractive Bradgate Park, about three miles away. Although the route was originally double track throughout till B.R. days, one set of lines was lifted, and for most of the journey trains operate along a single line.

Stock

Since the Trust was set up to preserve a Great Central Railway it is fitting to begin an examination of the locomotives operating along the line with one of its former engines. The only G.C.R. express locomotive which has survived for preservation is the 4-4-0 No. 506, *Butler-Henderson*. It was built at the company's Gorton works in Manchester in 1919 to the designs of John G. Robinson. The class were known as 'Improved Directors', as they were a revised version of the original Director class of 1913. No. 506 was named after the Hon. Eric Butler Henderson, a board member of the G.C.R. The engine has since been thoroughly repainted and is now resplendent in the green livery of the Great Central, lined out in white and black, with deep red frames and lower splashers. The engine does need a certain amount of mechanical attention before it can be put into service again; it is at present on loan from the national collection at York. In its career this loco must have headed many expresses through Lough-borough on its way to Manchester from London.

One steam engine actually working on the line is the former L.M.S. 'Black Five', No. 5231. Designed by Sir William Stanier, the class were first introduced in 1934. They are 4-6-0 loco-

motives produced for general duties, capable of hauling the heaviest passenger and freight trains. Unfortunately, they were not named, a curious fact given their popularity and impor-tance throughout the Midland system. They were the second most numerous class of engines in Britain (after the G.W.R. pannier tank), numbering 842. In 1976 at Quorn Station, No. 5231 was named *3rd (Volunteer) Battalion, the Worcestershire and Sherwood Foresters Regiment*. It is a good choice of name, as many of the larger L.M.S. express locomotives were named after regiments of the British Army.

Another loco, one representing the L.N.E.R., is No. 4744, an 0-6-2 tank engine. Built in 1921, she started life on the Great Northern, and was used for hauling suburban trains out of King's Cross. There were special condensers fitted (the pipes visible at the top of the side tanks are part of this apparatus) to reduce steam and smoke in the long tunnels to Moorgate. This engine, now restored to its L.N.E.R. livery, was formerly held on the Keighley and Worth Valley Railway.

The G.C. has a sufficiently generous loading gauge to allow the running of continental locomotives. One of the most unusual locos on the line is Norwegian State Railways No. 377. This 2-6-0 tender engine was built in 1919 by the

OPPOSITE, TOP: *On the Bluebell Railway, 0-6-0 tank No. 27, built in 1909, and now painted in full S.E. & C.R. passenger livery, hauls the 1700 from Sheffield Park to Horsted Keynes on a March afternoon.*

CENTRE: *Footplate view from L.B. & S.C.R. No. 55* Stepney *as it climbs towards Horsted Keynes. Built in 1875, one of the famous Stroudley 'Terriers' (A1X class),* Stepney *was the first engine to arrive on the Bluebell, in 1960, having been withdrawn from Eastleigh B.R. shed in May of that year (p. 38).*

BOTTOM LEFT: *No. 2* Northern Chief *was one of the original 4-6-2s built for the Romney, Hythe and Dymchurch Railway in 1927. It is being prepared for work at Hythe station (p. 45).*

BOTTOM RIGHT: *On the Severn Valley Railway, class 2MT 2-6-0 No. 46443 crosses Victoria Bridge, still in the red livery it was given for a part in the film* The Seven Per Cent Solution *(p. 88).*

Swedish locomotive builders Nydquist and Holm. The class were intended for light passenger and freight work. This engine has been named *King Haakon VII*, as it was reputed to be the engine which conveyed this monarch from Norway during the German invasion of 1940. It has been restored to the light green livery which pertained around 1919.

There are two 0-6-0 saddle tanks at work on the railway and they usually work in conjunction. No. 5 *Littleton* and No. 4 *Robert Nelson* were both built for the Littleton collieries in Staffordshire.

The Railway's passenger-carrying fleet consists of five standard British Rail carriages all completed in the 1950s. They are corridor coaches with one exception, a first-class restaurant car, which is used for special evening departures offering five-course meals. The carriages are being repainted in their original cream and maroon livery.

There are also two former L.N.E.R. catering vehicles. First, a buffet car built in 1937 to a Gresley design, which has since been modernized inside by British Rail. Secondly, there is a buffet/restaurant car built in 1938 for the Flying Scotsman train. This carriage has been rebuilt as simply a buffet. A full dining service is offered on two mid-day trains; the evening meals on the named trains in the summer.

In addition to running a regular steam service, the Trust has a programme of engine restoration in their yards at Loughborough.

OPPOSITE, TOP: *The 'Terrier' No. 10* Sutton, *now on the Kent and East Sussex Railway, celebrated its centenary on 26 September in 1976. The G.W.R. diesel railcar is being towed dead as the train rounds the curve out of Tenterden Town (p. 48).*

BELOW LEFT: *Rebuilt at the Boston Lodge workshop of the Festiniog Railway, 0-4-0 + 0-4-0 Double Fairlie locomotive* Merddyn Emrys *leaves Porthmadog Harbour station with a heavy summer train.*

BELOW RIGHT: *Former Penrhyn Quarry 0-4-0* Linda, *rebuilt by the Festiniog Railway as a 0-4-2 and adapted for oil firing, sits in Boston Lodge workshops (p. 117).*

They have four locomotives at present undergoing extensive repair and repainting. The largest is the Pacific No. 71000 *Duke of Gloucester*. The class 8 was designed after nationalization by R. A. Riddles. The engine was completed in 1954 and was intended as a prototype for a standard B.R. express locomotive. But a decision was then taken to switch to diesel and electric traction, and this was the only one of its type ever built. *Duke of Gloucester* saw good service on the West Coast line from Euston to Glasgow for some six years.

There is another 4-6-0 undergoing restoration, No. 34039 *Boscastle*. The engine was built for the Southern Railway in 1941 and numbered 21C139 as part of the West Country class. Some were rebuilt under B.R., involving the removal of the distinctive 'air-smoothed' casing. As a result of the modification, they were 4 tons heavier but much more reliable and economical. *Boscastle*, during part of its varied career, headed the Golden Arrow service to Dover from Victoria.

The Great Western is also to be represented on the railway. No. 6990 *Witherslack Hall* is one of F. W. Hawksworth's modified Halls, completed in 1948. They were medium powered general-purpose engines. This loco was selected in 1948 to take part in exchange trials and was run over the Great Central network to assess the efficiency of various company's locomotives. It spent most of its life in the Oxford area, before being scrapped in 1966.

There is an L.N.E.R.-designed 4-6-0, No. 1364, a class B1. This engine was built in 1947, five years after the class had been introduced by Edward Thompson. Like the Halls on the Western, they were general-purpose engines, and came to be a fairly numerous class - some 410 in all. For a few years in the late 1940s they were the staple express engine along the Great Central before being replaced by more powerful engines. This engine spent much of its working life based at Nottingham, before being scrapped in 1966. Another B1, No. 1306 *Mayflower* has recently arrived from Carnforth. The Society also has a wide range of industrial tanks, 0-6-0s and 0-4-0s.

By the beginning of 1979 the tally of locomotives at Loughborough had risen to 22. The latest acquisition, one due to the foresight

The restoration of the Duke of Gloucester *must be one of the largest projects ever undertaken by a preservation society, but the M.L.S.T. has always intended to preserve examples of main line engines, and the M.L.S.T. and the Duke of Gloucester Steam Locomotive Trust (who own No. 71000) are making steady progress. This is the official B.R.* photo taken on the engine's completion at Crewe in 1954. The photo (BELOW) shows it as it was in November 1968 at Barry scrapyard, the cylinder removed for display (sectioned) at the Science Museum, Kensington. Many parts are being manufactured from scratch for the restoration, which is following the original plans.

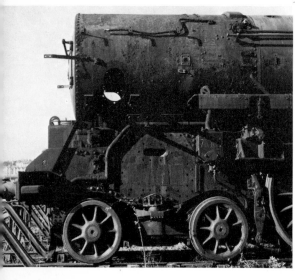

of a Nottingham businessman, is an ex-G.W.R. 2-8-0 No. 5224 with side water tanks. She is entering strange territory, going to the Great Central, although in the heyday of steam Great Western engines were no strangers to Leicester. No. 5224 and her sister engines were designed for the Great Western by their Chief Mechanical Engineer, George Jackson Churchward. Built in May 1924, she weighs over 82 tons, and spent most of her working life in the South Wales coalfield, working the short heavy-haul coal trains from the pits in the valleys to the ports and factories. With this acquisition, Loughborough's already wide variety of steam locomotives has received an interesting and useful addition.

ABOVE: Butler-Henderson, *built in 1919, is the only Great Central express loco to have survived. It is now back on loan from York.*

BELOW: Mayflower, *an L.N.E.R. 4-6-0 B1 class, undergoes servicing at the Loughborough engine shed of the M.L.S.T.*

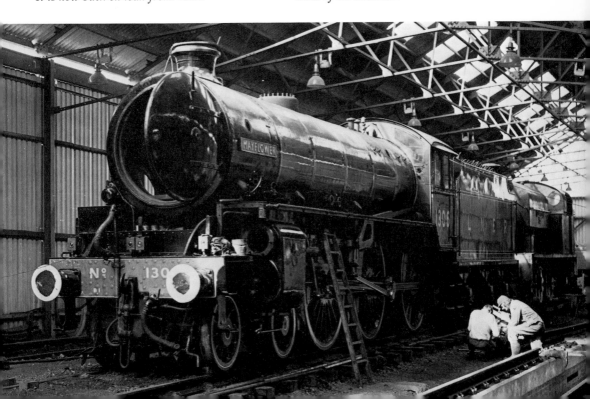

Bulmer's Railway Centre

In 1968, the cider makers H. P. Bulmer decided to establish a railway centre near their premises at Hereford. The show piece was to be the celebrated Great Western locomotive *King George V*, together with five Pullman coaches formerly used on the Southern Railway's Golden Arrow and Bournemouth Belle. These comprise the 'Bulmer Cider Train'.

For their centre, Bulmer's were able to make use of the Moorfield Depot of the former Midland Railway. The track layout is a triangle, which enables engines and coaches to be turned round. On the waste land enclosed by these lines are the remains of the original Midland sheds.

King George V was the prototype of a famous class. In July 1927, soon after completion, she was shipped to America to represent British locomotive design at the Baltimore and Ohio Railroad Centenary. She still has her large brass

No. 6000, King George V, is the pride of Bulmer's Railway Centre. Built in 1927, it was exhibited in America in that year at the Baltimore and Ohio Centenary Celebrations. The B. & O. presented an American locomotive bell to the engine, which is still carried over the buffer-beam. It frequently works steam specials, using preserved Pullman and G.W.R. stock.

bell on her buffer beam in commemoration of that visit. On her return to Britain *King George V* was restored for normal express running, and on occasion for royal trains and other prestige runs. When withdrawn from service in 1962, she had covered nearly two million miles, and, being scheduled for preservation, was stored at Swindon. In 1968 Bulmer's offered to pay for her complete restoration, provided she could then be housed and steamed at their Hereford headquarters. Since B.R. withdrew their ban on steam running, *King George V* has been able to work enthusiasts' specials over certain lines in the Western Region.

Since 1968 other preservation societies have based their locomotives here, among these being the Merchant Navy Class Preservation Society's Bulleid Pacific, No. 35028, *Clan Line*. A fine example of her class, she was built in 1948. Under B.R. she worked such famous trains as The Golden Arrow and The Atlantic Coast Express, and on one occasion, near Axminster, achieved an authenticated 104 m.p.h. She was withdrawn from service in 1967 and immediately acquired by the Society. She took part in the Shildon cavalcade in 1975, and now hauls enthusiasts' specials.

Another famous locomotive stored here is the London Midland and Scottish Railway's *Princess Elizabeth*, which belongs to the Princess Elizabeth Locomotive Society. Designed by Sir William Stanier, a 4-6-2, she is one of a class designed for the fast London–Glasgow trains, and introduced in the 1930s. In 1936 *Princess Elizabeth* ran non-stop from London to Glasgow (401 miles) in 353 minutes. She continued to work on this route till withdrawn in 1962 and bought by the Society: until 1976 she was kept at the Dowty Railway Preservation Society's premises at Ashchurch, but is now based on Hereford. On occasion she too hauls enthusiasts' specials.

These three are the star exhibits at Bulmer's, but there are other locomotives too: one steam tank engine, the 0-4-0 saddle tank *Pectin*; and two diesels, *Woodpecker* and *Cider Queen*.

The Worcester Locomotive Society store two of their locomotives here: the G.W.R. 0-6-0 pannier tank No. 5786, and a 0-6-0 saddle tank *Caernarvon*, which comes from Stewart and Lloyd's steel works at Corby.

Tyseley Railway Museum

The Birmingham Railway Museum at Tyseley, whose full title is the Standard Gauge Steam Trust, is not simply a place where visitors go to look at objects in glass cases; it is a working museum where fully operational steam engines are housed between runs and where rescued locomotives are restored and maintained. The museum is situated on a spacious site behind the existing British Rail diesel depot. It consists of two large sheds, the Upper Shed, which houses the toolroom, and the New Shed, which acts as the heavy workshop. The former contains a variety of powerful lathes, and milling and grinding machines, while the latter contains a huge wheel-turning and axle lathe weighing over forty tons. In addition there are various smithies. All this equipment, and the technical skills which it involves, has meant that Tyseley Depot is able to offer comprehensive repair and restoration facilities for steam engines.

Since B.R. ended steam running in the late 1960s, enthusiasts have been hard-pressed for lines and sheds to run and maintain their engines. This need produced a solution in Tyseley. It now contains a wide variety of locomotives from many companies. These include the Great-Western-designed *Clun Castle*, *Albert Hall*, and *Thornbury Castle*, together with a number of 0-6-0 pannier tank engines. Equally impressive, in its crimson livery, is the ex-L.M.S. express locomotive, Jubilee class 4-6-0 *Kolhapur*. From the London and South Western Railway, decked out in light green, is the 4-4-0 T9 class No. 120.* In black is the L. & Y.R. 2-4-2 tank engine No. 1008.* In addition to these locomotives, there is a fine collection of old coaches, including some replica vehicles from the Liverpool and Manchester Railway of the 1830s. Also notable amongst this collection are some magnificent chocolate-and-cream Pullman cars.

Besides these working remains of the steam age, there is a static museum. Included in the displays are locomotive models, sectioned parts and illustrations. Twice a year, very successful open days are held at the depot, with some of the engines in steam and run along a mile or so of track. Footplate rides are offered as a further attraction.

The railway museum stands as an example of enthusiast achievement. It also represents a degree of co-operation between B.R., the City of Birmingham, and amateur supporters: the first two bodies both have official representatives sitting on the governing trust of the museum.

The necessity of a depot such as this for the continued and successful running of steam is quite clear. In normal service a locomotive usually ran for about 100,000 miles before being thoroughly overhauled, which overhaul involved stripping the engine down and removing the wheels and frame. The process needs much heavy equipment and a high degree of skill. Engines selected for preservation, though the pick of the bunch, were obviously at the ends of their useful lives with B.R. Consequently, they have required either immediate attention, or were due for overhaul in the immediate future. Tyseley has been developed to tackle this maintenance and renovation for enthusiasts lacking expertise or equipment to do the work themselves. The sort of routine work which is undertaken at Tyseley includes the removal and renovation of all mudhole doors, washout plugs, water gauges, safety valves and boiler tubes. The boiler is then filled with steam to check its strength and the accuracy of the gauges. Other parts requiring special attention include the wheels and their flanges together with the brake and draw gear.

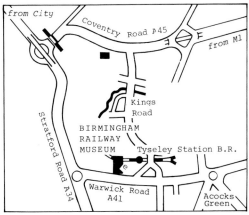

* These engines have now left Tyseley

Birmingham itself, as an industrial town, possesses many fine relics of industrial growth: the railway museum is but one. The Science Museum is the complement of Tyseley, and contains an early English steam engine built in 1784. It also houses a whole variety of the kind of mechanical apparatus which made Birmingham one of the most important manufacturing towns of Europe in the nineteenth century.

The Birmingham Railway Museum at Tyseley is built around a well-equipped workshop which has many pieces of specialized equipment, including a wheel tyre and electric wheel drop. The project which started it all was the preservation of Clun Castle, *the engine which worked the last steam train out of Paddington, seen here, fully restored to main-line condition, at Tyseley engine shed. Note the distinctive double chimney.*

Shackerstone Railway Society

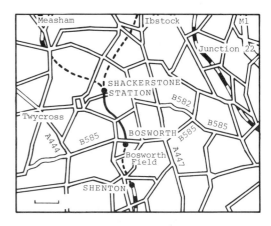

The Society, which specializes in industrial locomotives, owns the four-and-a-half miles of track between Shackerstone and Shenton, and operates the 2¾ miles from Shackerstone to Market Bosworth. The other section has been lifted, and it is hoped to re-lay track along this route shortly. The Society's headquarters at Shackerstone contain a fine museum. There are many relics on display including signal apparatus, signs, tickets, badges and photographs. The Society possesses a fine collection of industrial locomotives. There are four 0-4-0 saddle tanks, constructed by Borrows (1906), Hunslet (1925), Bagnall (1941), and two Pecketts (1951 and 1942), and one 0-6-0ST built by Hawthorne Leslie in 1938. There are two former B.R. coaches both completed in the 1950s, and a number of miscellaneous goods vehicles, mostly from the pre-nationalization period.

Shackerstone was once the junction station for the Moira West–Nuneaton line and a branch to

Coalville and Loughborough. In its heyday, six trains each way passed through, plus the Loughborough service operated by motor trains (1922), but passenger services ceased as early as 1931, except for excursions which continued until about 1960. The then Midland Railway Society acquired use of the charming but by then utterly derelict station at Shackerstone in 1970. The Society adopted the Shackerstone name in 1972. This 1974 view of the station shows clearly three of the Society's locos: Peckett 0-4-0 Herbert; *Robert Stephenson & Hawthorn 0-6-0 side tank No. 4; Hawthorn Leslie 0-6-0 saddle tank No. 21.*

The Foxfield Light Railway Society

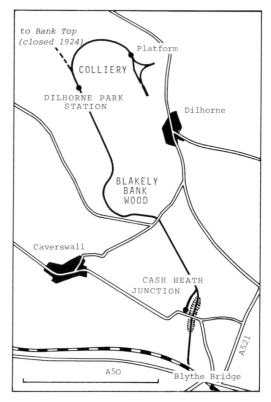

The Foxfield Light Railway is a 3-mile standard-gauge line running from the now-closed Foxfield Colliery, Dilhorne, to the former North Staffordshire (Stoke–Derby) Railway, which it joined at a junction four hundred yards west of Blythe Bridge station. When the colliery closed in 1965, the railway and mine were purchased by Tean Minerals. The railway is now operated with their permission.

The line is interesting: it was built with sharp curves and gradients as steep as 1 in 20, in order to minimize the expense of earthworks. From Foxfield, the line climbs steeply, curving left through Foxfield Wood and Pearcroft Wood to the line's summit (705 ft). The colliery is visible

Hunslet 0-6-0 Wimblebury *with a train at Foxfield station in the summer of 1978. In the foreground, coming off the storage siding, is* Lewisham.

Henry Cort, *built in 1903 and the oldest engine at Foxfield, hauls a one-coach train towards the line summit. The old colliery is visible.* Henry Cort *is now rarely used on passenger services.*

below to the left. Having swung round to the south-west, it straightens out through Dilhorne Wood, passing Stansmore Hall, a seventeenth-century building, and circles the foot of Blakely Bank Wood. The line then crosses the Caverswall–Dilhorne road at a gated level crossing, and runs into Cash Heath Junction. The line continues downhill through a deep cutting spanned by a bridge on the Caverswall–Blythe Bridge road.

At present, the passenger service is operated from Foxfield for $2\frac{1}{2}$ miles to Cash Heath Junction. The intermediate station, Dilhorne Park, has excellent picnic sites. Access to the railway is at present (1979) from Foxfield only.

Stock

Appropriately, the railway is operated with a number of industrial tank engines. The oldest is Manning Wardle 0-6-0 saddle tank *Rhiwnant*, built in 1895. There are four Bagnalls, two 0-6-0, *Topham* (1922) and *Lewisham* (1927), and two 0-4-0, *J. T. Daly* (1931) and *Hawarden* (1940). There are two Avonside locos, both 0-6-0STs; a Hunslett 0-6-0, a Stephenson & Hawthorn 0-4-0 side-tank crane *Roker* (1940), and two 0-4-0 Pecketts, *Henry Cort* (1903) and No. 11. There is a Barclay, No. 1, and also several diesel shunters.

For passenger services, the Society has two B.R. Mark 1 carriages (1957), but has older and more unusual stock, including four L.M.S. bogie scenery vans, two converted to observation cars and one to a refreshment van. There is a wide range of goods stock, including a Smith Rodley steam crane.

105

Chasewater Light Railway Society

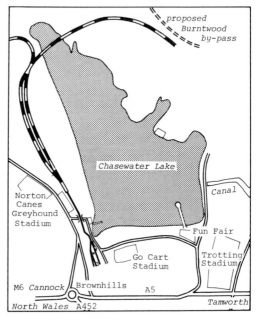

The Chasewater Light Railway was first leased from the National Coal Board in 1965. At the time it still constituted part of the truncated remains of the former Cannock Chase and Wolverhampton Railway, built in 1856, and an extension of the Midland Railway's Walsall Wood branch opened in 1884. The Chasewater Society is the operating group of the Railway Preservation Society. Trains normally run on Sunday afternoons between May and September, with pre-grouping stock, and are usually steam powered. The line runs around the edge of Chasewater Pleasure Park, which features a fine lake, go-cart stadium and fun fair. Ultimately it is hoped that the railway will operate along a 2-mile stretch (purchased from B.R. in 1978) with proper station facilities at each end to enable a regular passenger schedule to be introduced. A particular feature is a narrow quarter-mile causeway across the end of the Lake in the Park.

On the Chasewater Railway, 0-4-0 Neilson Alfred Paget hauls a d.m.u. trailer coach, used because of its good observation facilities.

Stock

Motive power is provided by a number of saddle tank locomotives. One engine which has been restored is *Asbestos*, a Hawthorn Leslie 0-4-0ST built in 1909. The oldest engines on the line are, No. 11, *Alfred Paget*, an 0-4-0ST built by Neilson in 1882, and No. 9 *Cannock Wood*, a former L.B. & S.C.R. 0-6-0T, built in 1877.* There are two Barclay and two Hudswell Clarke saddle tanks together with one Peckett loco, all of which are receiving attention.

The Society possesses a fine collection of vintage coaches. Recently restored is a Manchester, Sheffield & Lincolnshire Railway six-wheeler, which was taken over as a rotting hulk. It dates from about 1890. A superb example of restoration is provided by the sole surviving vehicle from the Maryport and Carlisle Railway, a six-wheeled carriage built in 1879. There is also a former Great Eastern full brake coach, No. 44, built in 1885. There are a number of other vintage coaches, mostly from the Midland Railway.

---

* This engine has now been sold to the East Somerset Railway.

Dean Forest Railway Preservation Society

The Dean Forest Railway Society was formed by enthusiasts in 1970 when the then goods-only branch from Lydney Junction to Parkend, in the Forest of Dean, first came under threat of closure. The Society began collecting funds and equipment, to be ready when the line actually closed, so that they could recommence a steam service. Norchard, the station to the north of Lydney, was selected as their headquarters. At this base, the Society has laid track back to the depot buildings (it had been lifted by British Rail), and the buildings have been restored for the public's use. At Parkend, now a true two-platform station, $3\frac{1}{2}$ miles from Lydney, the Society rents the old station, with a siding to accommodate preserved stock.* There is also a small museum here. The Society is actively raising funds for the actual purchase of the line, should B.R. decide to dispose of the branch. At present, B.R. retain it in case of the resumption of coal traffic. Restoration work is pushing ahead on the Society's Hunslet Austerity 0-6-0ST, No. 3806, built in 1953. They also possess an ex-G.W.R. auto-coach, No. 167, which is being worked upon, planned to be a passenger vehicle. In addition, the Society possesses a Peckett 0-4-0ST *Uskmouth 1*, built in 1952. Their rolling stock, including goods vehicles, is mostly from the Great Western.

* Since 1978, Parkend has been vacated, and all stock and relics concentrated at Norchard.

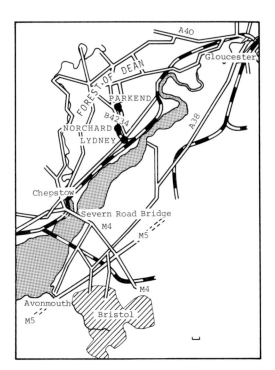

The Parkend site of the Dean Forest Railway Society: Peckett 0-4-0 Uskmouth 1 *gives brake-van rides.*

Dowty Railway Preservation Society

The Dowty Railway Preservation Society was formed in 1962 by enthusiasts of the Dowty Group's Sports and Social Society. Dowty manufacture mining machinery. (Non-employees can join as associate members.) The Society selected a group of sidings next to the company's works at Ashchurch, Gloucester-shire. Ashchurch arose as a junction on the 1840 Birmingham–Gloucester Railway, the junction lines being built to serve Tewkesbury and Evesham. The track layout was complicated, with a diamond cross-over being built to join the two branches which went in opposite directions from Ashchurch, which was con-sequently quite an extensive site. The sidings which Dowty R.P.S. use were built to serve the Midland Railway provender store, a large warehouse where feed for the Company's cartage horses was processed before being despatched to the towns and cities. Both branches – and consequently Ashchurch station – are long closed.

Apart from the standard-gauge lines, there is a 2 ft gauge railway, laid to give rides and earn funds on open days. Short standard-gauge rides are also possible.

Stock
The largest item is a Southern Railway Q class, No. 30541, a 0-6-0 tender locomotive. At present undergoing restoration, she will probably be moved to the Bluebell Railway before long.

The Society owns a number of tank engines. There are four and they are all 0-4-0 saddle tanks. The most distinctive is 'Cadbury No. 1', an Avonside of Bristol product, completed in 1925. This side tank was used at the Birming-ham Bournville works until 1962 when it was replaced by diesel power. The design is some-what unusual, resulting from the need to haul heavy trains on sharply curved sidings. It has outside Walschaert's valve-gear. The other three industrial locos were manufactured by Barclay of Kilmarnock, Scotland. One is oil-fired, one fireless.

There are two impressive former Great Western carriages here. No. 9635 is a first-class restaurant car, built in their centenary year, 1935, for work on the Cornish Riviera. This carriage is now undergoing extensive re-storation. When completed it will be used to serve teas on open days. The other G.W.R. carriage is the special saloon No. 9044, built in 1881. It was an early corridor coach, and is the oldest surviving complete carriage from the G.W.R. The saloon was used on Royal Trains, and it is believed the the Prince of Wales rode in it during his tour of Wales in the 1930s. Ultimately it was used as the Shrewsbury Engineer's saloon, and was purchased by the Society in 1964. It is now being restored to 1920s livery.

In addition, the Society has assembled an impressive number of narrow-gauge loco-motives. There is also a variety of rolling stock to provide rides. Several signal boxes have been acquired and moved to the site. There is a large collection of signs and name plates, together with a variety of signalling equipment.

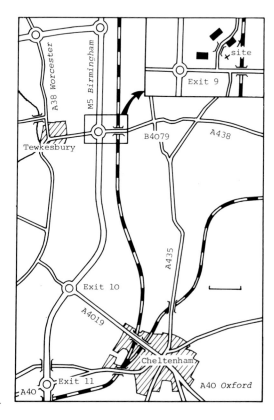

Quainton Railway Society

The Quainton Railway Society was formed in 1969 as a working railway museum of locomotives and rolling stock together with equipment of all kinds as used until the 1950s. The Society originated from the London Railway Preservation Society, formed in 1962. Over the years it has built up an extremely large and impressive array of exhibits. Quainton itself is of interest in that it was the place where the Great Central and Metropolitan Railways met. Many of the locos and some of the rolling stock reflect these two companies, but there are other main-line and industrial engines, for the aim of the society is to make their collection as comprehensive as possible.

Stock

From the Metropolitan Railway, there is a 0-4-4T, No. 1, built in 1898, renumbered as L.T.44. There is a former Great Western pannier tank, No. 7715, completed in 1930 and then purchased by London Transport and numbered L99. There is another pannier tank, built to Great Western designs in 1952 by British Railways, No. 9466. This is a 94XX class, and may be distinguished from earlier pannier tanks by the shorter tanks which leave the front of the smoke box exposed. Another historic loco at Quainton is the former L. & S.W.R. 2-4-0WT, No. 0314, built by Beyer Peacock in 1874. Besides these, there are a host of industrial locomotives of various types, and a number of Sentinel shunting engines. In all, there are around forty steam engines undergoing restoration here.

The Society has a very interesting and historic collection of coaches. There is a Great Northern six-wheeled third-class brake carriage, built in 1895.

Other historic carriages include an L.N.E.R. Gresley-designed BSK coach, No. 41384, built in 1936; an L.D.C.R. first-class four-wheeled coach built in 1880; an L. & N.W.R. first-class kitchen/dining car No. 77, built in 1901; and an

The London Railway Preservation Society formed in 1969 the Quainton Railway Society, based on the sidings at Quainton Road station (B.R. still uses the through line for goods), the place where the Great Central and Metropolitan Railways met. Its particular speciality is old coaches: this train of vintage G.N.R. and G.C.R. 6-wheelers is hauled by L. & S.W.R. 2-4-0 tank No. 0314, a well-tank loco (the water tank slung between the wheels) built in 1874.

L. & N.W.R. six-wheeled passenger brake, No. DM 279982, built in 1891.

The Society holds a number of open days on bank holidays. Rides are then available, when the engines are in steam. The nearest railway station is Aylesbury, and there is occasionally a charter d.m.u. service from there to Quainton station.

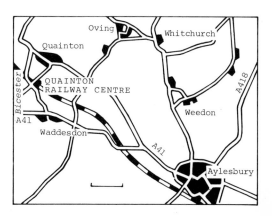

The Cadeby Light Railway

Cadeby is a small Leicestershire village not far from Market Bosworth (from which the famous battle of 1485 took its name). The narrow-gauge railway there is entirely the inspiration of the Rector, the Rev. E. R. Boston. It runs round the grounds of his rectory.

In 1962 he bought the Bagnall saddle tank *Pixie*, No. 2090, from Staveley Minerals who had no further use for her in their quarry. Following *Pixie*'s arrival, a track-bed was prepared and track laid. This involved clearing away vegetation and laying down ballast delivered from the nearby Cliffe Hill quarry. The railway was fortunate in receiving much of its track free, as a gift from Cadeby quarry. Track-laying went on from early summer through to September by which time a station and most of the upper curve had been completed. *Pixie* had not worked for some time; she therefore needed a thorough overhaul. New slide bars, new crossheads and fresh piston rings were fitted. The boiler was carefully examined and given a stiff hydraulic test. The first steam run was in April 1963, and the locomotive proved to be in fine working order. That summer witnessed the completion of the 400-yard line between Cadeby and Sutton Lane Stations.

Since then, many more locomotives have been acquired; part of the permanent way has been relaid with 40-lb rail replacing the lighter, original track. Besides the engine *Pixie*, the Railway now has two other steam locomotives: *Sergeant Murphy* and *Margaret*, both obtained from Penrhyn Quarries Ltd. *Sergeant Murphy* was built by Kerr Stuart, and is the only remaining example of the type they designed for work on military railways during World War I. After working a spell for the Royal Navy at Beachley Dock, she was purchased by Penrhyn Quarries. There, she was involved in a fatal accident, and was then regarded with a certain amount of superstition by the slate workers. A 0-6-0 side tank, she is at present being restored. The second locomotive bought from the Quarries is a Hunslet, No. 605, *Margaret*, completed in 1894. Built for the Quarries, she is of 0-4-0 design. She also is being restored.

In addition to these steam-powered engines, the Railway has acquired several diesel locomotives. These include Motor Rail 'Simplex' Diesel, No. 3874. This engine was built in 1929 and is of a class originally designed to run in France during World War I. No. 3874 was rescued from the Birmingham, Tame and Rea District Drainage Board in 1965. Another early 'Simplex' diesel owned by the Railway is No. 5853, constructed in 1934. It is universally known by the operating staff as 'The Diesel';

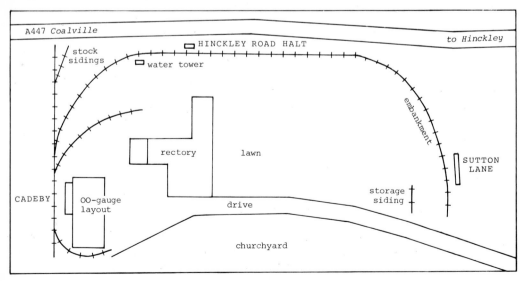

Pixie, *Bagnall 0-4-0 No. 2090 of 1919, on the Cadeby Light Railway.*

this is now an accurate description, as the original petrol engine was replaced in 1958 and a Dorman 20 h.p. diesel substituted. Also to be seen is No. 1695, *Lilleshall*, a Baguley petrol-driven engine finished in 1928; Motor Rail Diesel No. 5609, built in 1931; and a Hudswell Clark diesel No. 558, completed in 1930. This last engine is curious in that it was designed with a dummy chimney of a steam type. (It is rumoured that these were fitted to these locomotives because the works manager was a keen steam enthusiast and had very dogmatic views as to the proper appearance of engines.) The three open wagons which serve as passenger carriages have all come from the R.A.F. railway at Fauld. They have since been smartly turned out in grey-and-black livery with red fittings.

There are two bonuses to be found at the railway; one is a collection of traction engines and the other a fine model railway. The latter is housed in a wooden shed situated behind Cadeby station. It represents the South Devon section of the Great Western Railway between Newton Abbot and Totnes. The actual countryside around Dartmoor is faithfully reproduced, although the junction station of Olton Prior is imaginary. The main line is worked on the basis of the 1938 timetable, with the clock speeded up by a ratio of 8:1, permitting the day's schedule to be completed in only 3 hours.

The railway boasts a large number of G.W.R. locomotives, including Kings, Castles, Stars, Manors and Granges, together with the ubiquitous pannier tanks. Twenty engines are required to fulfil the demands of the timetable. The line has taken over a decade to build, so far, and much work still remains to be done. In the rectory itself there is a very comprehensive collection of railway relics ranging from nameplates to tickets and luggage labels.

The traction engine collection includes the steam roller *Thistledown*, built by Aveling and Porter, and *Fiery Elias*, a Foster traction engine built in 1929. Both are in full working order. *Fiery Elias* is a single cylinder 7-h.p. engine capable of hauling 16 to 20 tons, while *Thistledown* is a 5-h.p., ten-ton steam roller built in 1903. She worked for Leicester County Council until 1960, and has since been well restored.

The Cadeby Light Railway is probably the smallest steam-worked narrow-gauge railway in the world. It is the brainchild of Rev. E. R. Boston and his railway enthusiast friends – people who are fascinated by steam locomotives, and are prepared to work very hard to ensure their preservation. The line is open to the public on the second Saturday in the month, and other days by arrangement.

111

The Leighton Buzzard Narrow-Gauge Railway

During World War I supplies of sand from Belgium dried up, and pits near Leighton Buzzard were opened to meet the need. Increased output demanded improved transport, and 4½ miles of 2 ft gauge railway was laid down between Churchways and Pages Park and opened for traffic in 1919. Motive power was at first by steam but latterly till the pits were closed in 1969, petrol-driven ex-W.D. locomotives were used.

The Leighton Buzzard Light Railway Society was formed in 1968 in anticipation of the line's closure, and ran their first passenger train – diesel hauled – on 3 March 1968. In June their

Pixie, 0-4-0 *Kerr-Stuart on the Leighton Buzzard Narrow-Gauge Railway. Built in 1922, she is a saddle tank.*

first steam engine arrived, and was run along the line. (Trains now start from Pages Park Station in Billington Road.) This first engine was *Chaloner,* which has a vertical boiler and was built by De Winton & Co. of Caernarvon in 1877, for work in slate quarries in the Nantlle Valley, North Wales. She remained there until bought in 1960 by Mr Alfred Fisher, who overhauled her. She is claimed to be the oldest narrow-gauge engine in England, and the last working example of an industrial type once common in North Wales.

Chaloner is No. 1; No. 2 is *Pixie,* a 0-4-0 saddle tank, built in 1922, which worked in Devon County Council roadstone quarries till 1955. She was bought and overhauled by the Industrial Locomotive Society, and began service at Leighton Buzzard in 1969.

Rishra, No. 3, was built in 1921 for service in India. She hauled coal trains from a wharf on the Hooghly river to the boiler house of the Pulta Pumping Station at Barrakpore, north of Calcutta, and after long negotiations was restored by the apprentices of the Hooghly Dock and

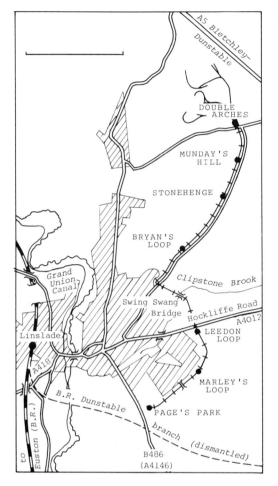

Engineering Co. She was then shipped back to England, and ran for the first time there in October 1972.

The Doll is No. 4. A 0-6-0 tank engine built by Andrew Barclay in 1919 for work in an ironstone pit in Oxfordshire, she was later transferred to a foundry in Bilston, where she had very rough treatment. Purchased by the I.L.S. in 1972, she is in process of being restored, in the hope that she may once again be steamable.

The Society has three other steam engines and eight diesels, mostly W.D. types, and offers a regular scheduled service on Sundays, Easter to September, and Bank Holiday Saturdays and Mondays in addition; there are 3 miles of track now in use.

Over one hundred years old, Chaloner *is a vertical-boilered De Winton, built for work in North Wales quarries in 1877. She is one of the oldest steam locomotives of any gauge still in regular use. The coaches were built by the Railway on bogie-wagon chassis.*

Future plans include the improvement of Pages Park station, the building of further passenger rolling stock, and the setting up of a museum of the local sand industry.

Besides being an ancient market town of considerable interest, Leighton Buzzard is also within reasonably easy reach of such places as Woburn Abbey, Whipsnade Zoo, the Stagsden Bird Gardens, and the Shuttleworth Aircraft Museum at Old Warden near Biggleswade.

113

Whipsnade and Umfolozi Railway

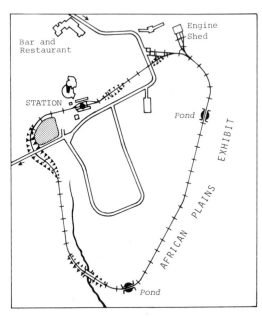

Opened in 1970, this splendid narrow-gauge railway was created from scratch as a commercial venture, and is operated by Pleasurail. It allows close-quarter viewing of species like white rhinos, bison and camels, uncaged in the animal paddocks of Whipsnade Zoo. It is an imaginative answer to the problem of helping visitors to the Zoo see as much as possible of the wildlife there.

The first stage went only to the white rhino enclosure. The rhino came from Umfolozi in Zululand, hence the railway's name. They soon grew used to the 2 ft 6 in. gauge steam locomotives, and so in 1973 the railway was extended to its present length of about 2 miles. (The animals are now so used to the railway that train crews often have to persuade sleeping rhinos that the best place to take a nap is not on the permanent way!)

The railway forms an irregular oval, with trains starting and finishing at the twin-

On the Whipsnade and Umfolozi, No. 2 Excelsior, a 1908 Kerr-Stuart saddle tank. At 14½ tons, she is only half the weight of Chevallier.

platform Whipsnade Central station next the dolphinarium. Fairly considerable engineering works were necessary (the Zoo is on top of the Dunstable Downs), and the line features a short tunnel, two level crossings, steep gradients, and several cuttings and embankments.

Much of the line's equipment and rolling stock came from the Bowater paper-mill railway at Sittingbourne (part of which has been preserved as the Sittingbourne and Kemsley), which was last used for industrial purposes in 1969. The three 0-6-0 tanks, *Chevallier*, *Conqueror* and *Superior*, were built by Manning Wardle, Bagnall and Kerr-Stuart respectively, in 1915, 1922 and 1920. (*Conqueror* fell into the dock at Bowater in the 1953 flood.) The fourth steam loco is the oldest (1908), the 0-4-2 *Excelsior*, built by Kerr-Stuart. Passengers are carried in coaches rebuilt from pulp wagons.

On static display is the 3 ft 6 in. gauge 4-8-0 No. 390 from the Zambesi Sawmills, built in Glasgow in 1896, and a Rhodesia Railways sleeping car. These items were presented to artist David Shepherd (of Cranmore) by President Kaunda, and then transported over 12,000 miles to Whipsnade.

The railway operates with steam most of the time, but two 100 h.p. Fowler diesels are used for shunting, and sometimes haul off-peak trains.

V
Wales

Introduction: Narrow-Gauge Railways in Wales

It was probably in North Wales that railways first became an attraction for visitors on holiday. There was a passenger coach, or coaches, to carry tourists on the 1 ft 11½ in. gauge Festiniog Railway as early as the 1840s, long before that line had steam locomotives. Horses pulled trains up the long continuous gradients, and gravity took them downwards.

The particular attraction of the F.R. for visitors was that fine views could be seen from its course high among the mountains. Later, steam locomotives were introduced, and regular passenger trains followed (the first in Britain on a gauge less than standard). The F.R. blossomed out into a small-scale main line which became a prototype for narrow-gauge railways throughout the world; visitors came to see it as an engineering marvel. By 1895 Baddeley and Ward's guide to *North Wales* was commenting '. . . though the wonder has somewhat worn off, still no orthodox tourist visits Wales without taking a turn . . . on the "Toy" railway.' The epithet 'Toy' was to be disdained by future generations of railway enthusiasts, but by 1895 several other narrow-gauge or 'Toy' railways had been built in Wales and were finding in tourism a useful way of supplementing ordinary goods and passenger traffic. More were to follow, and the Snowdon Mountain Railway was being built specifically for tourist traffic, to take holiday makers to the summit of the highest mountain in England and Wales.

During the 1930s Welsh narrow-gauge lines lost most of their local passengers to faster, more convenient, buses. Those lines that continued to run passenger trains did so almost entirely in summer only, for holiday visitors, to whom the twin attractions of small trains and mountain scenery were as enticing as ever. It was on lines known to holiday visitors, the Talyllyn and the Festiniog, that the railway preservation movement commenced in the 1950s. People on holiday started to come not only to travel on these railways, but also to help re-open and run them, voluntarily.

Most of the Welsh tourist railways have joined to form the Narrow Gauge Railways of Wales Joint Marketing Panel. This publishes a combined timetable sheet for the Festiniog, Welshpool and Llanfair, Talyllyn, Vale of Rheidol, Llanberis Lake, Snowdon Mountain, Fairbourne and Bala Lake lines. It also arranged for 'Narrow-Gauge Tourist Tickets' to be issued, which give seven days unlimited travel on all these lines except the Snowdon.

Many of these railways have links with the Association of Railway Preservation Societies. The preservation movement as a whole benefits greatly from the expertise provided by well-established undertakings such as the Festiniog and the Welshpool and Llanfair, and these in turn benefit from sound financing and safe operation and publicity of newer preserved railways.

Meanwhile, in north and mid-Wales, the 'Great Little Trains of Wales' (to use the collective name coined by the joint marketing panel) have become one of the Principality's most popular attractions for visitors.

They are all, those that operate a regular tourist service, *little* trains, that is to say, narrow-gauge. The standard-gauge preserved railway in this part of the world is limited to a scheme at Llangollen where work has already started re-laying a long-dismantled line. On the other hand, several British Rail lines in north and mid Wales have their own scenic attractions and are worth travelling for their own sake, although trains are not, of course, steam-hauled. Notable are the Conwy Valley line (from Llandudno Junction to Blaenau Ffestiniog) and the Cambrian Coast line (Dovey Junction to Pwllheli). The latter links several of the little trains.

Though small, most of the little railways that were built up to the time of World War I were not made that way to attract custom, like a later generation of miniature railways. They were made narrow-gauge because such railways can traverse sharp curves and this, in a mountainous region, meant smaller civil engineering works and, in turn, cheaper construction. Narrow-gauge railways also meant small, cheap locomotives and rolling stock and low running costs. Many of them were built to provide mines and quarries with an outlet.

The Festiniog Railway

The line and its history

The purpose of the Festiniog Railway was to link slate quarries around Blaenau Ffestiniog with the harbour at Porthmadog (or, as it was known until recently, Portmadoc). This is about 13 miles to the south-west and some 700 ft lower. The line was built by the Festiniog Railway Company, and opened in 1836. The first steam locomotives were introduced in 1863, two small 0-4-0 tanks with tenders for coal. Many strange designs had first been considered, for much contemporary opinion held that it was impracticable to build locomotives at all for so narrow a gauge. In 1865, four-wheeled passenger coaches were acquired, and the line passed by Board of Trade inspector for regular passenger traffic. This was a remarkable feat, for, since the 'gauge war' between 7 ft and 4 ft 8½ in. gauges, it had been illegal to construct a passenger railway of any gauge other than standard.

The Festiniog Railway really caught the public imagination, however, when rapidly increasing traffic obliged it to introduce more powerful motive power, *Little Wonder*, a double-ended 0-4-4-0 built to Fairlie's patent, carried on two bogies and having the appearance of two locomotives back-to-back – a compact but powerful machine. The type had been tried elsewhere, but it was on the F.R. that it was first really successful. Shortly afterwards the F.R. introduced the first bogie coaches to be used in Great Britain. Behind all this lay the Spooner family: James Spooner was the engineer who built the line, Charles Spooner, his son, introduced steam traction and developed the railway. The slate trade flourished and the railway prospered with it.

And when the slate trade eventually declined, the railway did too. Tiles became cheaper, and standard-gauge railways built direct to Blaenau Ffestiniog took much of what traffic was left. Local year-round passenger traffic (except for quarrymen's trains) ceased in 1930, and all passenger traffic was suspended at the outbreak of war in 1939. In 1946 the railway, overgrown, closed for freight too.

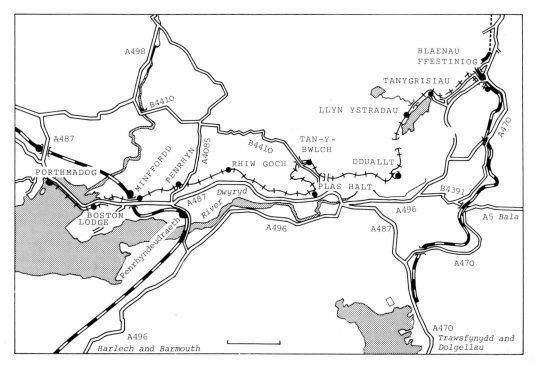

117

It became a lot more overgrown during the next few years, for the Act incorporating the Company was so old that it included no provision for legal abandonment and dismantling and the company could not afford to obtain such powers from Parliament.

The re-opening

The Festiniog Railway Society Ltd originated from a public meeting called by seventeen-year-old L. A. Heath Humphrys in Bristol in 1951. The intention was to re-open the railway with voluntary support. Investigations showed that the Company was heavily in debt, which would make it expensive to obtain control. The society sought a wealthy patron, and eventually found him in A. F. Pegler, who purchased a controlling interest in the Company in 1954, and then set up a trust to hold the controlling shares. The original trust was superseded in 1964 by the present one, called the Festiniog Railway Trust, which is a registered charity.

After Pegler obtained control, Company and Society agreed to work together to re-open the railway. This was not an easy task, for during

On the Festiniog Railway, double Fairlie Merddin Emrys *brings a down train into Tan-y-bwlch.*

eight years of dereliction, the railway had become so overgrown with brambles, rhododendrons, and even small trees, that it was for much of its length no longer possible to walk along it. The undergrowth had to be cut back, and this was done sufficiently for works trains, hauled by internal-combustion-powered locomotives, to traverse the whole line in 1955; to make the track safe for passenger trains, much more clearance and renovation work was needed.

Re-opening the F.R. has thus been done by stages: Porthmadog to Boston Lodge (1 mile) (which houses the railway's works) in 1955; to Minffordd (2 miles from Porthmadog) in 1956; to Penrhyndeudraeth ($3\frac{1}{4}$ miles) in 1957; and to Tan-y-bwlch ($7\frac{1}{2}$ miles), the half-way point, in 1958. There was then a pause for consolidation; the next station, Dduallt ($9\frac{1}{2}$ miles) was reached in 1968.

A big obstacle prevented re-opening of the next section. In 1955, after control of the

118

Blanche, built in 1893, heads a train along a dry-stone embankment typical of the Festiniog.

railway had changed but before any of it had been re-opened, electricity authorities obtained powers to submerge part of the course of this section of the line beneath a reservoir for a hydro-electric power station. The F.R. had an immensely long legal battle to obtain compensation: eventually, in 1971, it received £106,700 on grounds of lost operating profits.

This sum has not been enough to pay for building a deviation line. Work started, however, in a small way, in 1965, and in 1978 the line was re-opened to Tanygrisiau (12¼ miles). Other sources of money for it have been the Wales Tourist Board and the Manpower Services Commission. Equally significant has been that a large part of the work has been done voluntarily: this has meant that volunteers have excavated large amounts of rock to make cuttings and dumped the spoil to form embankments.

The railway proper is operated by a mixture of permanent staff, temporary staff and volun-teers. On any particular train the driver is almost certain to be on the permanent staff, the fireman is probably a volunteer, and the guard and buffet car attendants might be either permanent staff or voluntary, or temporary staff too.

A journey down the line
A trip on the Festiniog Railway generally starts at Porthmadog. As with all the railways in this section, the train service is geared to visitors on holiday, and so is most intensive in high summer, and less so in spring and autumn. Even out of season, there are trains at weekends and over Christmas; the only periods during which there is no public train service at all are from mid-November until Christmas, and from the New Year until mid-February.

Porthmadog station shows its origin by being at the harbour; the building is partly old, partly new-and-in-keeping. It includes the booking office, the railway shop which sells books, souvenirs and models, and the self-service restaurant. Immediately on leaving the station, the railway runs along the Cob, an early

119

nineteenth century sea wall. On clear days, the mountains of Snowdonia, including Snowdon itself, can be seen to the north. At the end of the Cob comes Boston Lodge Works: passengers get a brief glimpse of scenes of industry within. Minffordd is an interchange station with B.R.'s Cambrian Coast line; after another mile or so the railway takes up the hillside-shelf formation which continues, with few interruptions, as far as Dduallt. The line climbs gradually; the floor of the valley is eventually left far below, and the views are magnificent: wooded hillsides, mountain streams, steep slopes, rivers, lakes, the distant sea and a far glimpse of the silhouette of Harlech Castle.

The old line passed through a long tunnel beyond Dduallt. This is now blocked, and its far portal is submerged below the normal water level of Llyn Ystradau reservoir. So the deviation has immediately to gain height: it does so by a spiral, unique in Britain. It climbs round a curve of approximately 220 degrees, crosses over the original line by a new bridge at the approach to Dduallt station, and continues to curve and climb, taking up a new course parallel to the old but higher up the hillside. A new tunnel about 310 yards long follows, bored through rock by miners employed by the company during 1975–6; beyond it the route runs above the shore of the reservoir, past the power station, and falls gently to Tanygrisiau.

Work is proceeding rapidly on renovation of · the old line thence to Blaenau Ffestiniog.

Stock

Festiniog passenger traffic has grown rapidly: during the years 1940 to 1954 inclusive it was zero, but in 1975 there were 441,000 passenger journeys. Locomotives and rolling stock have increased in proportion. The first steam locomotive used by the new regime was the 0-4-0 tank, *Prince*. In theory this locomotive is one of the originals: in practice she (or *he* – it is difficult to conform to the usual convention of referring to locomotives as *she*, when faced with such a name) has been rebuilt so many times that little if any of the original remains. The 1946 closure interrupted one of the rebuildings: a new boiler, delivered but not fitted, was something of a godsend to the new regime, which completed re-assembly in 1955. A further rebuilding has just taken place.

The F.R. had three other double Fairlies after *Little Wonder*, and two of them survived in 1955. Both were subsequently overhauled and used and both, eventually, became due for rebuilding again. This has meant provision of two new double boilers. One of the locomotives, *Merddin Emrys*, was rebuilt in 1970; with the other, *Earl of Merioneth*, so much new work is being incorporated that she is regarded as a new locomotive incorporating some old parts. The original locomotive stock has been supplemented by two 0-4-0 saddle tanks, *Linda* and *Blanche*, from the Penrhyn Quarry Railway (which have been rebuilt as 2-4-0 saddle tanks, to make them ride better, and with superheaters and piston valves to make them more efficient); and by *Mountaineer*, a 2-6-2 tank built in the U.S.A. in 1917 for British military light railways in France: she subsequently ran for the Tramway de Pithiviers à Toury until 1964, when that line closed. She was then bought by the present writer and brought to the U.K. Like the other locomotives, she now belongs to the Festiniog Railway Company.

All steam locomotives in use have been converted to burn oil instead of coal. Conversion was almost immediately followed by the oil crisis and rapid escalation in the price of oil: this the railway has met by modifying the locomotives to burn a mixture of waste oil and diesel oil (instead of pure diesel oil). The conversions, prompted by the need to eliminate sparks which set fire to lineside forestry, proved their worth during the 1976 drought when, if the locomotives had still burned coal, trains would have had to have been cancelled beyond Penrhyndeudraeth so as to avoid the forestry area. Several small diesel locomotives are used for works trains and some off-peak passenger trains.

Mountaineer was saved from scrapping in 1964 when the Tramway de Pithiviers à Toury, in France, was closed. Built in 1917, this 2-6-2 Alco tank provides a fine show of smoke as it enters Tan-y-bwlch cutting. The smoke colour is partly due to the fact that Festiniog locos are oil-burning – a change forced because of the fire risk from sparks of coal-burners.

The great historic interest of the coaches on the line in 1955 was matched only by their state of dilapidation. They included four-wheelers from the 1860s and bogie coaches from the 1870s, but none had been used or maintained for the previous fifteen years. Those that were repairable (which eventually proved to be most of them) were gradually rebuilt and brought back into service. To them were added coaches from other long-closed lines – the Welsh Highland and Lynton and Barnstaple Railways – which had fortunately survived; subsequently, many new coaches have been built. F.R. coaches carry first- and third-class passengers: first is both more expensive and very much more comfortable. Many of the first-class seats in recently-built coaches came from withdrawn standard-gauge Pullman Cars. There are licensed buffet cars and observation cars included in most trains.

Photography

Despite the mileage of film exposed at it, the Festiniog Railway is not an easy line to photograph. It is particularly dangerous to attempt to reach vantage points by trespassing along the line, for clearances are tight – often only a few inches between train and rock cutting. But the line is unfenced across the Cob, with a footpath alongside. Main roads cross the line near Boston Lodge and Penrhyndeudraeth, and minor roads run near to it between these points. It seems likely that Dduallt will become a favoured photographic location. The little hill in the centre of the spiral belongs to the railway company, and is a picnic site with a viewpoint: photographers are able to alight at Dduallt to photograph the trains as they circle around them.

The area around

It is worth remembering that however impressive the Festiniog Railway may seem, it was originally but a small part of the distribution system of the slate industry. To put it into context, there are two other visits to make in the vicinity.

The Llechwedd Slate Caverns at Blaenau Ffestiniog show how slate was quarried or, to be precise, mined. Visitors enter the mine on a small train hauled by a battery-electric locomotive. Parts of the old workings are illuminated: life-size dummy miners appear to be hewing rock. Elsewhere the train emerges briefly into daylight before plunging underground again. The effect is dramatic.

Porthmadog was in the past as famous, if not more so, for its sailing ships as for its railway. These ships distributed Ffestiniog slate throughout the world. The Porthmadog Maritime Museum enables visitors to see something of this end of the industry: situated in an original quayside slate-storage shed are displays and artefacts, and alongside the quay (and accessible to visitors) is the ketch *Garlandstone*. She is not a Porthmadog-built ship (none is known to survive), but she did trade to Porthmadog, and her spars and black hull contrast markedly with modern yachts and motor cruisers, giving an idea of what the harbour once was like.

The Talyllyn Railway

The line and its history

James Winton Spooner, elder brother of Charles Spooner of Ffestiniog, was the engineer who constructed the Talyllyn Railway. This line of 2 ft 3 in. gauge was opened in 1866 to link slate quarries at Bryn Eglwys, near Abergynolwyn, with Tywyn, where an interchange station, now called Wharf, was built alongside a siding of the coastal standard-gauge line. This was itself then new – original Talyllyn plans were to go to Aberdovey harbour.

Like the Festiniog Railway, the Talyllyn Railway was laid out on continuous down gradient, but it does not seem that gravity was ever used regularly to power trains. However, the Talyllyn Railway Company did develop one delightful custom dependent on gravity: visitors who wished to return to Tywyn late in the evening, say after climbing Cader Idris, after the last train had gone, could arrange to have an empty slate wagon left for them at Abergynolwyn – and in this they would embark to trundle

gently homewards through the dusk.

From this it can be appreciated that the Talyllyn was not, for much of its life, a busy line. When it was built, however, it was well and substantially equipped with what were then modern locomotives and rolling stock, in anticipation of both heavy slate traffic and of passenger traffic. The railway company was a subsidiary of the Aberdovey Slate Co., which had been formed to exploit Bryn Eglwys quarry, and had re-equipped the quarry on a grand scale, in the belief that it held large reserves of good quality slate, and perhaps gold as well.

Both these beliefs proved to be unfounded, though slate quarrying on a limited scale continued until the late 1940s. The railway was still operating then, but since the 1860s no new locomotives or passenger carriages had been added, and the track too, except for one short section, was laid with the original rails. The railway had become a remarkable antique, and it was also very dilapidated indeed. Furthermore the railway company was not nationalized in 1948, unlike most other railway companies, for the T.R. was no longer considered important for transport. Its absence from the transport bill drew it to the attention of the author and engineer the late L. T. C. Rolt, who approached

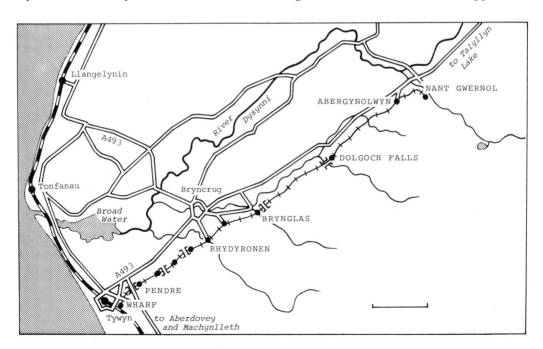

Talyllyn Railway No. 6 Douglas awaits departure from Tywyn Wharf station.

the owner to find out what could be done to perpetuate the railway.

The owner, of both railway and quarry, was Sir Henry Haydn Jones, who had purchased them in 1911 and intended, despite closure of the quarry, to continue to run the railway during his lifetime. This, sadly, was not very long, for he died in 1950.

The formation of the Preservation Society

The Talyllyn Railway Preservation Society was formed at a public meeting in Birmingham in October of the same year. A committee was appointed which included L. T. C. Rolt, J. H. Russell, P. B. Whitehouse, and P. J. Garland. The intention was to revive the railway by public subscription, and run it with volunteers. This concept was entirely novel, and the pioneers had no idea that they were starting a movement which would become national, and

indeed worldwide. Rather, they had a daunting task ahead of them, and were far from confident of success: P. J. Garland recently told the author that he agreed to become Honorary Treasurer because, as an accountant, he felt that someone with practical experience of liquidation would be needed before many months had passed! He is now President of the Society.

Lady Haydn Jones, Sir Haydn's widow, had inherited the railway company shares and she very kindly agreed to give them to a new holding company, called Talyllyn Holdings Ltd, controlled by the Preservation Society. In effect this meant that the Society was able to run the railway, without having to pay for it. This was fortunate, for there was much else to be paid for over the next few years.

Under Society operation, the numbers of passengers carried on the railway rapidly increased. This brought both revenue and problems: for a time equipment was deteriorating from wear and tear more rapidly than the Society could improve it. This vicious circle was

Douglas *again, heading a train of recently-built coaches near Rhydyronen.*

changed only when the Territorial Army relaid a mile of track as a training exercise.

The number of passenger journeys was 15,628 in 1951, and 165, 232 in 1977. Though there have been ups and downs, the figures have tended to increase, and this has meant many changes and improvements. Where once a single train, going up and down the line, could carry all the traffic, there are now sometimes three on the move at the same time. So, as well as additional locomotives and rolling stock well-suited to their task, this has meant heavy rail, proper ballast, passing loops, signal boxes, electric train staffs, colour-light signals and a telephone system – all things unknown in Sir Haydn's day. It has also meant re-equipped and extended workshops, and rebuilt stations. But the original locomotives and coaches, two and four in number respectively, are maintained to their traditional appearance, even though they

now incorporate many new parts, and the new buildings harmonize with their surroundings. The track, the gauge, the route, the scenery and the steam are still the same.

Actually the route is not quite the same: it has been extended. Beyond Abergynolwyn passenger station there continued the 'mineral extension'. For $\frac{3}{4}$ mile, to sidings at the foot of a rope-worked incline which led to the quarry, this extension ran along the hillside among forest-covered mountains, and it was an early ambition of the society to open this section for passenger traffic. But restoration of the Tywyn to Abergynolwyn section had to come first, and then much work was needed to rebuild the extension to passenger rather than freight standard. It was a proud day when, on 22 May 1976, the T.R.'s Nant Gwernol Extension was opened.

The Railway today

The Talyllyn Railway therefore now extends from Tywyn to Nant Gwernol. It is best to join trains at Tywyn Wharf, for Nant Gwernol has no road access (though footpaths are planned), and in any case the line is seen to best advantage during the journey into the hills rather than away from them.

At Tywyn Wharf the Railway Shop has an extensive range of books and souvenirs; refreshments are available, and the Narrow-Gauge Railway Museum contains many exhibits from narrow-gauge lines, both passenger-carrying and industrial. The museum is an entity distinct from the railway, but related to it.

The railway traverses Tywyn by a half-mile cutting, to reach Tywyn Pendre station. Here are the railway's works, and locomotive and carriage sheds. After Pendre the line climbs steadily through farmland past Rhydyronen station ($2\frac{1}{2}$ miles), while the hills close in gradually, as far as Brynglas ($3\frac{1}{4}$ miles). Here the route takes up a hillside shelf formation on the south side of the narrow valley of the stream called Afon Fathew. The hills on either side grow steadily higher, and just before Dolgoch Falls station (5 miles), the railway crosses a ravine by a three-span brick viaduct. At Dolgoch Falls station, locomotives usually take water, which gives photographers their opportunity, and many passengers leave the trains altogether to visit the waterfalls.

At Abergynolwyn ($6\frac{1}{4}$ miles) the grey-stone station building, though it looks old, was completed only in 1969; it includes a refreshment room. Many down trains from Nant Gwernol to Tywyn pause here for long enough for passengers to sample it.

The valley through which the T.R. runs from Brynglas almost to Nant Gwernol is straight, but as the train approaches Abergynolwyn the sides of the valley come closer together and the valley floor rises towards the railway. But then, when the train leaves Abergynolwyn, the valley is seen to widen again, and its floor falls away. The cause of the latter feature is an accumulation of glacial moraine, an ice-age relic; as a consequence of the two features together, the finest views on the railway, looking up the continuing valley to the mountains beyond, are revealed to passengers on the extension.

Stock

When the T.R.P.S. took over in 1951, all of the Talyllyn Railway's locomotives and passenger

coaches were over eighty years old. The locomotives were 0-4-0 tank *Dolgoch* which was (just) in working order, and 0-4-2 saddle tank *Talyllyn*, which was not and had been placed, worn-out, on a siding beneath a hay barn. There were four four-wheeled passenger coaches and one four-wheeled brake van, which included a ticket window from which the guard could issue tickets at stations en route. All these five vehicles could be entered from one side only and all station platforms were on the north side of the line, a feature which continues to this day.

Both *Dolgoch* and *Talyllyn* were in due course rebuilt, and they and the original coaches and van continue to operate. An immediate need to supplement the original stock was met by obtaining from British Railways two locomotives, a brake van and several coal wagons from the Corris Railway. This line, fortunately of the same unusual 2 ft 3 in. gauge, had been closed in 1948, but the stock had remained at its station at Machynlleth, not far from Tywyn. The locomotives, both 0-4-2 saddle tanks, were named on the Talyllyn *Sir Haydn* and *Edward Thomas*, after the T.R.'s former owner and traffic manager respectively. Another steam locomotive, a 0-4-0 tank of industrial type, was presented to the railway in 1953 and named *Douglas*. In 1969 a similar but larger locomotive, built only in 1950 and scarcely used, was purchased from the Irish Peat Board. It was a 3 ft gauge locomotive, and is being rebuilt as a 0-4-2 tank for the 2 ft 3 in. gauge. Several diesel locomotives are used, almost exclusively for works trains.

Corris Railway passenger coaches could not be obtained from British Railways, for the Corris line had lost its passenger service in 1931 and the coaches were then dispersed. But the body of one which had been used as a garden shed was eventually recovered, rebuilt and put back into use; and bodies of two coaches from the Glyn Valley Tramway (closed in 1935), which had also survived, were similarly obtained and rebuilt. The first supplements to the coaching stock were open toast-rack quarrymen's coaches from the Penrhyn Quarry Railway: these were in poor condition and did not long survive, but there are now several four-wheelers built by the T.R. and based on the Penrhyn design, with added roofs. More import-

No. 3 Sir Haydn, *a 0-4-2 transferred from the Corris Railway on its closure in 1948, crosses the major engineering feat of the Talyllyn, the Dolgoch viaduct.*

ant are several bogie coaches built at Tywyn to a handsome and substantial design which, though modern, complements the traditional lines of the locomotives.

Among all the stock new to the line, the original stock is now somewhat diluted. The flavour of the past can be recaptured, however, when the T.R. runs from time to time a special vintage train of the original stock.

The Vale of Rheidol Railway

The line and its history

Though the Talyllyn Railway was engineered by a member of the Spooner family, the Vale of Rheidol Railway vindicates better the techniques they demonstrated on the Festiniog. It was opened in 1902, to link Aberystwyth with Devil's Bridge 11¾ miles to the east, and for the final four of those miles its 1 ft 11½ in. gauge enables it to twist and turn along a shelf cut on the steep side of the Rheidol gorge. In this location a standard-gauge line would have been very much more expensive to construct.

The railway was built to carry minerals (lead ores and so on), tourists, and ordinary passengers and freight traffic, in roughly that order of importance. In those prosperous Edwardian times it prospered too, so much so that the independent Vale of Rheidol Light Railway Company was taken over in 1913 by the Cambrian Railways Co. So the V. of R. line descended to the Great Western Railway in 1922 and, in due course, to British Railways in 1948. By then it had long-since ceased to carry freight; passenger trains ran only in summer for tourists, and had been suspended completely from 1940 to 1944 inclusive. In 1968, when the rest of British Rail had gone over to diesel and electric traction, the V. of R. line became not only B.R.'s only surviving narrow-gauge section, but also its only surviving steam-worked line. And so it continues.

The V. of R.'s fortunes under B.R. have varied. In the 1950s with its main-line maintenance standards, and particularly its track, it was an example to volunteers on the Talyllyn and Festiniog Railways as they struggled to recover their railways from years of decay. But publicity for the V. of R. was conspicuous by its absence – for example, winter timetables, as I recollect them, regularly included in the V. of R. table the forbidding statement 'service suspended', without any indication that the service would start up again in the summer: 'service suspended', in timetable-ese, was generally a euphemism for 'line closed completely'. In the late 1950s, B.R.,

spurred on perhaps by the success of other Welsh tourist lines, started to publicize the Vale of Rheidol, named the locomotives, and re-introduced Sunday trains. Traffic increased.

Then in the 1960s, as a consequence of London Midland Region electrification, former G.W.R. lines in the Birmingham area were transferred from the Western to the London Midland Region, and so were their extensions to Chester and North and mid Wales. These routes soon afterwards suffered a decline in services from which they have never fully recovered. The Rheidol was included in the transfer, and by the end of the 1967 season was looking very down at heel. Locomotives which a few years before had been spotless were now filthy, and their nameplates had been removed for fear of theft. The last remaining passing loop, at Aberffrwd, 7¾ miles from Aberystwyth, had been lifted, and the increase in the number of passengers was levelling out just at a period when on the Festiniog Railway, for instance, passenger traffic was increasing more rapidly than ever.

A group of railway enthusiasts with practical experience on preserved lines negotiated with B.R. for purchase of the Rheidol, with a view to running it properly. B.R. was at first willing to sell; then, for political reasons, the proposed sale was cancelled.

However B.R. started to develop the line itself. A big improvement was made at Aberystwyth. The narrow-gauge line was diverted into

OPPOSITE, TOP LEFT: *Talyllyn Railway 0-4-2 saddle tank No. 3* Sir Haydn *waits for the right-away at Dolgoch Falls station with a spring morning train (p 123).*

TOP RIGHT: *On the Snowdon Mountain Railway, 0-4-2 tank No. 3* Wyddfa *(Swiss Locomotive and Machine Works No. 925 of 1895) starts the descent from Summit station with the 1540 to Llanberis (p. 136).*

CENTRE: *2-4-2* Katie *at the Barmouth Ferry end of the Fairbourne Railway (p. 139).*

BOTTOM: *On the Welshpool and Llanfair Light Railway, 0-6-0 tank No. 1* The Earl *(Beyer-Peacock No. 3496 of 1903) draws a 1600 Llanfair Caereinion–Sylfaen train into Castle Caereinion (p. 132).*

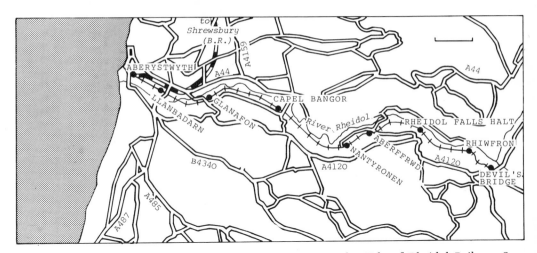

the main station, to terminate in the 'Carmarthen bay' formerly occupied by standard-gauge tracks used by trains for the closed Aberystwyth–Carmarthen line. At the same time, narrow-gauge tracks were laid into the former standard-gauge locomotive shed, a substantial building then standing vacant. This not only enabled the V. of R. locomotive shed – a cramped and isolated corrugated-iron building dating from the opening of the line – to be vacated, but also provided extensive undercover winter storage for coaches, which had previously been lacking. So the stock was better protected from both weather and vandalism.

Locomotives and coaches were repainted in B.R. blue livery (which suits them surprisingly well), locomotive names were replaced, and local railway management intensified publicity for the line. The idea for formation of the Narrow Gauge Railways of Wales Joint Marketing Panel came from B.R.'s area manager at Machynlleth, in whose domain the Rheidol lay. A souvenir and refreshment shop was opened at Devil's Bridge. The reward for all this has been an increase in the number of passenger journeys from 95,500 in 1969 to 179,000 in 1975, an all-time record for the line.

OPPOSITE, TOP: *2-8-2 River Mite on the turntable at Dalegarth on the scenic Ravenglass and Eskdale Railway (p. 152).*

BOTTOM: *'Lambton' tank No. 29 just above Beckhole, between Grosmont and Goathland, on the North Yorkshire Moors Railway (p. 172).*

In 1970 the Vale of Rheidol Railway Supporters' Association was formed to promote and popularize the line, and provides an unusual, possibly unique, example of B.R. and railway enthusiasts getting together for such a purpose. Its committee of eight members includes two appointed by British Rail and six elected by the Association's own members, who numbered 350 in 1976. Members publicize the line and organize party visits to it. They can visit the shed at Aberystwyth by arrangement, and have the use of a standard-gauge camping coach there.

The line today

The Vale of Rheidol line itself, after leaving Aberystwyth terminus, runs parallel to the standard-gauge for $1\frac{1}{2}$ miles, to Llanbadarn station. Then the main line bears away to the north and the V. of R. continues eastwards along the floor of the Rheidol valley, crossing the river by a timber viaduct. There are in total seven intermediate stations and halts at which trains call by request. In the first $5\frac{1}{2}$ miles, the steepest gradient is 1 in 105, but then stretches of 1 in 50 start to alternate with level sections, and from Aberffrwd the gradient is 1 in 50 continuously for 4 miles to Devil's Bridge. The line winds along a shelf cut on a steep and wooded hillside, and offers views of a cascading river far below, and traverses side gulleys by means of strikingly tight horse-shoe curves.

The phenomenon known as the Devil's Bridge is in fact three bridges of various ages, one above the other, spanning a chasm. To be

precise, the bridge attributed to the Devil is the lowest and oldest of the three. They are found by turning left on leaving the station and walking a few hundred yards along the road. There are also waterfalls to be viewed and visited.

Stock

Three locomotives work the V. of R.: No. 7, *Owain Glyndŵr*; No. 8, *Llywelyn*; and No. 9, *Prince of Wales*. All are 2-6-2 tanks, and powerful for the gauge. No. 9 is the oldest, and was built for the opening of the line. Nos. 7 and 8 were built for it by the G.W.R. at Swindon in 1923 and No. 9 (then G.W.R. No. 1213) was rebuilt there so as to be almost identical to them. The name *Prince of Wales* was carried by the locomotive when owned by the original V. of R. company, and re-instated by B.R. when the other two locomotives were named. The coaches now in use include bogie observation cars, with sides open above the waist, and closed bogie coaches. The latter were built by the G.W.R. as late as 1938, incorporating components from earlier coaches; the former also date from 1938 or, in some instances, 1923. The Vale of Rheidol line is operated entirely by paid staff, and drivers, for instance, alternate between driving steam locomotives on the narrow-gauge line and diesel trains on the standard.

Photography

The course of the upper part of the railway makes it difficult to reach and photograph, but there is an overbridge at the approach to Devil's Bridge station, and elsewhere a rough road leads to the level crossing and station at Aberffrwd, where locomotives take water and provide a photographic opportunity. Between Llanbadarn and Aberffrwd several minor roads run close to the railway and also offer photographic potential.

OPPOSITE: *A descending train winds round the sharp curves near Devil's Bridge on the Vale of Rheidol Railway. The loco is Owain Glyndŵr. Note the check-rail.*

The Welshpool and Llanfair Light Railway

The line and its history

The early history of the 2 ft 6 in. gauge Welshpool and Llanfair Light Railway has much in common with that of the Rheidol. Both came under the wing of the Cambrian Railways, and so passed in due course to the G.W.R. and then to British Railways.

The W. & L. was opened in 1903 and linked Welshpool, where there was an exchange station with the standard-gauge, with Llanfair Caereinion, 9½ miles to the west. It was built and owned by the independent Welshpool and Llanfair Light Railway Company, but was operated from the start by the Cambrian. The G.W.R. therefore started to work the line in 1922, and absorbed the local company the following year. Passenger services ceased in 1931; although the countryside through which the railway passes was and is very pleasant, it lies outside the main tourist area of North and mid Wales. General freight traffic continued: the line eventually became the last non-preserved narrow-gauge railway to carry public freight traffic in Great Britain. It was finally closed in November 1956.

Preservation

Following the Talyllyn and Festiniog examples, a preservation society was formed the same month. Support was slow in coming forward and negotiations with B.R. and the Ministry of Transport were long drawn out, though working parties of volunteers were permitted on the line from 1959. In 1960 the preservation society was replaced by the Welshpool and Llanfair Light Railway Preservation Co. Ltd, and in 1962 B.R. was authorized to lease to the preservation company the line from Raven Square, on the western edge of Welshpool, to Llanfair. The company has since been able to purchase it outright.

One of the causes of delay had been that the line, commencing at the standard-gauge station on the east side of Welshpool, had to traverse the town and in doing so crossed several streets on the level without gates. Authority to reopen this section could not be obtained and it has been dismantled. The preservation company was able to use it for a time for works trains.

So the preservation company based itself on Llanfair, and in 1963 re-opened the 4¼ miles to Castle Caereinion. In 1964 it re-opened a further 1¼ miles to Sylfaen, though towards the end of the season trains had again to terminate at Castle Caereinion because of poor condition of the track beyond. The following winter floods severely damaged the viaduct over the River

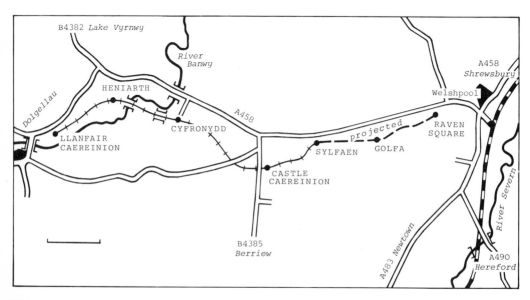

The W. & L. has an unusual variety of continental locos. No. 10 Sir Drefaldwyn *came from Austria in 1970. The train is of Austrian and British stock.*

Banwy, about $1\frac{1}{2}$ miles from Llanfair, a disaster, for the company could ill afford repairs. During the 1965 season a shuttle train service ran between Llanfair and Heniarth Gate ($1\frac{1}{4}$ miles) only, until viaduct repairs were completed in mid-August. The train service was then resumed as far as Castle Caereinion; resumption of trains to Sylfaen had to wait for a full overhaul of the track throughout, and was delayed until 1972. Work continues on the section from Sylfaen to Raven Square, Welshpool.

The line today

The railway is now operated almost entirely by volunteers, who are members of the preservation company, with only a few paid staff. It is not as busy as some of the other Welsh lines, which makes it pleasant for people who do go to it. Train services are not so extensive either, but

there are two or three trains each way daily throughout the summer, at weekends in spring and autumn, and daily during the Easter and Spring Bank Holiday periods. Road travellers can conveniently include a visit to the W. & L. while going to or returning from lines further west, and unlike those lines, the W. & L. is within easy range of the Midlands.

Llanfair Caereinion station has a buffet and railway shop, and locomotive sheds and repair works, built by the preservation company because the original shed was located on the section now dismantled, in Welshpool. Most of the way to Heniarth Gate, the line close by follows the tree-lined north bank of the River Banwy, and an isolated watering point enables locomotives to take water. Beyond the viaduct, the line follows the south bank of the river, crosses a tributary by a stone-built viaduct and reaches Cyfronydd ($2\frac{1}{4}$ miles). Here the river diverges to the north, and the railway continues in an easterly direction up a side valley. The countryside is typical of the Welsh borders – no mountains, but cultivated hills and valleys interspersed with woodland – not spectacular, but pastoral and pleasant. Castle Caereinion was originally the mid-point of the line. At Sylfaen the railway comes alongside the main road from Llanfair to Welshpool (though parking space is limited, and intending passengers are advised to park at Castle or Llanfair); Raven Square, Welshpool, the eventual eastern terminus, is about $2\frac{3}{4}$ miles further on.

The railway was one of the first to be built under the provisions of the Light Railways Act 1896, and is in many ways a typical light railway. It has few bridges, but many level crossings (without gates across the road), and it has few earthworks but many sharp curves and steep gradients, which enable it to follow, so far as possible, the lie of the land. Even where the line runs alongside the River Banwy, there is a sudden short stretch of 1 in 33, and near Welshpool the gradient is 1 in 29 for over half a mile.

Stock

Two locomotives, identical 0-6-0 tanks, were built by Beyer Peacock for the opening of the line, and worked it alone throughout its pre-preservation existence, until 1956. Fortunately both survived closure and, after a period in store, first one and then the other were obtained by the preservation company and returned to the line.

The original passenger coaches were less fortunate: they were scrapped a few years after passenger services were withdrawn. This meant that the preservation company had to obtain coaches from elsewhere, and it also judged it necessary to augment the locomotive stock. Without main-line maintenance facilities to fall back on, it has to rely on members working in their spare time, so locomotive overhauls are inevitably protracted. In any event, additional locomotives have been an attraction to visitors.

There were no other public railways of 2 ft 6 in. gauge surviving in Britain to form a source of supply. Fortunately for the W. & L., though, the Admiralty ceased to use its 2 ft 6 in. gauge Lodge Hill and Upnor Railway in Kent in 1961, and the W. & L. was able to obtain from it rolling stock which included five bogie coaches. Four of these were rather primitive, of covered toast-

rack type, but the fifth was a comfortable saloon coach built only four years previously!

More coaches were obtained in 1968. These are four four-wheeled coaches which came from the Zillertalbahn, a 760 mm gauge railway in the Austrian Tyrol. Short and tubby in appearance, with slatted wooden seats, these coaches are pleasant, but typical of a railway tradition very different to that of Britain. They did, however, solve the W. & L. railway's immediate passenger-carriage problem, and a fifth similar coach has since been obtained from the same source.

The first additional steam locomotive suitable for passenger trains was *Monarch*, an articulated 0-4-4-0 tank obtained from Bowaters' paper-mills railway in Kent by a member of the preservation company in 1966, and then donated to the railway. Large and powerful – too much so for light trains – she spent several years first stored and then under overhaul, but she entered revenue-earning service in 1974, and can be expected to be particularly useful when the steeply graded section from Sylfaen to Welshpool is re-opened.

Before *Monarch* entered service, another steam locomotive was already hauling passenger trains. This was 0-8-0 tank No. 10, *Sir Drefaldwyn* – the name is Welsh for Montgomeryshire, in which county the W. & L. was situated before the recent re-organization of local government. She complements the Austrian coaches for she was purchased in 1969 from the Styrian Provincial Railways and entered service on the W. & L. in 1970. She was built in France in 1944, to a German military railway design; she spent her working life up to 1969 in Austria.

British builders of steam locomotives formerly had a thriving export business, particularly with British colonies and the W. & L. has now brought back to Britain two locomotives representative of the trade. The first is *Joan*, a 0-6-2 tank built in 1927 by Kerr-Stuart, and bought by a group of W. & L. members from the Government Sugar Factory of Antigua in the West Indies; the second is 2-6-2 tank No. 85 of the Sierra Leone Government Railway. That system is now closed, but No. 85 was built by Hunslet as recently as 1954; with her the W. & L. was able to obtain four modern bogie coaches built in England in 1961.

The preservation company has also had a

succession of diesel locomotives, large and small, for works trains.

Photography
Running through an open countryside, the W. & L. is not a difficult line to photograph. There are vantage points at or near most stations

No. 1 The Earl nears Llanfair Caereinion with a ballast train on the Welshpool and Llanfair.

and level crossings. Other tourist attractions in the neighbourhood include Powis Castle, and boat trips on the Shropshire Union Canal at Welshpool.

The Snowdon Mountain Railway

The line and its history

Of all the old-established railways in this section, the Snowdon Mountain Railway has the least complex history. This rack railway was built in the 1890s, on principles developed in Switzerland, to carry tourists from Llanberis to the summit of Snowdon. It continues to do just that. The company owning and operating the line, originally the Snowdon Mountain Tramroad and Hotels Co. Ltd, is now Snowdon Mountain Railway Ltd.

The railway has always been unique as the only mountain rack railway in the British Isles, and it has gained distinction by sticking to steam power while most Swiss rack railways have been electrified.

Oddly enough, there was an early intention to electrify the Snowdon. That same 1895 guide book referred to in the introduction to this section, published while the railway was being built, describes it as 'the new Electric railway' and adds 'powerful steam locomotives are to be used *at first*' [author's italics]. They still are!

In the Abt rack system used on the Snowdon railway, pinions beneath the locomotives engage with two toothed racks laid between the rails, to propel the locomotives onwards and upwards, up gradients too steep for normal adhesion working. On the Snowdon railway, the gradient is in places as steep as 1 in $5\frac{1}{2}$, which is another British record for a locomotive-worked line. Descending locomotives are braked by the rack and pinion, too.

The opening day in 1896 was marred by a disaster. The locomotive of the first descending train left the rails, possibly at a point where frost had distorted freshly laid track, and became disengaged from the racks. It fell into a ravine and was damaged beyond repair. The driver and fireman jumped clear and were unharmed, and the carriages forming the train, which as a safety precaution had not been coupled to the locomotive, were stopped safely by their own brakes – but not before a passenger had jumped out and been fatally injured.

The line was closed, and guard rails, of inverted-L shape, were laid on either side of the racks; grippers were fitted beneath the locomotives which would engage with the guard rails, should a locomotive attempt to leave the rails, and prevent pinions from disengaging from racks. The railway re-opened for the 1897 season and there has been no similar incident subsequently.

The line today

To avoid disappointment, it is essential to consider what weather conditions are likely to be at the summit before making a trip up the Snowdon Railway. The summit is 3,561 feet above sea level. On a fine day it is a superb place with magnificent views; on a wet, windy, cloudy day it is most unpleasant. On any day, conditions are more severe than in the valley below.

The starting point, the Snowdon station at Llanberis, is at the south-east end of that village; it has a restaurant, a shop and a buffet. Trains comprise a single coach and a locomotive (which, on the uphill journey, pushes it). Each coach carries up to about 60 people, and at busy times trains run in convoy, but there is still sometimes a queue of passengers at Llanberis. The train leaves the station past the locomotive shed and works; the first few hundred yards, on a gradient of 1 in 50, are deceptively easy: one wonders what all the fuss is about. Then the coach rears up as it reaches the first steep section, where the gradient is 1 in 6, and the locomotive starts to work in earnest, with appropriate sound and fury (although travelling at about 5 m.p.h.). The Snowdon Railway is a

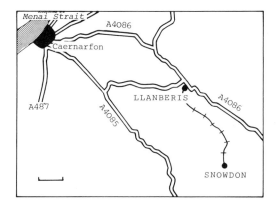

A train arrives on Snowdon summit. Coach and engine are always uncoupled for safety reasons, and so the engine is always below the coach. The racking is clearly visible.

fine line for locomotive noises: sitting in a down train at a passing loop and listening to an up train approaching, one would suppose it to be the Cornish Riviera at 90 m.p.h.

That first steep section takes the line across a stone viaduct; then the railway, which has so far been heading south-west, curves gently through 90 degrees to take up the south-easterly alignment which continues most of the way to the summit. There are three intermediate stations (none of which serves any built-up area) which have loops for trains to pass. At places where the gradient eases, passengers looking ahead sometimes experience the curious optical illusion that the track goes over a hump and then downhill. In fact, the upward course is continuous, and as the train climbs, ever more spectacular views are (on a fine day) revealed, to culminate in the very extensive panorama of mountain and sea obtainable from the top. The summit station is of course the highest station in

the British Isles; a café adjoins it.

The distance from Llanberis to Snowdon Summit is about $4\frac{3}{4}$ miles, with a vertical climb of 3,140 ft, and the journey takes one hour, up or down. Fares are not cheap: rack-railway fares never are, anywhere. Such lines are expensive to run. In spring, when ice and snow still cover the top of the mountain, trains terminate short of the summit, and fares are comparatively inexpensive. Trains do not run in winter.

Stock

The seven locomotives used on the Snowdon Mountain Railway were all built by the Swiss Locomotive Works of Winterthur, Switzerland. They are typical of rack locomotives built by that company, even to the gauge, which is 80 cm (2 ft $7\frac{1}{2}$ in.). They came in two batches, Nos. 2 to 5 built in 1895 and 1896, and Nos. 6 to 8 built in 1922 and 1923. All have boilers inclined in relation to the frames, so that boilers are approximately level when going uphill. No. 4, *Snowdon*, was rebuilt by Hunslet Engine Co., Leeds, in 1961–2, and in the process almost all the main components were renewed.

The coaches are all bogie coaches. Originally

137

This portrait of Snowdon Mountain locos taken at the Llanberis shed clearly shows the slope of the boilers on the 1895-design Swiss-built engines.

all were open-sided above the waist, with curtains to keep out the worst of the weather. In recent years all have been given glazed windows.

There is no other tourist attraction in the immediate vicinity to compare with the Snowdon Mountain Railway: but a visit to it can well be combined with a visit to the Llanberis Lake Railway and the North Wales Quarrying Museum, both described later.

Photography
The footpath from Llanberis to the summit follows the railway fairly closely, so photographers can ascend by early trains and descend on foot to photograph following trains. For car-borne photographers, a rough, narrow and steep road from Llanberis leads to an under-bridge about a mile up the line. At Llanberis station, the upper section of the car park overlooks the locomotive shed and provides a vantage point for photographing locomotives standing on its approach tracks: it is normally only here that it is possible to take a photograph which shows clearly the front of a Snowdon locomotive, unobscured by a coach.

The Fairbourne Railway

The line and its history

The Fairbourne Railway, two miles of 15 in. gauge line, originated as a 2 ft gauge horse-drawn tramway in 1890. At this time the village of Fairbourne was being built as a seaside resort, and the initial purpose of the tramway was to carry building materials. Very soon, however, it started to carry passengers also, between Fairbourne station on the Cambrian Railways, Fairbourne Beach, and Penrhyn Point at the foot of the Mawddach estuary, whence there was, and still is, a ferry to Barmouth. The line functioned in useful but unspectacular manner with horse-drawn trams for the next twenty-five years or so.

In 1916 the horse tramway was purchased by Narrow Gauge Railways Ltd. This company was associated with Bassett-Lowke Ltd the famous model engineers and, in spite of its name, built and operated miniature railways: that is to say, small railways whose size was intended to attract custom, using locomotives which were, more or less, scale models. Favoured locations were seaside resorts and, prior to World War I, international exhibitions. In 1915 N.G.R. Ltd had taken a lease on the closed Ravenglass and Eskdale Railway in Cumberland, and was by stages narrowing the gauge to 15 in. and re-opening it. It repeated the operation at Fairbourne. The line was relaid to 15 in. gauge and became known as the Fairbourne Miniature Railway. A Bassett-Lowke miniature 4-4-2 and open-air four-wheeled coaches were provided to work it.

The miniature line passed through several changes of fortune, operator and rolling stock until the start of World War II. During that War the line was closed; it was badly damaged by the weather and the military.

What was left was purchased in 1946 by new owners from the Midlands. Track was relaid, the locomotives (one steam, one petrol) and the coaches were overhauled, and the line was re-opened in 1947. The venture was successful and since then there have been a great many

developments: more and better locomotives, both steam and internal combustion, more and better coaches, some open-air, some closed, and much-improved stations. In 1976 an extension at Penrhyn Point was opened to bring the line closer than ever to the ferry landing.

In 1958, after several years of improvements, the word 'miniature' was dropped from the title, and the operating company became Fairbourne Railway Ltd.

The Railway today

Visitors arriving by road and rail encounter the Fairbourne Railway at its Fairbourne station. This immediately portrays the scale of improvements under the present ownership. The earlier station, a roadside run-round loop from which tracks continued into a locomotive shed, is now reduced to the status of sidings. Intending passengers first cross its tracks by board crossing and then cross a bridge over a stream to enter the new station, built in 1956. An overall roof spans four tracks, and the whole building is used to store rolling stock under cover in winter. A buffet and shop are adjacent, and those parts of the station area not covered by track or building have become a garden of traditional railway-station smartness.

After leaving the station, trains cross

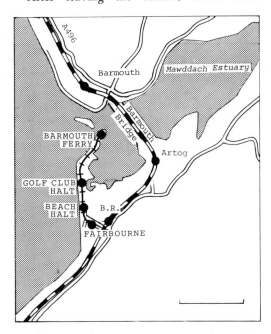

Siân departs from Fairbourne for the two-mile journey to Barmouth Ferry station.

another bridge over the stream and then run alongside a straight road in a westerly direction for about a quarter of a mile to the beach. There the line turns sharply northwards. The juxtaposition here of seaside holiday houses, beach, and 15 in. gauge railway is reminiscent of the Romney, Hythe and Dymchurch Railway. There are request halts at Bathing Beach and Golf House, and a passing loop, installed in 1952 at approximately the mid-point of the line to enable a frequent train service to be run, with two trains in use simultaneously. Beyond the passing loop the railway runs by sand dunes and shingle beds to Penrhyn Point, which has fine views up the Mawddach Estuary to the east, with Barmouth Bridge in the foreground and the mountains beyond.

Stock

The stock of steam locomotives, which before World War II was never more than two, and often only one, is now four. Pride of the line are two handsome 2-4-2 tender locomotives: *Siân* (Welsh for *Jane*) which was built specially for the line in 1963, and *Katie*, built in 1950 but purchased by the F.R. only in 1965. They are similar in appearance and, appropriately for a line which has dropped 'miniature' from its title, are scarcely miniature machines. Certainly they have no known prototype, and are way

over scale for models of standard-gauge locomotives built for 15 in. guage. The proportions of their cabs are such that the driver, sitting in the tender, is as likely to look forward over the cab roof as through the cab windows, and the design represents perhaps a half-way stage between a miniature locomotive and a full-size locomotive for the gauge. In any event, they are handsome, well-proportioned machines, well suited to their work.

The other two steam locomotives are miniature locomotives. One of them, the Bassett-Lowke-built 4-4-2 *Count Louis*, has been on the Fairbourne line since 1925. The fourth steam locomotive is 4-6-2 *Ernest W. Twining*, built in 1949.

Since the 1930s some trains have been hauled by internal combustion locomotives; there has been a succession of these, of which the survivors are 0-6-0 diesel *Rachel* and Bo-Bo diesel *Sylvia*.

Coaches are a mixture of open-air and fully-enclosed types. Some of the open-air coaches have end screens to protect passengers from locomotive exhausts, and some are articulated in rakes of three. A buffet car is taken to Penrhyn Point each day to serve refreshments there.

Photography

Absence of fences alongside the railway makes it easy to photograph. The combined trip from Barmouth Quay by ferry (motor boat) and then over the railway makes an unusual excursion.

The Llanberis Lake Railway

The Llanberis Lake Railway, though opened only in 1971, has antecedents of much more extensive history. It was built on the track-bed of part of the 4 ft gauge Padarn Railway, which from 1843 to 1961 carried slates from Dinorwic Quarry, Llanberis, to Port Dinorwic on the Menai Strait. Railway and port were owned by the quarry company, which also had an extensive system of 1 ft 10¾ in. gauge lines serving the Quarry itself. This was claimed to be the largest slate quarry in the world, and its railway system, operated by attractive little 0-4-0 saddle tanks, most of them built by Hunslet, was well-known to railway enthusiasts.

The locomotives, rolling stock and track of the 4 ft gauge line were sold for scrap after closure (with the exception of a few items which went to museums), but the first two miles of its route lay alongside the attractive lake called Llyn Padarn, and this gave rise to ideas of using it for a tourist railway. Matters became urgent in 1969 when the quarry company went into liquidation and its assets were put up for auction. A. Lowry Porter, a physiotherapist with experience as a volunteer on the Festiniog Railway, called a meeting which set up the Llanberis Lake Railway Society. This made successful bids at the auction for three of the surviving steam locomotives and one diesel, all of 1 ft 10¾ in. gauge.

In the meantime the old Caernarvon County Council had placed a preservation order on the Quarry's very extensive Victorian workshops, with a view to turning them into a museum – as has subsequently been done. The locomotive shed, forming part of the works, has been made available to the new railway, providing it with the valuable feature of ready-made covered accommodation for storage and repairs. The county council also acquired the track-bed of the old 4 ft gauge line alongside the lake and made it available to the railway.

Promoters of the new line decided it should be built to the common gauge of 1 ft 11½ in., rather than the quarry's unique gauge of 1 ft

10¾ in., to suit any further locomotives and rolling stock which might be obtained. The locomotives obtained from the quarry company were in due course modified to fit, when they were overhauled. Coaches were built at Llanberis. Just over a mile of the old track-bed was cleared of bushes and trees, and 1 ft 11½ in. gauge track was laid on it. The Llanberis Lake Railway Co. Ltd was formed, with the intention that local capital and local labour (in an area of high unemployment) were to be used.

Opening day was fixed for 28 May 1971 and the railway was ceremonially opened on that day by T. Mervyn Jones, chairman of the Wales Tourist Board. But the opening train carried no passengers: shortly before the ceremony a coach had become derailed. Examination showed that new track had settled under the weight of locomotive *Dolbadarn*, and that the suspension of the new coaches was not flexible enough for them to pass over the defective section safely. There was no time to check the whole line before the opening ceremony, so to avoid risk of a further derailment, to a passenger train, it was arranged that the opening train would make a demonstration run, empty – which it did,

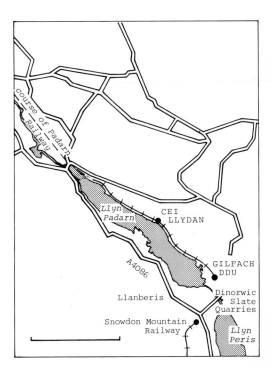

141

without trouble. Subsequent examination of the track showed no further defects and a pre-booked passenger special ran the following day. But it was decided to rebuild the coaches to a better design and at the same time operate a diesel locomotive up and down the line to iron out any further weaknesses.

Public passenger train services eventually started on 19 July 1971. During the following winter the line was extended to its full length, and more locomotives and coaches have been added at intervals. Steam locomotives on the line in 1978 included three from Dinorwic quarry and two 0-4-0 tanks imported from Germany. Recently, too, the railway has had much winter freight traffic in connection with a hydro-electric power scheme, for which electric cables were laid in a trench alongside the line.

The line today
Visitors to the Llanberis Lake Railway turn off the main road almost opposite the mountain railway station at Llanberis, down a side road which leads to the lake railway's terminus at Gilfach Ddu.

For almost its entire course the railway runs close to the lake. Despite the proximity of old quarries, the railway runs through rural sur-roundings, with a steep hillside on one side of the line and the lake on the other. There is no road along this shore of the lake, so only rail passengers get the very fine view back across the lake to the Snowdon range of mountains. There is a passing loop at Cei Llydan and the line

Dolbadarn, a 0-4-0 from Dinorwic Quarry, hauling a train of Railway-built coaches, stands at Cei Llydan on the Llanberis Lake Railway.

OPPOSITE: *Leaving Gilfach Ddu. That the track-bed was built for the 4 ft gauge is clear.*

terminates at Penllyn: there is no station here and visitors join trains only at Gilfach Ddu. Return trains do, however, call at Cei Llydan where passengers may alight, and there is a lake-side picnic place.

Photography and the area around
Visitors to the Llanberis Lake Railway should certainly not miss the North Wales Quarrying Museum in the former quarry workshops adjoining Gilfach Ddu station. The Museum is a joint venture of the County Council (formerly Caernarvonshire, now Gwynedd), the Depart-ment of the Environment and the National Museum of Wales. Original equipment of the workshops forms the bulk of the exhibits, much of it in its original location. The fitting and blacksmith's shops, iron and brass foundries, pattern makers' workshop and store, and an enormous water wheel, combine to give a vivid impression of the interior of a Victorian en-gineering works.

Pleasant footpaths starting from Gilfach Ddu have been laid out through the oak woods which cover the hillside here. One of these crosses a bridge over the railway, which is a useful vantage point for photographers. The Cei Llydan halt is also useful for photography.

The Bala Lake Railway

The line and its history

Closure under the Beeching Plan of the very picturesque standard-gauge line from Morfa Mawddach (Barmouth Junction) to Ruabon prompted several ambitious proposals for preservation. These eventually resulted in two separate undertakings, only one of which is at the time of writing open for passenger traffic.

This is the Bala Lake Railway, which runs from Llanuwchllyn for four-and-a-half miles, mostly alongside Bala Lake (the largest natural lake in Wales), to Bala (Llyn Tegid) station at the lake's north-eastern extremity. This railway is notable among Welsh tourist lines as being primarily the result of local initiative. It originated with a public meeting held at Bala in April 1971. A company was formed: Rheilffordd Llyn Tegid Cyf, or in English Bala Lake Railway Ltd, and £10,000 was raised from shares sold locally. A supporting group, the Bala Lake Railway Society, has also been formed.

The new railway was laid to a gauge of 1 ft $11\frac{1}{2}$ in. on the track-bed of the old line. Work started at the station of Llanuwchllyn, and the first section, a little over a mile to a temporary terminus at Glanllyn, was opened on 13 August 1972. The line was subsequently extended by

stages: Bala (Llyn Tegid) was reached in 1976. There are hopes of extending the line still further towards Bala town.

The line today

Llanuwchllyn station includes the platforms, station buildings and signal box of the former standard-gauge station. New sheds for storage and maintenance of locomotives and rolling stock have been added. The station building includes the original booking office, which still displays the last (1965) timetable of the former standard-gauge line, and a new refreshment room. Here, after train time, the author found a relaxed atmosphere – nothing much happening and a murmur of Welsh in the background – reminiscent of the Talyllyn of twenty years ago.

Train services run throughout the summer and at weekends in spring and autumn. Generally, steam locomotives are used only at weekends. Leaving the station, the railway has a long stretch of straight track; then it comes beside the lake shore which it follows, more or less, as far as the other terminus. Hills rise up from the south side of the line. At Llangower, $2\frac{1}{4}$ miles from Llanuwchllyn, is a picnic place with access to the lake. Bala (Llyn Tegid) station comprised in 1978 little more than a platform and run-round loop, close to the B4391 road from Bala to Llanfyllin.

Stock

When the Bala Lake Railway was opened, it

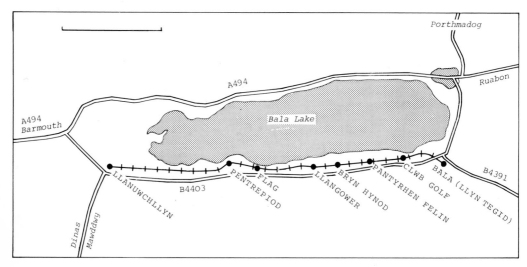

The Bala Lake Railway also makes use of old track-bed built for a different gauge, in this case the standard-gauge Barmouth-Ruabon. The purpose-built Meirionydd *prepares to leave Llanuwchllyn. Steam haulage is also used.*

used a small four-wheeled diesel locomotive. In 1973, however, a handsome Bo-Bo diesel locomotive was built for it by Severn-Lamb Ltd, with a Leyland engine: this is named *Meirionydd*. Regular steam haulage started in 1975 after the arrival of the 0-4-0 saddle tank *Maid Marian*. This locomotive was built by Hunslet in 1903 for Dinorwic Slate Quarries Ltd and is typical of her type: she was bought for preservation in 1968 by the Maid Marian Locomotive Fund and ran on the Bressingham and Llanberis Lake railways before coming to Bala. Her performance on the B.L.R. has been good, and she has been joined by sister

locomotive *Holy War*, on loan to the railway.

The first coaches were two bogie toast-rack coaches with open sides. They have been joined by three closed bogie coaches, all built for the line. These coaches are of limited size and comfort compared with, say, the new coaches of the Festiniog and Talyllyn Railways, and appear to represent practical economy rather than any attempt to exploit the possibilities of the gauge.

Photography and the area around
The line is not difficult to photograph, for it runs in many places close to the road along the south shore of the lake. Apart from the lake itself there are few other specific attractions for tourists in the vicinity, but Bala is a pleasant small town in an attractive hilly district. If one wished to have a holiday staying in a central location to visit all the 'Great Little Trains' in turn, Bala would be as good a base as any.

145

Llangollen Railway Society

The Llangollen Railway Society, originally formed in 1972 as the Flint and Deeside Railway Preservation Society, is the only standard-gauge steam line operating in North Wales. It is based at Llangollen Station, and was on the former Great Western Railway from Ruabon to Bala, which then connected with the Cambrian Coast line at Barmouth. The connection at Ruabon was with the company's main line from Paddington to Chester and Birkenhead. The Bala Lake railway, as it was originally called, connected at Corwen with the L. & N.W.R.'s line south from Rhyl and Denbigh. Unfortunately both of these routes were scheduled for closure under the Beeching report, and the line to Llangollen stopped passenger running in 1965. The track was lifted shortly afterwards, and the land sold to the local authority.

It was felt by local enthusiasts that this famous Eisteddfod town situated in the picturesque valley of the River Dee would be bound to attract sufficient visitors to make a steam railway financially viable. It would also provide an interesting transport comparison with the Welsh branch of the Shropshire Union Canal which had its dock and turning point in the town. (An interchange should also be possible at Berwyn Halt.) Accordingly, money was raised and negotiations opened. The first plan was to purchase the station at Llangollen and the $3\frac{1}{2}$ miles of track on the way west to Corwen. The Society's ultimate aim is to re-lay the line to this junction, via Carrog, Glyndyfrdwy and Berwyn. Berwyn, $1\frac{1}{2}$ miles out from Llangollen, is the terminus for the initial passenger service planned. This would be a journey of some ten miles through some of the remotest Welsh uplands. It is an ambitious project, but would be a marvellous ride if it were completed.

The Society received the keys for Llangollen Station in June 1975. Since then much work has been focused on the restoration of the station

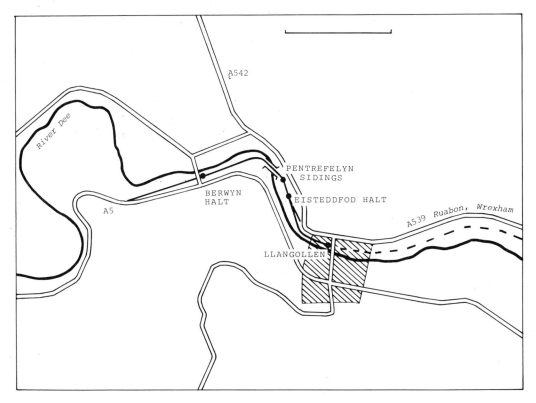

buildings. When the Society took over, they were dilapidated in the extreme. Today they are smart, and in good order, and a refreshment room and shop have been provided. In addition, the station and goods areas have been re-laid with track, which has been extended for half a mile in the direction of Corwen with track donated by Shell Oil. The original signal box, situated at the end of Platform 1, has been preserved, and controls the points and movement of trains in the area. The station was officially re-opened on 13 September 1975, after months of intensive clearance work, when a diesel ran the length of one section of track.

Stock

The Society has acquired a number of saddle tanks and a deal of rolling stock. Most of the locomotives have arrived as gifts from firms who have switched to diesel traction. The first steam engine to be restored on the line is the unusual 0-6-0 saddle tank *Austin 1*. It is a Kitson loco, built in 1932 and acquired from British Leyland at Longbridge, Birmingham, hence its name. This is one of the largest which Kitson manufactured, and was probably a one-off job. It has been suggested that the company adapted one of their standard industrial locomotives for a customer who required a loco with a bigger capacity. In addition, there are the following locomotives undergoing restoration on the railway: Hudswell Clarke 0-6-0T, *Richboro*, built in 1917; Hunslet 0-6-0T, No. 1234, built in 1917; Peckett 0-4-0ST, No. 2084, built in 1948. The Society also possesses a Sentinel tank engine No. 9596. These box-shaped shunting locos were designed by the L.N.E.R. in 1925 but were still produced under B.R. Indeed this engine was completed in 1955, after nationalization. The first train to be hauled on the Society's line was headed by the Fowler diesel, 0-4-0 named *Eliseg*.

Although the Society has applied for a Light Railway Order, it is still, in early 1979, being considered. They do hope to be able to run a regular passenger service and to that end have acquired two carriages. There is a former G.W.R. brake third, No. 5539, which was constructed in 1938, and the Society has recently purchased a non-corridor second-class brake No. E43182. This coach was built at

The attractive Llangollen station (the Dee is just to the left of the picture) has regained much of its G.W.R. splendour. Austin 1 *stands at the plaform; the Fowler diesel is nearer the camera.*

Doncaster in 1954 and operated on the suburban service from King's Cross. Having been sent to York for repairs, it was decided that it was excess to requirements and was sold in January 1977. The Society also has a former G.W.R. 'Toad' goods brake van, No. 17407, built in 1940.

There is a Llangollen Railway Rolling Stock Group. Membership is open to the public and is available by purchasing one or more shares in any item of stock subsequently purchased by

Austin 1 in a close-up: the result of five years of restoration work, during which the loco was completely re-tubed, and vacuum brakes fitted.

the Society. A number of locomotives and passenger coaches have been selected for possible preservation, when they and the funds become available. Regular steam open days are planned for the future, and it is hoped that passenger running may be permitted soon.

The area around
Llangollen, besides being the site for the International Musical Eisteddfod, every summer, has a number of historic buildings. On a hill overlooking the town are the remains of Castle Dinas Bran. There is a beautifully decorated eighteenth-century timbered house, Plas Newydd. It was the home of the 'Ladies of Llangollen', two Irish women who settled here, drawing famous visitors because of their eccentricities.

The River Dee which flows through the centre of the town is spanned by a fine fourteenth century stone bridge, built by a Bishop of St Asaph.

The Gwili Railway

The line and its history

While steam 'tourist' railways originated and indeed proliferated in North Wales, South Wales remained something of a blank on the preserved-railway map. This blank was partly filled with the opening in 1978 of the first section of the Gwili Railway.

Historically the line has respectable antecedents. It commenced its existence not on the narrow gauge but, by contrast, on the broad. Brunel's broad gauge is so much associated with the West Country and the lines thither that one tends to forget that it extended also far into South Wales, and when the Carmarthen and Cardigan Railway was promoted in the late 1850s, it was built on the broad gauge. So much of it as was built, that is: for the line never

reached Cardigan, and at this stage got no closer than Llandyssul. In due course, however, the Manchester and Milford Railway was opened and extended, despite the ambitions indicated by its name, from Pencader, on the C. & C. near Llandyssul, to Aberystwyth: later still, the standard-gauge C. & C. and the M. & M. were successively taken over by the Great Western Railway, and Carmarthen to Aberystwyth became one of that company's secondary main lines.

Its passenger service was eventually withdrawn about 1964, but much of the southern part of the line remained in existence for freight traffic for several years thereafter. So when the Gwili Railway was promoted to bring back the nostalgia of steam to this part of South Wales, it

Peckett 0-4-0 Myrddin/Merlin *(the engine is bilingually named, one each side) was built in 1939. This inaugural train, one d.m.u. trailer, ran on the Gwili Railway in March 1978. A regular passenger service is now running.*

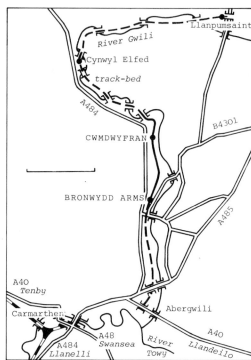

The Gwili Railway is in hilly but open country.

was able to purchase nearly 1½ miles of track northwards from Bronwydd Arms (the first station out of Carmarthen), and 8 miles of track-bed extending from Abergwili, on the outskirts of Carmarthen, past Bronwydd Arms to Llanpumsaint. This purchase was completed on 8 November 1977; the Gwili Railway Co. Ltd's Light Railway Order, covering the whole of this section, had come into force five days earlier. Supporting the company is the Gwili Railway Preservation Society.

The line today

The section over which train services run at present is from Bronwydd Arms northwards for

about a mile to a new halt made at Cwmdwyfran. Throughout its length, the line follows the attractive valley of the River Gwili. During the summer of 1978, frequent trains ran at weekends only; the first public services between Bronwydd Arms and Cwmdwyfran started on 30 April, although they had run since 25 March over just half a mile of track. During that first season, 20,000 passenger journeys were recorded.

Stock

During 1978 the train was a stumpy 1939-built Peckett 0-4-0 saddle tank named *Merlin* (or *Myrddin*), hauling a single coach which was formerly a British Rail d.m.u. trailer car. The latter was the line's only passenger vehicle in use, though the popularity of the service suggested more would be obtained. Locomotive stock included two other tank locomotives of industrial origin, and there were several goods wagons used for works trains. It is hoped that in the long run, locomotives of Great Western origin will re-appear, for examples of several classes which once worked over the line have been preserved.

VI
Lancashire and the North-West

The Ravenglass and Eskdale Railway

This fascinating 15 in. gauge line links two valleys, Miterdale and Eskdale in West Cumbria, and runs from Ravenglass on the coast, to Dalegarth, some three miles from the celebrated Hard Knott Pass.

The line and its history
It was opened in 1876 as a 3 ft gauge line, to serve a group of iron mines in Eskdale. The output of these mines did not come up to expectations and the line was bankrupt less than a year after it had been opened. It remained thus until the closure of the last mine forced complete abandonment in 1912.

The line lay derelict till 1915, when its remains were leased by Narrow Gauge Railways Ltd, a concern in which Messrs Bassett-Lowke, the model-makers, had a large interest. N.G.R. re-gauged the track from 3 ft to 15 in., and a train service was resumed using miniature locomotives built by Bassett-Lowke, together with locomotives and coaches built some twenty years before by Sir Arthur Heywood for his private railway at Duffield in Derbyshire. The Bassett-Lowke engines were scale models built for exhibition, and proved to be too lightly constructed to stand the hard slogging needed on the switchback R. & E. line. The Heywood engines, though strongly built, were already some 20 years old and past their prime. However, one of the Heywood engines, a 0-8-0 named *Muriel*, was rebuilt in 1926–7 as a 0-8-2 using *Muriel's* chassis with a new boiler and firebox. She was renamed *River Irt* and is still in regular service.

In 1925 the line was taken over by Sir Aubrey Brocklebank, Chairman of the Cunard Steamship Line. He expanded the quarries at Beckfoot, and enlarged the crushing plant at Murthwaite to provide extra revenue from freight for the little line. After his death however, his successors took little interest and the line deteriorated. They sold it to the Keswick Granite Co. in 1948. The Granite Co. ran down the quarries but kept the railway running. In

1958 they put it up for auction. It was eventually bought by Mr Colin Gilbert, a Manchester stockbroker, who put up the bulk of the money on behalf of the newly formed Ravenglass and Eskdale Railway Preservation Society. Since then freight traffic has been abandoned, and an all-the-year-round passenger service run.

The line is operated by a permanent staff under the Manager, Mr Douglas Ferreira, assisted by voluntary help from Preservation Society members.

A journey down the line
The time allowed for the 7-mile journey is 40 minutes. This may seem excessive, but it must be remembered that this is a miniature railway, and the line abounds in sharp curves and stiff gradients. Drivers have to know the road thoroughly in all weathers, and the peculiarities of their engines too, if they are to get the best out of them and keep time.

Leaving Ravenglass we drop down to Barrow Marsh alongside the River Mite, dive under the main road and reach Muncaster Mill Halt. The mill waterwheel has been restored and will probably be turning as we pass. The interior machinery is being gradually restored too, and is open for visitors' inspection.

From the Halt, a stiff climb begins on a long S-bend through Miteside woods; our engine begins to bark with effort up gradients varying

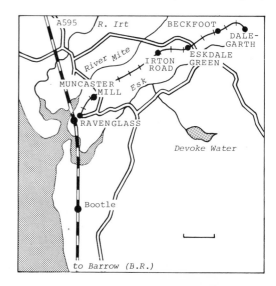

In the fine surroundings of the valley of the Mite, 2-6-2 Northern Rock *heads for Ravenglass with a train of modern enclosed bogie stock.*

sharply between 1 in 42 and 1 in 79. The scenery is striking, and the local names fascinating not only here but all along the line. Beyond Miteside Halt, with its shelter made from a boat, we come to Katie Caddie Gates, Katie Caddie Curve, Creep Cutting, and then a minor summit known to enginemen as 'The Top'. It is not line summit by any means; merely one of the many with which this line abounds. A gentle drop to Murthwaite follows. On the right, built into the hillside and now heavily overgrown, is all that remains of the stone-crushing plant and former workshops of the R. & E.R. The plant is now demolished, and scrub has taken over, but ten and more years ago the place was, so to speak, littered with history, relics of former locomotives and rolling stock, now put aside for proper preservation.

From Murthwaite there is a gentle climb through Horsefall Wood to Rocky Point, where the line circumnavigates an outcrop. Our engine works hard again up the 1 in 47 to Walk Mill summit, where, ahead, Scafell looms up in the distance, and our track, straight for once, dips and rises like a fairground switchback. Down, down we go to the Big Stone, then up again and sweep round into Irton Road Station, some four miles from Ravenglass. This is the half-way point, and there is usually a train from the other direction waiting to pass us.

From Irton Road to Eskdale Green is a half-mile – but a very pretty one – and in this short distance we pass from Miterdale into Eskdale. Eskdale Green is now a charming station, made so by the work of the Yorkshire Branch of the Preservation Society. It was not always thus however. It was once a ramshackle place with a dilapidated hut and grass-grown platform. Local legend has it that a neighbouring farmer went to a sale and bought a second-hand hen house. It was to be delivered by rail on a certain day. On the appointed day he sent a boy to fetch it. Arrived at the station the boy loaded up the only hut he could find. . . .

Leaving Eskdale Green, the line curves under the road, and climbs sharply to Hollinghow Woods, over 1 in 36. With a heavily loaded train, a good start is needed to avoid stalling on the bank, particularly in wet weather. We twist and turn through the woods on a ledge, higher than and some distance from the valley road. About a quarter-mile further on, and still in the woods, we reach Fisherground Corner, so called because the farm of that name is below us on the right. A short sharp gradient follows, and on the left, supported by two concrete columns, is a water tank made from an old steel wagon body which is filled from a hillside stream. This still serves as an emergency water supply for thirsty locomotives.

On again past Spout House Farm, we come to Gilbert's Cutting. In pre-preservation days the line made a sharp S-bend here to get round an outcrop. It was a splendid place for photography, but bad for railway operation, as the curve had to be negotiated carefully. In 1963, Mr Gilbert paid for a cutting to be dug through the outcrop.

From this point on, we are near to, and still above, the road which keeps us company for the next half-mile or so. Soon we pass the former Beckfoot quarry, long abandoned and shrouded in trees. A quarter of a mile ahead is Beckfoot Halt. This request stop is mainly used by visitors staying at the former Stanley Ghyll Hotel, which is now a centre run by the Y.H.A. It is the building on our right as we pass the Halt and on the other side of the road. Beckfoot Wood lies ahead, and the line runs beside a lane leading to Dalegarth Cottages. Drivers say this can be a tricky stretch. The gradient is stiff (though not the stiffest on the line) and it can be slippery in wet weather. Little sunlight can penetrate the trees, and even if the rest of the line be dry this part is apt to remain damp and greasy. Leftward among the trees on the other side of the lane are the remains of bothies in which miners of the 1870s lived before proper accommodation was built for them.

Once at the summit, we coast down past Dalegarth Cottages and into the terminus first opened in 1926. There are two tracks in the station, with a turntable at the end. The main platform is on the right, with a building housing a refreshment and waiting room, a shop and the booking office. A spacious car park and picnic area is in the field behind. This is one of the many improvements put in since preservation. That the Railway is now a go-ahead concern is obvious. During the last ten years two new locomotives have been built, the greater part of the line relaid. The track layout at Ravenglass has been greatly improved and effectively signalled, saloon coaches provided to ensure passenger comfort during bad weather, and an awning erected to provide much needed shelter on the bleakest part of the station at Ravenglass. The greatest advance of all has been in the matter of train control.

Train control by radio. Through the years the R. & E.R. has tried many methods, but none, however satisfactory they may have been elsewhere, was really suited to the conditions under which the R. & E.R. has to work. Then someone came up with the idea of radio control. A scheme was evolved, and it has been in use successfully for some years now.

The system briefly is this: each locomotive is equipped with a radio transceiver and there is another unit in the control cabin at Ravenglass.

Between the two terminal stations are three loops where trains can pass each other, at Miteside, Irton Road Station, and Fisherground. Some distance ahead of each loop, a disc with a zig-zag line on it is prominently displayed on a post beside the line. On reaching this, the driver calls up Control, identifies himself, states his position, and asks for instructions. He may be told to pass through the loop without stopping; on the other hand if the controller has another train approaching in the opposite direction he will instruct the driver to halt in the loop and let it pass. This process is repeated for every train in each direction throughout the day's timetable.

From his timetable graph before him on the desk the controller knows where every train *ought* to be at any given moment. Now, with his radio telephone, he knows where they all *actually are* – which can sometimes be a very different thing. With this system, emergencies can be anticipated and prompt action taken so

Irton Road station on the R. & E.R., with River Esk *awaiting departure.*

that mishaps do not in fact happen. The system is still in its infancy. The R. & E.R. is the pioneer of it in this country.

Stock

The Railway now has four steam locomotives. When in the early 1920s it was clear that the Bassett-Lowke models were not really up to the job, Henry Greenly designed *River Esk* as a freight engine to handle the stone traffic. She is a 2-8-2, the first engine of that wheel arrangement ever built in this country. She was built by Davey Paxman of Colchester in 1923. She is a miniature locomotive built to a scale of 4 in. to the foot. At one stage in her career she was given a steam tender with a 0-8-0 chassis. This was not a success, so the tender was mounted on two four-wheeled bogies instead, and the steam chassis stored away in case it might some day come in useful. *River Esk* has been a capable performer ever since, and is a very handsome engine. Until 1966 she wore a green livery, but in 1967 she was given a coat of blackberry black

lined out with red and white, and now looks even better.

For some twenty-five years, *River Esk* and *River Irt* carried the brunt of the traffic, for they were the only two steam engines on the line. *River Irt* is the oldest 15 in. gauge locomotive in active service anywhere; for she, as we mentioned above, is a rebuild of Sir Arthur Heywood's *Muriel* of 1894. She was powerful and reliable but certainly no beauty! Her miniature cab gave her driver little protection. She was given a larger one in 1972, and her chimney was lengthened in proportion. This gave a bonus of better steaming, and it also improved her looks. She wears her former green livery with red and black lining.

In 1967 *Esk* and *Irt* were joined by *River Mite*. She was built by Clarkson of York on – wait for it! – *River Esk*'s steam-tender chassis which had been thriftily stored away 33 years before. Naturally she had her teething troubles, but ten years of service has proved her worth. She was first painted Indian red – but is now a shade of vermilion.

The centenary year of the railway saw yet another locomotive added to the stud. This is

Northern Rock, designed and built at Ravenglass. The only part not made there was her R. & E. R. standard boiler, supplied by an outside firm. She went into service in April 1976, and has been at work ever since, and shown herself to be a powerful engine. She is painted in a yellowish shade of green known as muscat, and lined out with red and black.

Since the early 1920s the R. & E.R. has used internal combustion locomotives (i.c.l.'s) alongside their steam engines. In fact one of the Heywood engines, a 0-6-0 named *Ella*, was, when withdrawn, cannibalized into a petrol locomotive. The remains, now a tool van, are usually to be seen on a siding just outside Dalegarth station.

The i.c.l.'s were used as standby locomotives for hauling relief trains in summer and works trains in winter. They still perform these functions, and in addition tackle the winter passenger service, for at that season the steam engines are regularly under repair.

The i.c.l.'s most in evidence to summer visitors are three: first *Shelagh of Eskdale*. She is named after a local historical character, and is a diesel-hydraulic locomotive built in 1968 by Curwen and Severn-Lamb, painted royal blue.

A petrol-driven engine built in 1929 has given yeoman service. She was built to resemble as far as possible a steam tank engine and her exhaust was surrounded by a steam-engine-type chimney. Not unnaturally she was known as *Pretender*. Not long ago it was feared that her much-repaired engines were past further repair and that she would have to be scrapped. The R. & E.R. engineers however are nothing if not resourceful. They replaced her ailing petrol engine with a diesel salvaged from a boat sunk in Ravenglass harbour. This has given her a new lease of life and everyone now calls her *Perkins*. She is painted Brunswick green with orange and black lining.

A twin-car diesel set can generally be seen during the day in Ravenglass station. The cars are painted aluminium colour, and both carry the Silver Jubilee device. This is the R. & E.R. Silver Jubilee train, added to stock during 1977.

The train is very successful, and is used for light relief trains, small party bookings, and V.I.P.s visiting the line. The cars are excellently sprung, and their riding has to be experienced to be believed.

The coaches found at Ravenglass are a mixture of opens and saloons. The latest batch of saloon coaches were built and delivered between 1966 and 1974; the opens are mostly older. In fine weather, trains are made up of opens, with saloons used on rainy days. More often than not it is wiser to use both, but it is noticeable that the opens fill up first. The saloons have excellent observation windows, but the open coaches give by far the best view of the countryside during the run.

The area around
Ravenglass, Irton Road, and Dalegarth are ideal centres from which to set out by car or on foot, to explore the countryside.

Muncaster Castle is one mile from Ravenglass. The castle itself is mainly Victorian, but parts of the medieval castle remain. There is a fine collection of furniture and pictures, ornamental gardens to wander in, and a nature trail to follow.

Ravenglass itself was a Roman port; a 'Roman Trail' has been laid out to follow.

A *Roman road* ran from Ravenglass over Hard Knott Pass and Wrynose Pass to the Roman station near Windermere, and there was a Roman fort still to be seen on the slopes of *Hard Knott*. Not too far away by car is *Wastwater*, and further away in an easterly direction are *Coniston* and *Windermere*, and the beauty spot of Tarn Hows.

In the same neighbourhood, but 2 miles south-east of Hawkshead is Hill Top, Sawrey, the home of Beatrix Potter. From there it is not far by car to Grasmere and Rydal Water. Rydal Mount was the house in which the poet Wordsworth lived for the last 37 years of his life.

Grizedale Forest Wild Life Centre is well worth a visit. It is 3 miles south of Hawkshead on the road to Satterthwaite.

The Lakeside and Haverthwaite Railway

The line and its history

The Lakeside and Plumpton Branch Railway was opened by the Furness Railway Company on 1 June 1869; after almost a hundred years of continuous running, it was closed at the end of 1965.

From the beginning it was associated with Windermere tourism. This business reached a peak during the inter-war years, when special excursions were run from London, Blackpool and Leeds. After World War II, the traffic became narrowly seasonal; lack of winter trade led Dr Beeching to recommend the closure of this line to passengers in the early 60s; a freight service continued until 1967. The Lakeside Railway Estates Company was formed in that year in the hope of reviving the whole line. Later, when this was found to be impossible, they settled for the three miles between Lakeside and Haverthwaite. In 1970 they were granted permission by British Rail to start renovating the permanent way; from then on locomotives and coaches began to arrive. On 2 May 1973, the line was opened for the conveyance of passengers by the late Bishop of Wakefield, the Rt Rev. Eric Treacy.

The line today

The actual line now open to the public runs from the terminus station, Lakeside on Windermere and runs roughly south-west to Haverthwaite. Between these two lies Newby Bridge Halt, recently restored by the Blackpool Branch of the Society. There are two short tunnels at Haverthwaite; both are unlined, being cut through solid rock. Haverthwaite is the headquarters of the line, having not only spacious goods yards for storage of stock, and car parking, but being alongside the main A590 road. The railway is single-track throughout, with a run-round loop at each terminal station.

Stock

Most of the actual hauling on the line is performed by the 0-6-0 tank engines of which there are four, together with one 0-4-0, *Caliban*. This last loco has been numbered '1'. She was built by Alfred Peckett and Sons of Bristol in 1937 and worked for Courtaulds in Preston, until purchased by the Society in 1967. So that *Caliban* can pull (and more importantly, stop) passenger trains effectively, she has since been fitted with vacuum brake equipment. In addition, the Railway has an 0-6-0 Hunslet saddle tank now named *Cumbria*. She was built in 1953 for the Army to replace similar wartime engines. *Cumbria* was not worked particularly hard at the depot at Long Marston, and so arrived at Haverthwaite in very fine condition. Her Army number, '94', has been retained and vacuum brakes fitted to equip her for passenger service.

Another regular tank steamer is No. 14, *Princess*. She is an 0-6-0 saddle tank manufactured by W. G. Bagnall of Stafford in 1942. On completion, *Princess* was sent to perform shunting duties for the Preston Corporation on the banks of the River Ribble. She has since been renovated and had vacuum braking gear fitted. Unlike the Hunslet, this tank has outside cylinders and visible driving gear. Similar in external appearance are the two Hudswell-Clarke 0-6-0s, now numbered '5' and '6'. No. 5 was built in Leeds in 1929, and No. 6 at the same

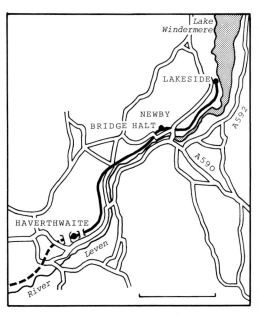

place some ten years earlier. They have both had chequered careers, but came together in the 1960s to work at the Byfield Ironstone Company's pits in Scunthorpe; when these pits were closed down in 1969, the locos were purchased for the Lakeside Railway.

Larger and more powerful are the two 4MT class 2-6-4 tanks. Designed by Charles Fairburn for the L.M.S. in 1944, they were intended for light passenger and goods duties. No. 2073 was built in 1950, and No. 2085 in 1951. They were built in Brighton for work on the Southern Region. No. 2073 did not require much re-storation, being ready for service within six months. No. 2085, however, needed more extensive repairs, and complete re-tubing. She was not ready for five years. No. 2073 has been painted in the livery of the London and North Western Railway, that is blackberry black. No. 2085 has been repainted in the livery of the Caledonian Railway, a bright mid-blue.

In addition to the steam locomotives, there are three diesel engines. No. 2 is a 0-4-0, *Fluff*. The bodywork was constructed by Hunslet of Leeds in 1937 but the engine is a Fowler 44 h.p. diesel. She is used for shunting, and for light works trains. Larger, and consequently more powerful, is the British-Rail-built Gardner 0-6-0. She was purchased in 1972 as a standby locomotive. These locos were built at the Swindon workshops, and this last engine (B.R. No. 2117) was completed in 1959. She was withdrawn from service in 1971, having completed much work, first on the Western Region and then in the Midlands. She arrived on the Lakeside Railway in April 1972. Finally, there is the tiny petrol-driven four-wheeled *Rachel*, No. 9 on the Railway. Manufactured in Bedford by the Motor Rail and Tram Car Company in 1924, she was originally used as a shunter in a paper mill in Burneside. She was purchased by a member of the Lakeside Railway Society and transferred to the line in 1973. *Rachel* is an exceptionally compact loco; she is powered by a 40 h.p. Dorman engine, and weighs a mere 10 tons.

The Railway also possesses ten coaches. These, with two exceptions, are all of British Railways origin. The Society purchased eight standard coaches to run their passenger service. There are six regular side-corridor second-class coaches; four are numbered E24248, E24377, E24381, and E24731 and were built in 1953; the others, E24449 and E24799, were built in the following year. In addition, they have purchased a 'BSK' and a 'BSO'. The former, No. E34181 built in 1951, matches the other six, but has only four compartments and a luggage and guard's brake compartment as well. The 'BSO', E9218 built in 1953, is of similar design to the 'BSK' except that it has a central corridor with open seating, with a guard's and luggage compartments. This carriage has now been converted into a buffet car. The luggage compartment is used as a bar, and the guard's compartment as a kitchen. There are two older coaches. One is a former L.N.E.R. Gresley-designed parcels van with a brake and guard's compartment, built at York in 1936. (It is significant in that it was one of the first of his carriages to be constructed in metal; previously teak had been used.) Lastly, there is a riding van and brake. Built at Derby for the Midland Railway, in 1913, this coach was originally a clerestory-roofed compartment carriage. It was later stripped and converted into a mess and tool van for gangers working on B.R. It has now been repainted and fitted with bunks for overnight workers on the Lakeside Railway.

There are many and various wagons on the Railway. One of the more outstanding is the Esso oil tank. It was presented by the Esso Company who had previously restored and repainted it. It is now used as an emergency mobile water tank in case of fire. In 1972 a goods brake van was purchased for £120. It was formerly used on the L.M.S., constructed at Derby in 1947, and has since been painted grey with a black frame. There are also some box vans, including a G.W.R. van and a Southern Railway van, both of 12 tons. There is also a bogie bolster wagon capable of handling long and heavy loads, together with a Conflat wagon and a general-purpose five-plank wagon.

The area around

Lake Windermere itself is well worth visiting; it is England's largest lake, being some ten miles from north to south. During the nineteenth century, the lake became noted for sailing, and a number of yacht clubs were established. B.R. boats run a service between Lakeside and

Ambleside, and provide a fine way of viewing the lake. The railway runs in connection with these sailings with a daily timetable from June to mid-September, and a weekend service from May to the end of October.

One of the pair of L.M.S. (Fairburn) 2-6-4 tanks on the Lakeside and Haverthwaite Railway. The two, one built in 1950 and the other in 1951, both at Brighton, worked on the Southern Region before further electrification there.

159

Steamtown

What Steamtown is

Steamtown Railway Museum is located at Carnforth in Lancashire, six miles north of Lancaster and Morecambe. Carnforth was once an important railway junction: three important pre-grouping Companies met here, the London and North Western, the Midland, and the Furness Railways. Built on the site of the formerly large marshalling yard and locomotive depot, Steamtown covers some twenty-three acres, including over three miles of track. Besides the sheds for storing the locomotives, there are good facilities for servicing and running them. The working coaling plant is capable of holding 150 tons of coal; there is an ash disposal plant, a seventy-foot vacuum turntable (particularly valuable in view of the limited space available), and a 75,000-gallon water storage tank. There are also carriage and wagon works, and a machine shop. The whole system is controlled from a restored Midland Railway signal box removed from the Settle and Carlisle line. For the visitor there is a gift shop and a cafe and ample free car parking. Steamtown has a fine collection of engines and carriages selected from a wide area. Main line express locomotives have been preserved from the L.N.E.R., G.W.R. and Southern Railway Companies, while the L.M.S. is prominent among the unnamed engines. The company has also succeeded in building up a fine collection of smaller industrial locomotives and their more modern diesel counterparts. In addition, they have acquired an interesting group of steam engines from Europe. Ever since the ban on steam-hauled trains was lifted by British Rail in 1971, the Steamtown depot has repeatedly supplied the locomotives required to haul these specials. Their authorized route is from Sellafield, through Barrow, Carnforth, Skipton, Leeds, Harrogate and York, to Scarborough on the east coast.

Locomotive stock

Probably the best-known engine housed at Steamtown is No. 4472, *Flying Scotsman*. After finishing her time with British Rail, *Flying Scotsman* was purchased by Alan Pegler in 1963. He had her extensively overhauled and re-painted in her apple-green L.N.E.R. colours, and she worked private excursion trains for six years. He then took her to America on a trade mission promoting British goods. Though she successfully travelled over 15,000 miles around the United States, the crossing to the West Coast and San Francisco produced financial difficulties for Mr Pegler. In 1973 Mr W. H. McAlpine purchased No. 4472, and since her return to Britain, she has been shedded here, and has powered numerous steam specials. *Flying Scotsman* was completed in 1923 and exhibited at the Wembley Exhibition. In 1928 she became famous for hauling the first non-stop train from King's Cross to Edinburgh. On a trial run in 1934, she became the first British steam engine to achieve an officially recorded 100 m.p.h. This famous engine has carried as many as six numbers in her lifetime. She was Great Northern No. 1472, then L.N.E.R. No. 4472, named *Flying Scotsman*. In 1946 she was re-numbered '502', then '102'. On nationalization in 1948 her new number was '60103'. Up to her official withdrawal from B.R. in January 1963, she had travelled 2,080,000 miles, most of this along the L.N.E.R. East Coast main line in express passenger service.

Until recently, another L.N.E.R. exhibit was the 4-6-0 class B1 *Mayflower*, No. 1306. *Mayflower* is now the only working survivor of a once numerous class of express engines, 410 being built originally. The first *Mayflower*, No. 61379 (B.R. numbering) commemorated the 300th anniversary of the Pilgrim Fathers and the name was transferred to 1306 when she was purchased privately. She is a

OPPOSITE, TOP: *On the Lakeside and Haverthwaite Railway, 1953-built Hunslet 0-6-0* Cumbria *awaits departure with a Haverthwaite-Lakeside (Windermere) train on an August Saturday afternoon (p. 157).*

BELOW: *This replica of* Locomotion No. 1 *built for the 'Rail 150' Shildon cavalcade now operates at the Beamish Open Air Museum. The original is at Darlington North Road Museum (pp. 196, 202).*

magnificent locomotive, now restored to her original apple-green livery. She has recently been moved to the M.L.S.T. at Loughborough (see p. 94). The other famous L.N.E.R. engine is a Gresley Pacific, No. 4498, named after her designer Sir Nigel Gresley. The A4 class were among some of the first streamlined locomotives produced for the fast East Coast run to Scotland to rival the L.M.S. in the west. This class of locomotive holds the world speed record for steam, 126 m.p.h. This was achieved by No. 4468 *Mallard*. *Sir Nigel Gresley* has often topped 100 m.p.h. and also holds the British record for post-war steam running with passenger trains.

In addition to these, Steamtown also has a fine Great Western engine, namely the Collett-designed Hall, No. 6960, *Raveningham Hall*, completed at Swindon in 1944 and then based at Oxford. These twin-cylindered 4-6-0s were designed for a whole range of duties, ranging from fast passenger to goods trains. After languishing at Barry scrapyard in South Wales, *Raveningham Hall* has been restored at Carnforth and has since taken part in several steam parades, including that at Shildon 1975.

Representing the Southern Railway, and immediately recognizable by her smoke deflectors, is No. 850, *Lord Nelson*. Designed by R. E. Maunsell in the 1920s, this 4-6-0 class was introduced to supersede the under-powered *King Arthur* locos. They suffered some teething troubles, however, and it was not until after World War II that they ran really smoothly, when fitted with multiple blast pipes. These were the engines which hauled the famous boat trains from Waterloo to the South Coast and pulled the excursion trains crowded with Londoners seeking the sun and sea.

Equally well-known, but not as glamorous, are the two 'Black Fives'. These 4-6-0 locomotives were designed by Sir William Stanier for the L.M.S. to work all kinds of train. They were first introduced in 1935, and from then on worked goods and passenger trains. These engines were superbly designed and popular with their drivers. They were un-named and wore a plain black livery with red lining. The two at Steamtown are Nos. 44871 and 44932. Both were built in 1945, No. 44871 at Crewe and No. 44932 at Horwich. The side view of a 'Black Five' has been adopted as the symbol for Steamtown. A particularly eye-catching locomotive at the Museum is No. 6441. Painted in L.M.S. maroon-and-black and lined in yellow, this engine is a striking exhibit. The 2MT 2-6-0 class was originally designed by H. G. Ivatt for the L.M.S. for secondary duties, but was so successful that they continued to be built by B.R. after nationalization. In fact, No. 6441 was not built until 1950, at Crewe. She then spent most of her working life in Lancashire on local passenger services, including the 'Lake Windermere Cruise' starting from Morecambe. (The engine was purchased by a Mrs Beet, who used to watch the loco running past her house when running between Carnforth and Hest Bank.)

In addition, Steamtown also has a comprehensive collection of tank engines designed for shunting duties, suburban and branch-line passenger trains and light goods work. Included in this category is their oldest exhibit, No. 1122. Built in 1891 for the Lancashire and Yorkshire Railway, this 0-6-0 tender locomotive is now undergoing extensive restoration to return her to full working order. The museum also possesses a Collett-designed G.W.R. 0-6-2 tank engine of the 56XX class.

Three Continental steam engines are preserved at Carnforth, two German and one French. The latter is No. 231K22, a 4-6-2 express locomotive built by the Paris, Lyons and Mediterranean Railway as early as 1914. Originally shedded at Avignon, she hauled expresses between Paris and the Riviera. Later in life, having been rebuilt in 1937, thereby increasing her efficiency, she was used to pull the 'Flèche d'Or' between Calais and Paris. The

OPPOSITE, TOP LEFT: *An impressive exhaust on a frosty January afternoon from 0-4-0 Peckett saddle tank No. 1999 (built 1941), and former Manchester Ship Canal 0-6-0 side tank No. 67 (Hudswell Clarke), as they head for Oxenhope on the winter steam service from Haworth.*

TOP RIGHT: *B.R. 4MT No. 75078 pilots 0-6-0 saddle tank No. 57* Samson *on a mid-December 'Santa Special', between Damems and Oakworth.*

BOTTOM: Samson *again, at Oakworth station. (All Keighley and Worth Valley Railway, p. 181.)*

Steamtown – the former Carnforth Motive Power Depot adjacent to Carnforth B.R. station – is now a centre with a wide range of locos. In this general view of the yard are the French 4-6-2 La France (1914, rebuilt 1937); G.W.R. Pendennis Castle, No. 4079 (built 1923, now in Australia); L.N.E.R. 2-6-2 No. 4771 Green Arrow, L.N.E.R. No. 1306 Mayflower *(built 1948: it also appears on the G.C.R.); German 4-6-2 No. 01.1104 (built 1940).*

external piping and gadgetry visible around the boilers of all these three engines are notably absent from British steam engines; they are air and water pumping apparatus, preheaters and generators, all devices added to try to improve running. The German express engine is No. 012 104-6. Again a 4-6-2, she was completed in 1940 by Schwartzkopf in Berlin as a streamlined express engine. Having been damaged by British bombing in 1944, the streamlined casing was removed in 1951 and she was converted to oil firing in 1957. She is noticably German, particularly distinguished by the shape of her

smoke deflectors. The engine is painted black except for the wheels, buffers and driving gear which are bright red. The colour scheme is the same for the other German loco, a 0-6-0 tank engine. This two-cylinder shunter was finished in 1927 and put into service at Bremerhaven, later working in Essen and at Mohne Dam.

There is also a fine collection of smaller, industrial locomotives collected from various sites throughout the country, twenty in all. The locos in regular use are No. 1, *Fina* (now renamed *Coronation*), and No. 2, *Cranford*. This engine is fitted with vacuum brake gear and so is suitable for hauling passenger coaches. One of the more unusual is *Gasbag*, an engine formerly used by Eastern Gas; it is particularly curious in that the four wheels are linked by chain drive. One of the – literally – more colourful is *Jane Darbyshire*, a 0-4-0 steam-powered tank loco built in 1929. She is now painted purple with red fittings and wheels. She was meant to be called 'J. N. Darbyshire', but the signwriter working on her name boards misheard his instructions and named her 'Jane' instead! Of

Since Carnforth was one of the last steam M.P.D.s in the country, retaining facilities up to the final withdrawal in 1968, the Museum company were able to take over equipment in good condition. The coaling stage is invaluable. Carnforth has two L.M.S. 5MT 4-6-0s: No. 44932 (1945) and No. 45407 (1937).

similar design is *British Gypsum*, another 0-4-0 tank completed in 1953; she is bright red. Also of note is *Glenfield*. Completed in 1902, *Glenfield* is a 0-4-0 tank loco with a crane mounted on top of her boiler. She is a working engine, and performs many useful functions in the Steamtown Museum. She is painted in black and light green, and lettered in cream.

Rolling stock

Steamtown has a fine collection of coaches, selected from many companies to complement their steam engines. They have a particularly fine collection of 'official' coaches, saloon coaches fitted with observation sections, dining facilities and lounges, so that senior railway

officials and directors could inspect their companies in a comfortable fashion. The North Eastern Railway's Directors' Saloon No. 305 is now in its original bright maroon. It still has the original carpets and upholstery on the armchairs and sofa. It has a clerestory roof, and is a fine example of Edwardian coach building.

It was also possible to purchase or hire a private saloon from railway companies. One of these is also preserved here, Great Western saloon 'Stapleford Park' No. 9004. It is a particularly attractive coach finished in the classic chocolate-and-cream livery of the Great Western, with a whitened roof and gold lettering along the sides. Steamtown also houses a Great Eastern teak-finished Chairman's saloon, complete with balcony, lounge, diner, kitchen, toilet and shower bath; a luxurious coach indeed. The Museum also has a Pullman car, 'Rosalind', which formerly worked on the South Eastern and Chatham Railway. Dating from the early twentieth century, this coach has been rebuilt several times and now serves as a passenger coach.

163

L.N.E.R. No. 4472 Flying Scotsman *is perhaps the most famous locomotive in the world. Now based at Carnforth, she often operates steam specials. Here on the main East Coast line, this is as she was before the tour of America, complete with double tender.*

OPPOSITE: *L.N.E.R. A4 Pacific ('Pacific' refers to the 4-6-2 wheel arrangement)* Sir Nigel Gresley, *No. 4498, is of the same class as* Mallard *which achieved the world steam locomotive speed record of 126 m.p.h. in 1938.*

Not to be missed either is the Museum's model railway display. This aims to suggest what some of the actual exhibits would have looked like when in regular use in various parts of the country. The display is designed to represent Berkhamstead on the L. & N.W.R. and L.M.S. main line at two different periods – first in the 1920s, and second in the late 1930s. Both models have appropriate locomotives and rolling stock. There are approximately fifty locomotives, a hundred coaches and around two hundred wagons operating on the model: it is a fine scenic display.

The area around
Not so far from Carnforth itself there are two old houses of historical interest. Borwick Hall is a fine Elizabethan manor house standing within its own grounds and has not been altered substantially since its construction, in 1595, around an earlier structure. It also possesses some fine gardens. Leighton Hall is a later construction. It consists of an eighteenth-century core, on which is superimposed the then fashionable Gothic style, in the early nineteenth century. The house is still in the possession of the Gillow family who have resided there for many generations; the house contains a fine collection of domestic furniture and pictures.

Steamport (Southport Locomotive and Transport Museum Society)

Steamport is a railway depot. It consists of a railway shed for storage and restoration, with three tracks leading into it. A fourth is planned

Steamport Southport was also once an M.P.D.–Southport Derby Road. Stanier L.M.S. 5MT 4-6-0 No. 44806, named Magpie *after an association with the television programme, stands in the shed behind some of the industrials.*

for 1979. With the help of a team employed under the Job Creation Scheme, restoration has been accelerated.

The largest locomotive preserved here is the former L.M.S. Stanier-designed 4-6-0 No. 44806, *Magpie*, built in 1944. More modern is the Riddles 2-6-0, No. 76079 (4MT class), completed in 1957. In addition, there are four saddle tanks, two Pecketts (a 0-4-0ST and a 0-6-0ST), a Hudswell Clarke (0-6-0ST, *Waleswood*) and a Hunslet (a 0-6-0ST, No. 9 *Kinsley*). There is a non-corridor second-class coach; (B.R. No. M12244) built in 1950 to an L.M.S. design. There are two cranes, and a number of goods vehicles.

Hudswell Clarke 0-4-0 saddle tank Waleswood
was built in 1906, worked at Waleswood colliery
near Sheffield until 1962, then spent 10 years on
standby duty in nearby Kiveton Park. Arrived at
Steamport in 1974, she is regularly in steam.

The Isle of Man Railway

The Isle of Man Railway features some of the oldest narrow-gauge steam engines in Britain. Originally the island had an impressive network of lines. Steam was operated from Ramsey in the north around to Kirk Michael and St Germains on the west coast. The line divided at St John's, where one branch ran to Peel, another to Foxdale, and the third to Douglas. From here another route continued down the east coast, around to the terminus at Port Erin. There is an electric railway from Douglas to Ramsey along the east coast. The other, longer, route to the west has been closed down. The steam section is between Port Erin and Douglas. There are six intermediate stops, at Port Soderick, Santon, Ballasalla, Castletown, Colby and Port St Mary.

Work began on constructing this historic railway in 1870. The first section was completed between Port Erin and Ballasalla in 1874. The Manx Northern Railway, from St John's to Peel and Ramsey, was built in 1878. The track is 3 ft gauge. Rail traffic remained high till the 1950s but then started to fall off. Different parts of the railway were permanently closed after 1968. In

1965 so much maintenance was necessary that the whole system was temporarily closed down, and did not re-open until 1967. After 1968, operation was concentrated on the Port Erin line, with the backing of the Manx Government.

Besides some of the fine coastal scenery, the locomotives themselves are some of the most interesting features of the railway. They were built between 1876 and 1926 by Beyer Peacock of Gorton, Manchester. Most locomotives are in existence, though not necessarily working. The following are still operational: Nos. 4 *Loch*, 5 *Mona*, 8 *Fenella*, 10 *G. H. Wood*, 11 *Maitland*, 12 *Hutchinson*, and 13 *Kissack*. They are all 2-4-0 tanks, painted in a mid-green livery and lined out in black on white. They have polished brass domes and their numbers on the chimney stack, also in brass, with name plates on each water tank. They are designed to run faster than most narrow-gauge locos, and are fitted with 3 ft 9 in. driving wheels which enable them to run up to 45 m.p.h.

The coaches in use on the railway are also of historical interest. There were originally as many as seventy-five, the first narrow-gauge carriages to be lit with electric lights in Britain. They are brightly painted in red and cream, and date from 1926. There is a permanent staff of about twenty, and in the winter the footplate staff assist the fitters on maintenance, while the others work on the track. At one point, the

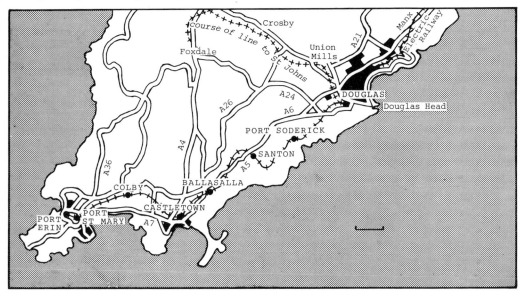

The distinctive design of the Isle of Man Railway 2-4-0s is clear in this picture taken in 1968, but the sidings on which they stand are less used now, and only two platform faces of Douglas are used.

management, realizing the appeal of this historic railway, provided its staff with Victorian uniforms. Station masters wore gold-braided uniforms, top hats, and capes. After 'nationalization', the Railway reverted to normal uniform.

There is a railway museum at Port Erin. The line's first engine, *Sutherland*, laid down in 1873 is there, as is the last, *Mannin* (1926). There is also the Royal Carriage, together with a host of memorabilia, including tickets, photographs, signs and signals. There is another railway museum on the west coast, in the former station village of Kirk Michael.

The 3 ft gauge track on the Isle of Man Railway is slightly unusual and worth notice. Like most narrow-gauge lines, the rails are flat-bottomed and attached directly to the sleepers without chairs. The difference is that a seating is cut into the wooden sleeper so that the rails are inclined inwards. The staff claim that this reduces wheel and rail wear and tends to stop

rails spreading on curves. The ballast is sprinkled with the residue from the bottom of coal-fired gas retorts in order to prevent the growth of weeds. It is the bright blue powder which may be seen over the track-bed, giving off a faint smell of gas.

Other railways and attractions
Since 1893, a Douglas–Ramsey electric railway has run. It is in fact the largest tramway in the British Isles, with over 17 miles of double track. It is a particularly picturesque route, moving inland before Laxey and crossing a large viaduct, which provides a clear view of the famous Manx waterwheel. The cars are brightly painted in red and white with light brown, with the large side panels in varnished teak. Trains are usually arranged as a motor car with a trailer.

At Laxey there is a mountain railway, a 3 ft 6 in. gauge electric line running up to the summit of Snaefell. There is a centre rail to help prevent derailment and assist braking.

Castletown has a transport museum of a different kind. It is a nautical collection, and is housed in a three-storeyed boat-house almost 200 years old. Among the exhibits is a schooner-rigged yacht, the *Peggy*, which dates from 1791.

Dinting Railway Centre

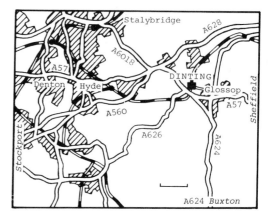

The Dinting Railway Centre, otherwise known as the Bahamas Locomotive Society, is based in the former Great Central engine shed, at Dinting on the B.R. line between Manchester Piccadilly and Glossop. The society was formed early in 1967 in an effort to secure the L.M.S. Jubilee class 4-6-0, No. 5596 *Bahamas*, for preservation - hence the title. The loco was purchased, and then sent for restoration by the Hunslet Engine Company of Leeds. *Bahamas* is now housed there and on display to the public. Since then then, the Society has acquired a considerable number of exhibits. On loan from the Manchester Museum of Technology (off the Oxford Road) is the former Great Central 2-8-0 No. 102, completed in 1911. In addition, there are a number of tank engines.

Bahamas, No. 5596, an L.M.S. 4-6-0 Jubilee class (1935), was the cause of Dinting Railway Centre, an ex-G.C.R. depot. No. 5690 is also a Jubilee. Just in the picture to the right of Bahamas is Southwick, a 0-4-0 crane tank.

The Society also has several coaches, most of which originated with the L.M.S. They include a medical officer's saloon, No. 45017 (1923) and an open third No. 7991 (1926). (The latter is, at the time of writing, on the Severn Valley.) The Society's plans for the future aim to provide the North-West with a fully operational steam locomotive museum, and a stabling point for preserved locomotives which can then be used for specials on British Rail's territory. The centre is open most weekends and weekdays throughout the year, while special steam open days are arranged at Easter and on Bank holidays in the summer. Brake-van rides are offered when locos are in steam.

VII
Yorkshire and the North-East

The North Yorkshire Moors Railway

Yorkshire is a very fortunate county; not only does it have Britain's largest static railway collection, in the National Railway Museum at York, but it can also boast of having two of the country's six major preserved standard-gauge railways within its bounds.

The line and its history

The larger of the two is the North Yorkshire Moors Railway, whose beginnings can be traced back to the tiny seaport of Whitby a century and a half ago. In those days, the only connection between Whitby and the rest of the country – other than by sea – was the often impassable turnpike road over the bleak and desolate moors. By the time that the Whitby and Pickering Turnpike Road Act became due for renewal in 1826, the more far-sighted residents of Whitby were thinking of a railway as an alternative. Various schemes were suggested, one of them being for a line to connect Whitby with the newly opened Stockton and Darlington Railway. Robert Campion, the author of this scheme, had a route surveyed and reported on it at a meeting early in 1831. It was discussed at another meeting two months later together with a further scheme, favouring a line to Pickering. A committee was formed to look into both and Campion's surveyor, Thomas Storey, was engaged to survey this alternative route.

Not being entirely satisfied with Storey's surveys, the committee finally called in George Stephenson, the 'father of British railways', and asked him to examine and report upon the two schemes. Stephenson reported in favour of the Pickering route at a meeting held a year later at Whitby's Angel Inn. The report was received with great enthusiasm; a share list was opened on the spot, and before the close of the meeting, £30,000 of the estimated £48,000 cost of construction had been subscribed. Unhappily, Stephenson's estimate was to prove wildly inaccurate, and the final cost of the line came to a staggering total of over £105,000. In the Angel Inn that day hopes ran high, and on the crest of

the wave of enthusiasm the committee pressed on. Application was made to Parliament, and on 6 May 1833, the Whitby and Pickering Railway Act received the Royal Assent. The first step forward had been made, despite the fact that the legalities seem to have been done in such haste that one section of the Act approved the use of steam locomotives, and another one forbade it!

Work now started in earnest. The first sod was cut in September 1833, and by June 1835 sufficient progress had been made for a regular service to be started from Whitby to Grosmont. Finally, on 26 May 1836, the ceremonial opening of the whole line took place. Church bells and a procession through the streets of Whitby started the day, and when the first train arrived at Pickering it was greeted by a crowd of no less than seven thousand people supported by the music from five bands. That is no mean feat for a quiet country town. After the celebration lunch at the Black Swan, the official

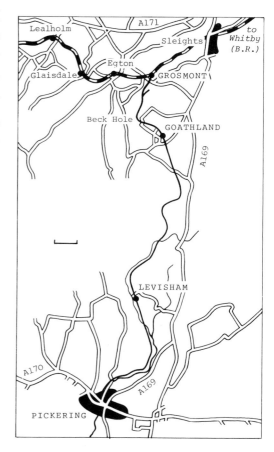

Grosmont Motive Power Depot on the North Yorks Moors Railway, with, from left to right, N.E.R. 0-6-0 No. 2392 (built 1923, now at the National Railway Museum); a Lambton 0-6-2 tank (1904); No. 2005, an L.N.E.R. K1 class 2-6-0 built in 1949; 'Black Five' (L.M.S. 5MT 4-6-0) No. 5428, named Eric Treacy *after the former Bishop of Wakefield, the railway photographer.*

party returned to the Angel Inn at Whitby, and the celebrations went on until the early hours of the following day.

The first trains bore little resemblance to their steam-hauled counterparts of later years. Horses provided the motive power, and passengers travelled in what was virtually a road coach on railway wheels. (One of these is pictured in oils in Whitby Museum.) Freight was carried in horse drawn wagons too; the stones for Waterloo Bridge, Somerset House and many other famous buildings travelled the first few miles of their journey to London over the metals of the Whitby and Pickering Railway.

During the first few years of its existence, the line prospered, carrying some four thousand people each month at a fare of four shillings (20p) inside or three shillings (15p) outside. One of them, Charles Dickens, described it as a 'quaint old railway along part of which passen-

gers are hauled by a rope'. He was referring to the 1500-yard-long incline between Beck Hole and Goathland: since its gradient of 1 in 15 was too steep for horses, the coaches were hauled up by means of a cable.

In 1836, Whitby solicitor Henry Belcher published a book entitled *The Scenery of the Whitby and Pickering Railway*. Three years later he persuaded the railway company to run special trains to Grosmont in connection with a fête to raise funds for a new church there. The trains from Whitby started at 9.00 a.m. and ran at hourly intervals. The fare was reduced from 9d to 6d ($3\frac{3}{4}$p to $2\frac{1}{2}$p). Trains in the opposite direction ran as required, the first one leaving Pickering at 5 a.m., and the fare was 1s 6d instead of 2s 3d. The first cheap railway excursions had arrived.

Despite these promising beginnings, the fortunes of the line began to decline in the early eighteen forties. A network of railways had rapidly spread over the country; the 'Railway Mania' had begun. The outstanding figure in the railway world at this time was George Hudson, a financial manipulator whose dubious dealings had given him control over an empire of small railways. One of Hudson's companies, the York and North Midland Railway, opened a line from York to Scarborough in 1845, with a branch to

Pickering. In the same year, the directors of the W. & P.R. sold the line to the Y. & N.M.R. for £80,000.

Hudson was not the sort of man to let the grass grow under his feet, and the line from Whitby to Pickering was soon doubled and joined to the York and North Midland. Steam engines were introduced to the line in 1846, and the first reached Whitby a year later. Having been designed for horse-drawn traffic, the line abounded in sharp curves; special short-wheelbase engines, known as 'Whitby Bogies', were built to work the line, together with four-wheeled coaches (instead of the six wheeled ones by then coming into use). Rapidly acquiring the nickname of 'Whitby Bathing Machines', these coaches ran from Whitby through to London and became notorious for their rough riding. Further amalgamations took place over the ensuing years, both before and after the collapse of Hudson's empire in 1849. By 1854, both the W. & P.R. and the Y. & N.M.R. had become part of the newly formed North Eastern Railway.

The Beck Hole incline remained a thorn in the

During the Jubilee weekend of 1977, Lambton No. 29 leaves Grosmont for Goathland, over the level crossing.

side of the railway operators. The N.E.R. decided to bypass it, by building a deviation between Grosmont and Goathland. This was completed in 1865. The hindrance to through locomotive working was thus eliminated, although the 1 in 49 gradient which replaced it was and still is one of the steepest in the country. In 1872 the incline once again came into use, when a 750-yard length of 43 in. gauge track was laid on it, in order to test a mountain railway locomotive built at Leeds and destined for Brazil.

In 1908 part of the old line was re-opened, from Grosmont to the foot of the incline. A summer service of railcars was introduced. This ran until the advent of World War I in 1914, carrying holiday-makers from the coast to the moors.

After the war, the railways were merged into four groups: in 1923, the N.E.R. became part of the London and North Eastern Railway. When

Lambton and train start to climb the Esk Valley from Goathland on the N.Y.M.R. Former courses of the railway can readily be seen on the valley floor.

the four groups were nationalized the L.N.E.R. became British Railways (Eastern Region). Nationalization did not lead to continuing prosperity for the Pickering and Whitby line. In 1964, the Beeching Report recommended that all three lines to Whitby should be closed. A very strong case was made for the retention of rail connection to Whitby, and extremely vigorous local opposition was aroused. Finally, only a modified form of the Beeching plan was adopted. The lines from Whitby to York and to Scarborough were abandoned in 1965; the line to Middlesbrough was left open. For the first time in one hundred and twenty-nine years, trains no longer ran between Whitby and Pickering. The short length between Whitby and Grosmont, however, was kept open, since it is part of the line to Whitby from Middlesbrough.

Preservation

The Whitby–Pickering line lay neglected for two years. The track became rusty and overgrown; paint peeled from deserted stations and signal boxes. But in June 1967, Mr Tom Salmon of Ruswarp called a meeting at his home. From this small beginning emerged the North Yorkshire Moors Railway Preservation Society, with the avowed intention of re-opening the line. Public meetings were held, and membership grew. Its prestige and status became such that even British Rail was prevailed upon to grant a six-month reprieve on the lifting of one line of the track. The membership continued to grow, area groups were formed, and in the first year of the Society's existence, £8,000 was raised. By now B.R. was prepared to give permission for restoration work to begin. One Sunday in November 1968 the level crossing gates at Grosmont were repainted; three months later a small saddle tank locomotive, on loan to the society, steamed proudly from Pickering to Goathland, cheered on its way by hundreds of well-wishers. The Whitby and Pickering Railway was coming to life again.

Steam open day at Goathland in 1976. No. 2392 in the foreground; Barclay 0-6-0 saddle tank Salmon (1942) in the background. The railbus used for the 'National Park Scenic Specials' is behind No. 2392.

Negotiations with B.R. continued. The society was reconstituted as the North Yorkshire Moors Historical Railways Trust. With the support of the local authorities and the English Tourist Board, it was able to purchase the track-bed from Grosmont to Pickering, together with the actual track as far as Ellerbeck. Thanks to the many individuals and organizations who lent locomotives and rolling stock to the railway, the Trust was now able to run privately chartered steam-hauled trains between Grosmont and Ellerbeck. These boosted both the membership and the income of the railway. By 1973 the Trust, with a membership then of 9,000, had managed to purchase the track from Ellerbeck all the way to Pickering. With the transfer of a Light Railway Order from B.R., all was in order to run a public service.

Eight years previously, Mr and Mrs F. F. Clough had travelled on the last train to Pickering; on Easter Sunday 1973, they came from North Wales to ride on the first public train on its return from Pickering to Grosmont. The Whitby and Pickering Railway, under its new name of North Yorkshire Moors Railway,

was well and truly back in business.

Nine days later, on 1 May, the railway was officially opened by H.R.H. the Duchess of Kent. At Whitby the Duchess unveiled a plaque at the Angel. She went on to unveil a further one at Grosmont station, and then journeyed to Pickering on the inaugural train. A large crowd awaited her, and she there unveiled a third plaque at the Black Swan.

Access

The journey time by rail from Whitby to Grosmont is seventeen minutes; from Middlesbrough it is one hour. Visitors arriving at Grosmont find it very easy to change from British Rail to the North Yorkshire Moors Railway as both railways use the same station. (In the days of horse traction, the station was a stone building to the east of the present line: it is

The other tank from Lambton Colliery, No. 5 (built 1909) nears Beck Hole on the North Yorkshire Moors Railway.

still there and, although it is now the local Post Office, the doors of the old stables can still be seen. The present station was built when the line changed to steam. For some years before the town's first Methodist Church was opened in 1867, Station Master Robert Ingham allowed the station to be used as a place of worship.

A journey down the line

Leaving Grosmont the train passes over the level crossing where the gates were so enthusiastically painted in 1968; it then crosses the River Murk Esk and plunges into a short tunnel dating from 1845. Alongside the line is a foot path, which after crossing the river passes through the narrow tunnel originally used by the old horse-drawn railway. To the left of the tunnel entrances is the church of St Matthew; it was in aid of the building fund of this church that Henry Belcher organized the first excursions. His work is recalled by the east window, which is dedicated to his memory.

Once through the tunnel and past a newly built engine shed, Deviation Signal Box marks the start of the notorious Beck Hole incline, part of which can still be seen on the right-hand side of the railway. Up to this point the train has been proceeding fairly gently, but now the bark of the exhaust increases as the engine begins to climb. The Murk Esk is crossed once more and as the train leaves the valley floor and the wooded banks of the Esk behind, it turns sharply to the left into the valley of a tributary, the Eller Beck. Still climbing, it crosses the Beck three times in rapid succession. One bridge, at Water Ark, crosses a separate footbridge over the river at the same time. Sweeping on below a road bridge and past the tiny village of Darnholm, the railway enters a cutting blasted from the solid rock. The staccato beat of the exhaust echoes back, until the driver shuts off steam and with a rumble of wheels and a screech of brakes, the train rolls to a halt at Goathland. Many steam trains terminate here but those who wish to may change to a modern diesel railcar for the rest of the journey to Pickering.

The epitomy of the N.Y.M.R.: a 1947 'Black Five' – the only one with Stephenson link-motion, No. 4767 – approaches Eller Beck with a train from Pickering on a late October afternoon.

South of Goathland, the route of the original line appears to the right and joins the present one, still climbing towards Summit Signal Box, the highest point on the line. Over the moors to the left, the majestic scenery is topped by the three radomes of Fylingdales Early Warning Radar Station, like a row of gigantic golf balls.

Once past the signal box the line descends, crossing Lyke Wake Walk, a forty-mile trail across the moors between Osmotherly and Ravenscar, and enters the environmentally unique area of Fen Bog, and the valley of Newton Dale. Some 22,000 years ago, water escaping from glacier lakes in Eskdale built up in Fen Bog before bursting forth and scouring out the deep trench of Newton Dale. To the average traveller, the tiny stream gurgling through the woods and the reedy swamp of Fen Bog, where the water laps up against the railway embankment, give little indication of the awesome deluge that once thundered along carrying millions of tons of earth and rock. The geologist, however, can find ample evidence of what happened from the strata exposed in the valley sides: rocks from pre-glacial times to modern Oxford clay can readily be identified.

No road runs along Newton Dale, and the wide panoramic windows of the railcars provide the best way to see the unspoilt countryside and the wildlife that it supports. Man has left some interesting items too: there are the ruins of Carter's House, which served as an inn to the navvies who built the line and Skelton Tower, an architectural folly built by the Rev. Thomas Skelton, a local eccentric. A little further south, the Raindale Inn served as a changing point for horses. Today it is used as a field study centre, and has been renamed 'The Grange'. Part of Levisham station, on the edge of Levisham Moor and the railway's first road contact since leaving Goathland, is also used as a field study centre; after that the only buildings before Pickering are a few cottages at Farwath, built to house the platelayers who maintained the track. Drivers were instructed to stop there to pick up and set down platelayer's wives as required; it was their only contact with the outside world. Newton Dale widens out here to become the Vale of Pickering, taking its name from the market town eighteen miles by rail from Grosmont. Pickering is the southern terminus of the North Yorkshire Moors Railway (as it was of the Whitby and Pickering) and is headquarters of the Railway Trust. The station is listed as a building of special interest, and like the stations at Grosmont and Goathland contains a gift shop and has refreshment facilities.

Stock

It is perhaps appropriate that a line which was engineered by George Stephenson should have running on its metals an engine named after the great man. This engine, No. 4767, was one of the last of the famous L.M.S. 'Black Fives', built in 1947. Together with several other N.Y.M.R. engines, it took part in the Rail 150 celebrations

Driver's eye view of Levisham station from No. 29, about to cross with No. 2005 (which is reverse-running) with the North Yorkshireman.

of the 150th anniversary of the Stockton and Darlington Railway at Shildon in 1975, where it was named *George Stephenson* by the Rt Hon. William Whitelaw, M.P. The choice of this name for this particular engine was apt as it is the only one out of a class of 842 engines that was built with Stephenson's link-motion valve gear. Like many of the engines on the line, No. 4767 is privately owned, but it is in the care of the North Eastern Locomotive Preservation Group, whose engines form the backbone of the railway's motive power, and whose volunteer members form the nucleus of the railway's locomotive staff. As its name implies, the Group's main interest lies in its North Eastern Railway locomotives, typical of goods engines in the north-east during the last fifty years of steam.

No. 2238 is an enormous eight-coupled engine of class T2, built in 1918. No. 2392, of class P3, with its six coupled wheels is not much smaller: although of N.E.R. design, it was

actually completed in 1923 by the L.N.E.R. History has a habit of repeating itself and the group's third engine, a K1 class 2-6-0, No. 2005, although an L.N.E.R. engine, was actually built by British Railways in 1949.

Other engines in which the group takes an interest are two 0-6-2 tank engines which were built for the privately owned Lambton Colliery Railway in the first decade of the century. They are bigger than the small shunting engines normally associated with industry, and their greater power and larger coal and water capacity enabled them to haul long trains of coal wagons from the inland collieries to the coast. They are easily distinguishable by their low semi-circular cab roofs, designed to enable them to negotiate the narrow tunnels of the colliery railway system.

No. 5428 is a sister engine of *George Stephenson* but with standard Walschaerts valve-gear. It has been named *Eric Treacy* after the former Bishop of Wakefield, the well-known railway enthusiast with many railway photographic books to his credit. The oldest engine on the line is a 0-6-0 saddle tank built for the Great Northern Railway in 1899 and still going strong, and there are several more interesting locomotives to be seen of industrial origin. Some are steam engines, a few are diesels: some are in working order, others have yet to be restored. Amongst those that are in the process of being restored are three locomotives of main-line origin; a 2-8-0 engine from the former Somerset and Dorset Railway, an 0-6-2 tank engine from the Great Western Railway, and a standard class 4 2-6-4 tank engine from B.R.

There is a large collection of coaches and other items of rolling stock. The observant visitor will find many vehicles of interest, ranging from B.R. diesel multiple units, and B.R. coaches built in the late fifties, to a Great Northern Railway coach of 1898; from a Shell-Mex tank wagon built during World War II to a snow plough from Edwardian days.

In addition to the regular services (see A.R.P.S. listings) many special trains are run. These include evening 'National Park Scenic Specials' from Pickering to Goathland, and specially chartered 'Disco Specials', which provide musical evenings to cater for all tastes. Licensed buffet cars are included on all special trains as well as on many service trains.

Combined rail/coach tours to the North York Moors National Park Centre at Danby Lodge are available in various forms and include catering services at several levels for those requiring them.

The Keighley and Worth Valley Light Railway

The line and its history

Sixty miles south-west of Grosmont, the town of Keighley lies astride the main line between Leeds and Carlisle. The Leeds and Bradford extension of the Midland Railway reached Keighley in 1847 and two years later was extended to meet the East Lancashire Railway at Colne. A scheme for a Manchester, Hebden Bridge and Keighley Junction Railway, which would have run through Haworth and down the Worth Valley to Keighley, had been put forward in 1845 but this, like many others proposed during the years of the Mania, came to nothing.

In 1861 a civil engineer, John McLandsborough, visited Haworth, and was surprised to find that the Worth Valley had no railway line. He drew up plans for a line connecting Keighley to Haworth and Oxenhope which were so well received by a number of influential men in the area that a deputation was sent to meet the directors of the Midland Railway and discuss the scheme with them. There were fifteen mills in the Oxenhope area and many more along the proposed route, all of which were potential customers. Knowing this, and anticipating the opening up of slate and free-stone quarries in the valley, the Midland directors gave the plan their blessing, and agreed to operate the line in return for half of the receipts. The deputation reported back to a meeting at Haworth where it was revealed that the building of the railway would take about a year and would cost some £30,000. The subsequent prospectus issued by the newly formed Keighley and Worth Valley Railway Company very prudently specified a share issue of £36,000. In a similar way to that of the inaugural meeting of the Whitby and Pickering Railway, a share list was opened on the spot. By the end of the meeting, a sum of £31,340 had been subscribed; almost identical to the one subscribed twenty-nine years earlier in Whitby. By another coincidence the ultimate cost of the K. & W.V.R. equalled that of the W. & P.R.: £105,000. Parliamentary approval for the line was duly sought and granted; the company was incorporated by the Keighley and Worth Valley Act of 1862. Mr J. S. Crossley, C.E., F.G.S., engineer of the Midland Railway, was appointed engineer for the line; it was, however, John McLandsborough, whose services had been retained by the company, who did most of the work.

The next stage began; land was purchased for a double-track railway, although only a single line was planned in the first instance. Tenders were invited for its construction; of the ten subsequently received, that of John Metcalfe of Bradford (£21,940 7s. 4d.) was accepted. Work commenced with the ceremonial cutting of the first sod at Haworth by Isaac Holden, the company Chairman on 9 February 1864. However, the contractor was to have difficulty in getting possession of the land. Prices ranged between eighty and one hundred pounds per acre, but even at these figures the owners seemed reluctant to part with their property. In the end it took three years to build the five-mile line. There were three further causes for delay. The most quoted reason is that a cow 'ate the plans': two surveyors working on the line adjourned for lunch, leaving what were reputed to have been the only set of plans in existence in the corner of a field; on their return they were

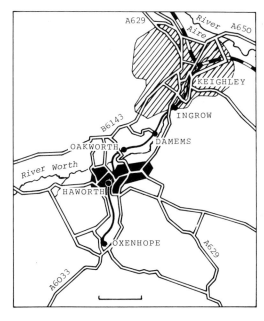

Just how 'uphill' the K. & W.V.R. line is, is shown in this picture of Polish Railways 2-8-0 No. Tr 203.474, climbing towards Haworth with a six-coach Easter Monday train.

Finally, early in November 1866, the line was completed throughout. Two weeks later, the West Riding of Yorkshire suffered from storms of extreme severity. Forty yards of embankment were washed away at Damems; there was a landslip at Haworth Station, and much more minor damage. After repairs the date was set for the Grand Opening on Saturday 13 April 1867. It rained!

The flag-bedecked engine rumbled out of Keighley station with the inaugural train of seven coaches and a guard's van. Once out of the station and on the steeply graded curve over the river, the engine slipped to a standstill on the wet rails (this was to be repeated many times over the years). The resourceful driver ran the train back through the station, and making a running start succeeded in climbing the bank. Again between Oakworth and Haworth the engine slipped to a halt: this time the train had to be split and taken to Haworth in two sections.

So started the Keighley and Worth Valley Railway. It was solid and dependable, hard-working and prosperous.

In 1883 Keighley Station was rebuilt on a new site to accommodate the Great Northern Railway's double-track line from Halifax, which ran alongside the Worth Valley line for its last mile into Keighley. In 1892, the somewhat suspect wooden viaduct over Vale Mill Dam between Oakworth and Haworth was replaced by a deviation over several new bridges and through the newly constructed Mytholmes Tunnel.

The heyday of the line was the years just prior to World War I. By the time of the grouping in 1923, when the Midland Railway became part of the London, Midland and Scottish Railway, the decline had already set in. Coal traffic to the mills dwindled as steam power gave way to electricity; materials began to come in by road and finished goods left the same way. After nationalization in 1948, the line became part of British Railways (Midland Region), although later transferred to the North Eastern Region.

Preservation

By the mid 50s, the line running at a loss, the question of its closure was referred to the Transport Users' Consultative Committee in

horrified to find that a cow had trampled their theodolite beyond repair, and had reduced the plans to an indecipherable pulp.

A far more serious delay occured during the digging of a tunnel under the Halifax road at Ingrow. A vein of shifting sand was struck. So much sand ran out of the workings that one end of the newly built Wesley Place Methodist Church, which stood nearby, subsided. (The chairman of the railway company, Isaac Holden, was doubtless embarassed by this, since he had laid the church's foundation stone a couple of years previously!) The building had to be demolished and re-sited further away from the tunnel. A legal wrangle followed and after four years, some £2000 damages were awarded against the company. Finally, the contractors failed to supply an adequate labour force: the company had to enforce a penalty clause in the contract, claiming for 309 days at £20 per day.

The Keighley and Worth Valley Railway is unusual in running through both heavily industrial landscapes and open countryside. The sharp gradient out of Keighley is always the cause of spectacular smoke, and here L.M.S. class 8F 2-8-0 No. 8431 (built 1944) double-heads with Swedish Railways 2-8-0 No. 1931. British-built, this loco reached Sweden in 1953 via the Netherlands, to whom it was sold at the end of the War.

1959. The Keighley Borough Council persuaded the Committee that a more intensive passenger service would be more remunerative. In June 1960 diesel multiple units took over the line, giving an extra sixty-six trains a week. But this did not have the desired effect, and the last passenger train ran on 30 December 1961; freight services lasted for a further six months. Strong local feelings were aroused by the withdrawal of the passenger services, and three months after the last passenger train ran Mr G. R. Cryer called a public meeting. Encouraged by the example of the Bluebell Railway in Sussex, where for two years a dedicated group of amateurs had been successfully running a steam

operated public service over five miles of former British Railways track, the meeting formed the Keighley and Worth Valley Railway Pre-servation Society, with the object of re-opening the line.

Preliminary approaches were made to B.R., and Haworth Station was rented as a headquart-ers and museum. A special train was chartered to run over the branch just before the freight service was withdrawn; then followed a series of lengthy negotiations with British Railways. By early 1964 the Society was given permission to carry out maintenance work on the line. Later on it was allowed to keep rolling stock there, and the first locomotive (a diminutive saddle tank) arrived by road in January 1965. More items arrived and British Railways authorized the running of works trains to haul them up the branch and to facilitate track clearance and maintenance. An operating company, the Keighley and Worth Valley Light Railway Limited, was formed in 1966 and finally reached agreement with B.R. to purchase the line for £45,000 and to lease Platform 4 at Keighley Station for a period of 25 years. A Light Railway

The kind of work that goes into restoration. LEFT: *looking along No. 75078 (a Standard B.R. 4MT, built 1956) in July 1973, and* OPPOSITE *the same loco being prepared for a boiler inspection at Haworth Yard in June 1978.*

the A650 to Keighley will find a large free car park close to the station. The A6033 from Hebden Bridge passes through Oxenhope and joins the A629 from Halifax and Huddersfield near Haworth. From this junction the A629 continues down the Worth Valley, through Keighley, to Skipton. Car parking is available free at Oxenhope and Oakworth, and for a small charge at Haworth.

As might be expected in a town of sixty thousand there are plenty of places to eat in Keighley. The station itself has a buffet in the summer months and similar facilities are provided at Haworth and Oxenhope during busy periods. When the railway buffet car is not running in one of the trains, it is open for service in Haworth yard, whilst inside the station a confectionery counter sells sweets, crisps and minerals and there is a well stocked bookshop. The same sort of services are available on a reduced scale at Keighley and Oxenhope.

A journey down the line
'Uphill' is the key word; once out of Keighley station, the line climbs continuously on an average gradient of 1 in 75 all the way to Oxenhope, 330 feet above its starting point. From the station, the line curves sharply to the right over the River Worth, on a gradient of 1 in 66 which for a short length steepens to 1 in 58, the steepest gradient on the whole line. The gradient eases appreciably after about half a mile. Shortly after this a gap appears in the industrial back streets which have bounded the line so far: this marks the site of the junction with the old Great Northern line, closed in 1967. The brick then closes in again, and almost at once Ingrow station is reached. The one-hundred-and-fifty-yard Ingrow Tunnel follows, above and to the east of which stands the second Wesley Place Methodist Church. After the tunnel, the built-up area is left behind, and the track winds and climbs as it follows the River Worth to Damems. The station here was reputed to have been the smallest on the

Order was obtained in due course, and the Inspecting Officer of the Ministry of Transport gave approval for the line to be re-opened on 29 June 1968. A short ceremony was held at Keighley, at which the Mayor cut a tape and declared the line again open. The inaugural train double-headed by two beautifully restored steam engines, stormed up the gradient from the station in splendid style (unlike its predecessor of a hundred and one years previously). The faith of the founders of the K. & W.V.R.P.S. had been vindicated; once again the valley echoed to the sound of steam engines working hard uphill.

Access
The Railway is easily reached by both public and private transport. Keighley Station is served by local rail services from Leeds, Bradford, Skipton and Morecambe, as well as by some of the Leeds–Carlisle expresses. West Yorkshire bus services from Bradford and Leeds to Keighley pass the station, and other bus services connect directly with most towns in the area. Visitors by car from Bradford and Leeds using

Midland Railway; it can only accommodate one coach. Beyond it, on a gradient of 1 in 64, the new company has built a passing loop to allow up and down trains to pass enabling a more intensive service to be worked in peak periods. Train movements through the loop are controlled by a signal box brought from Frisinghall on the Bradford–Shipley line. On becoming redundant the complete box was transported by road to Oakworth before being taken by rail to Damems.

Beyond the loop, the line enters a narrow cutting, emerging to run into Oakworth Station. The station is half a mile below the village, and is typical of that of a Midland country branch line; it has been kept in Edwardian condition, complete with gas lamps. It achieved fame in 1968, when the B.B.C. used it to film Edith Nesbit's book *The Railway Children*; E.M.I. used it too when making the film of the story. Leaving Oakworth over a level crossing, the line curves first to the left and then to the right, crosses a three-arch viaduct over the River Worth and plunges into Mytholmes Tunnel. It emerges in the valley of the Bridgehouse Beck,

which it follows for the rest of the way through Haworth to Oxenhope.

Haworth has achieved fame out of all proportion to its size, for the Rev. Patrick Bronte became curate of the Church here in 1820. Here, on the remote windswept moors, in a village of grim stone cottages, the three Bronte sisters, Charlotte, Emily and Anne, lived. Haworth attracts thousands of people every year to visit the Bronte Museum in the old Parsonage, and to see the old village.

Haworth Station is the headquarters of the railway, and the old goods yard is now the maintenance depot for the line's rolling stock. From here onwards the curves in the line become generally less severe as the valley opens up onto the barren moors, although the final bend tightens as it takes the railway into Oxenhope. This is the terminus, and there is a large museum where coaches and locomotives not in service are displayed.

Stock
The K. & W.V.R.'s collection of over thirty locomotives is one of the largest in the country.

B.R. No.43924 (Midland Railway No. 3924) is a 4F built in 1920. Fully overhauled in 1977, it is seen here in early 1978 hauling a freight on an enthusiasts' weekend.

The two oldest main-line locomotives in the collection are both 0-6-0 engines from the former Lancashire and Yorkshire Railway; the elder of the two, No. 752, was built as a tender engine in 1881, but rebuilt as a saddle tank fifteen years later. The other, No. 957, was not built until 1887, and survived in its original form to become British Railway's 52044. No. 957 is a veteran of the cinema screen; she appeared in *The Private Life of Sherlock Holmes* and again as the *Green Dragon* of the fictitious 'Great Northern and Southern Railway' in *The Railway Children*. There are two other L. & Y.R. engines on the line, both tiny 0-4-0 shunting engines known colloquially as 'Pugs'. One has been restored to its original L. & Y.R. livery whilst the other retains its B.R. unlined black.

The Midland Railway is represented by one of its standard 4F goods engines built at Derby in 1920. This engine, No. 3924, deserves a place in the annals of preserved steam locomotives. Not only was she the first of many engines to be

rescued from the Barry 'Graveyard', but she was also the first engine from there to be restored to working order. One other pre-grouping engine is to be found at Haworth. Originally No. 85 of the Taff Vale Railway, she became No. 426 of the Great Western Railway in 1922. Five years later she was put up for sale and being of a similar size and type to the Lambton engines, two of which (see above) are operating on the North Yorkshire Moors Railway, she was purchased for use at the Lambton colliery, her cab and bunker being cut down to conform with the restricted loading gauge.

Pannier Tank L89 came from the Great Western Railway by way of London Transport. Built at Swindon in 1929 as one of the 862-strong 57XX class she was bought by London Transport in 1963 and worked engineers' trains over the London Underground System until acquired by the K. & W.V.R. in 1970. Painted light brown for her appearance in *The Railway Children*, she has since reverted to the maroon livery that she carried under London Transport ownership.

The later class 5s, the famous 'Black Fives', are represented by No. 45212. One of the equally numerous and very similar looking heavy

This Lancashire and Yorkshire Railway 0-6-0 No. 52044 kept in B.R. livery, was built in 1887, and is the oldest main-line engine on the K. & W.V.R. Seen here between Haworth and Oxenhope.

freight engines of the class 8F 2-8-0s completes an L.M.S. trio. During World War II, hundreds of Austerity 2-8-0 freight engines based on the 8F class were built for army service overseas. After the war one of these, along with nearly two hundred others, was sold to the Netherlands. She was re-sold in 1953 to the Swedish State Railways and equipped by them for work north of the Arctic Circle. She returned to Britain and the Worth Valley in 1973. She is the only remaining member of her class in Britain.

Another Austerity type built during and after the war was a heavy 0-6-0 saddle tank. Many were later sold to the L.N.E.R. where they were known as class J94; the Worth Valley has several, together with three similar but heavier engines, known on the railway as 'Uglies'.

A further wartime mass-produced design, this time of American origin, was the U.S. Army 0-6-0 'switcher' or shunting engine. Many were shipped to this country for service on the continent. After the war the Southern Railway bought fourteen and modified them for use in the Southampton Docks. One of these, No. 72, resplendent in light-brown livery with a silver smoke box, helped to haul the society's inaugural train. Still wearing her colourful livery she has since been equipped for oil firing and named *Vulcan*, after her builders, the Vulcan Ironworks of Pennsylvania. The other engine on the first train was No. 41241, a 2-6-2 class 2MT tank engine, of L.M.S. design built by B.R. She wears a striking red livery, and carries the lettering 'KWVR' and the railway's crest on her side tanks.

During the first few years of its existence British Railways built many engines to pre-nationalization designs. One of these, of Southern Railway origin, is the semi-streamlined West Country class No. 34092, *City of Wells*, which is being restored for use on the line. Her 4-6-2 or 'Pacific' wheel arrangement makes her the railway's largest engine. British Railways standard engines have not been barred from the collection, and examples of class 2 and class 4 tender engines and a class 4 tank engine are included.

The Yorkshire Dales Railway

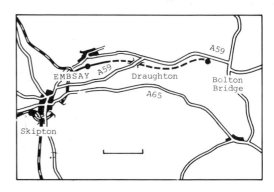

The line and its history

The Midland main line from Leeds to Carlisle passes through Skipton, some nine miles north-west of Keighley. During the last century proposals were made in 1846, 1856 and again in 1858 for a 'Wharfedale Railway' to link Skipton with Ilkley. These came to nothing, although in 1865 the Otley and Ilkley Joint Railway did reach Ilkley from the opposite direction. The Skipton–Ilkley route was proposed again in 1873, received Parliamentary approval in 1883, and was finally built and opened by the Midland Railway in 1888. A nine-mile branch to Grassington, from a junction near Embsay, was approved in 1897 and built in 1902. It lost its regular passenger service as early as 1930 although holiday excursions continued to run until 1967, the line having been kept open to

Embsay station on the former Skipton-Grassington branch is the centre for the Yorkshire Dales Railway.

serve the limestone quarries at Swinden.

The Embsay Junction–Ilkley line closed in 1965 under the auspices of the Beeching plan, and three years later, when it seemed likely that the line to the quarry would be closed, the Embsay and Grassington Railway Preservation Society was formed to try to save it. Changing its name a year later to the Yorkshire Dales Railway Society, it rented the eighteen-acre site at Embsay Station. With the arrival of its first locomotive in 1970, the Embsay Steam Centre came into being. The quarries at Swinden have since been extended, giving the Grassington Branch a new lease of life. Consequently the Society has had to change its aims and is now

In this 1975 photograph, Hudswell-Clarke 0-6-0 tank No. S100 heads a former Manchester, South Junction and Altrincham Railway coach. The limestone workings are clearly visible. Since 1975, the track has been rationalized, and is now single at this point.

extending eastwards along the old track-bed towards Ilkley. The ultimate hope is to reach Bolton Abbey, some five miles away, in easy stages; the first stage is the one-and-a-half miles to Holwell Bridge; the second a further mile to Draughton. Meanwhile the Society is actively raising money to enable it to purchase the site at Embsay and is in the process of transforming itself into the Yorkshire Dales Historical Trust.

Stock

Although specializing in 0-6-0 industrial tank engines, one of the Centre's more noteworthy items is of British Railways origin. This large loco is No. 48151, one of the L.M.S. class 8F heavy freight engines, sister to No. 8431 on the Keighley and Worth Valley Railway. Acquired as a long term restoration project, this engine is not likely to be in service for some years to come.

Most industrial engines are saddle tanks but S 100* and S 140 are conspicuous at Embsay because of their side tanks. Built by Hudswell-Clarke, they were originally supplied to the National Coal Board, from which they were subsequently purchased. Saddle tanks built by Hudswell-Clarke also feature in the collection, as well as representatives from the Yorkshire

Engine Company, Hunslet and Peckett. A further length of non-standard gauge track is of only 9½ in. gauge, the home of *King Tut*, a 'freelance' working model which is a firm favourite with children of all ages.

Side by side with a six-wheeled coach built in 1896 as the personal saloon of Sir Vincent Raven, Locomotive Superintendent of the North Eastern Railway, are two coaches of what is basically an L.M.S. design. Built for the electrification of the independent Manchester, South Junction and Altrincham Railway in 1931, they belong to the Altrincham Electric Railway Preservation Society. They have been joined by a standard British Railways coach and a Pullman car.

The area around

With Bolton Abbey, Skipton Castle and the beautiful Yorkshire Dales as nearby attractions, Embsay Station can be found off the A59 Skipton–Harrogate road, about 1½ miles out of Skipton. There is ample parking space at Embsay for visitors arriving by car and buses run at roughly hourly intervals from a bus station just round the corner from Skipton railway station. Light refreshments are obtainable on most Sundays throughout the year and a well-stocked shop sells books, souvenirs and model railway equipment on Saturday and Sunday afternoons.

---

* Now moved to the Chasewater Railway.

The Middleton Railway

The line and its history

In the Hunslet area of the great industrial city of Leeds can be found the Middleton Railway. Conceived originally in 1755 as a wooden tramway to carry coal, the various private agreements between the colliery owner Charles Brandling and the local landowners were superseded in 1758 by the first Act of Parliament to sanction the building of a railway.

In 1808, John Blenkinsop was appointed to be Brandling's agent; three years later he patented a rack-rail method of locomotive traction. Mathew Murray of the Round Foundry at Holbeck near Leeds was commissioned to build a locomotive incorporating the patent, and in June 1812 the resulting engine was tested and found to be capable of doing the work of sixteen horses. Together with a similar engine it worked successfully for over twenty years, even though one of them had to be rebuilt after blowing up in 1818 and killing the driver. (According to George Stephenson, who gave evidence about the accident, the driver had been 'in liquor' and had overloaded the safety valves.) The Brandling collieries changed hands in 1834, and shortly afterwards the new owners reverted to horse traction. Steam reappeared in 1866 after a further change of ownership although it was still on the original gauge of 4 ft 1 in.; the change to standard gauge was not made until 1881.

The National Coal Board inherited the Middleton when the mines were nationalized after World War II. In 1958 when the track needed wholesale renewal and the collieries were losing money, it was decided to close the line. Whilst haggling over the future of the railway went on between the N.C.B. and the City Council, who opposed the closure plan, the railway celebrated its bi-centenary in June 1958 with a special passenger train. The protagonists finally reached a compromise which led to the section of the line from Parkside Junction to Broom Pit being retained and restored; when, in 1959, the Leeds University Union Railway Society was

looking for a stretch of line to use as a railway museum, the disused part of the Middleton was an obvious choice. The University authorities were not too keen on the idea, but the enthusiasts, led by Dr R. F. Youell, persevered and founded the independent Middleton Railway Preservation Society. The ownership of the abandoned section had passed into many hands and much further negotiation was required before agreement was finally reached. Notwithstanding this, the line was re-opened in June 1960 (giving free rides at the traveller's risk) making the Middleton the first preserved standard-gauge railway to run a passenger service; it beat the Bluebell Railway to the title by just two months.

Although not the original intention, the idea began to develop of restoring the line to its original role as a goods carrier. Two of the companies who had previously used the rail-

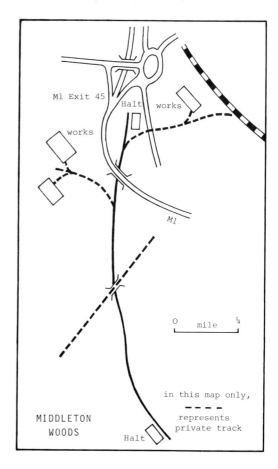

A line-up of Middleton stock, with a typically industrial background. Bagnall 0-4-0 Matthew Murray *(built 1943);* Hudswell Clarke 0-4-0 Henry de Lacy II *(built 1917);* Hawthorn Leslie 0-4-0 No. 6 *(built 1935);* Peckett 0-4-0 No. 2003 *(built 1941).*

way, Claytons and Robinson & Birdsell, agreed to support the venture in return for a regular daily service. This started in September 1960 and has run ever since. Diesel-hauled freight trains run every evening during the week, and a steam-hauled passenger service runs on Saturdays, Sundays and Bank Holidays from Easter until the end of October; trains leave at half-hourly intervals between two and five p.m. The part of the line now operated for passengers is a one-mile section starting at Tunstall Road Halt. Travelling south from there the line to the B.R. exchange sidings trails back on the left, and then the railway plunges through a tunnel under the M1. Emerging the other side, a further line trails back, this time to the right, leading to Robinson & Birdsell's scrap yard and to Claytons' works yard where the Middleton's locomotives have been kept since the railway's inception. A little further on the track goes under the bridge which formerly carried the G.N.R. branch to Beeston Junction and then passes the site of that railway's

exchange sidings on the left, used by B.R. locomotives up until 1967. The line terminates at Middleton Park.

Stock

The Middleton has several basically similar 0-4-0 saddle tank industrial engines. These include Peckett No. 2003, Hudswell-Clarke No. 1309 *Henry de Lacy II*, and Bagnall No. 2702 *Matthew Murray*, named after the line's first locomotive builder. Also to be found are two former L.N.E.R. engines, Sentinel No. 59 (which ended its 'main-line' career as B.R. No. 68153), and an 0-4-0 tank, No. 1310, built for the N.E.R. in 1891. This latter engine belongs to the Steam Power Trust 65 as does a rather quaint-looking tank engine built for the Danish State Railways in 1895.

Diesel locomotives used for freight workings include one of the original prototype shunters built on a steam engine frame for the L.M.S. in 1932, now named *John Alcock** after the Managing Director of its builders, the Hunslet Engine Company. *Carroll, Courage* (alias *Sweet Pea*), No. 3900002 (alias *Dumbo*), together with an assortment of wagons and cranes, complete the collection of this unique railway, which since 1962 has been protected by the National Trust because of its historical value.

* Now at N.R.M., York.

National Railway Museum York

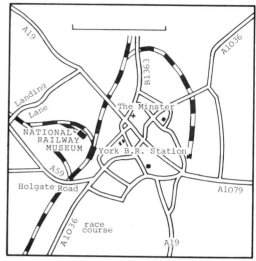

Even though it is not a working line, no account of steam railways could possibly omit the National Railway Museum at York. A Museum was started in part of York Station following the Stockton and Darlington Railway Centenary. It was opened in 1928, but the exhibits were later moved to an old engine shed in Queen Street, and most of them stayed in those rather cramped quarters till the opening of the N.R.M. in 1975. After nationalization, the British Transport Commission set up a museum, at Clapham in South London, containing both road and rail transport exhibits. Under the Transport Act of 1968, the Museum became the responsibility of the Department of Education and Science as an

outpost of the Science Museum, and the British Railways Board was directed to provide a single home for the railway collections at both Clapham and York.

Originally, York North Loco Shed consisted of four adjacent roundhouses, but two were demolished in 1957–8 to make way for a new diesel depot. The other two remained unaltered

The National Railway Museum, York. On the turntable is N.E.R. 0-6-0 No. 2392, built 1923. Mallard, the record-breaking A4 Pacific is back right.

and have now been converted into the museum's main display hall; the larger exhibits are stationed around its two turntables. The twenty-four roads around the larger table are used to display locomotives and one of them has had its pit deepened to enable visitors to walk upright beneath the engine on show above. The turntable itself has been kept in its original open form, with one road connecting it with the smaller twenty-road table, which has been decked in to give better public access to the items of rolling stock grouped around it. Direct connection to the main line through the diesel depot enables the exhibits to be changed from time to time. An associated new building has been erected on the Leeman Road frontage, and this provides an entrance hall, lecture theatre, refreshment room, shops for souvenirs and books, offices and stores as well as a gallery running the full length of the main hall.

Stock

It is only possible to mention a few of the items in the Musuem's vast collection. The loco-motives range from the Shutt End Colliery's *Agenoria* of 1829 to *Evening Star*, the last locomotive to be built for B.R. (in 1960). Pride of place must go to the L.N.E.R.'s streamlined *Mallard*, holder of the world speed record for a steam locomotive, 126 m.p.h. The N.E.R.'s No. 910 also holds a record: built in 1874 at Gateshead, she is the only engine to have taken part in the 50th, 100th and 150th anniversary celebrations of the Stockton and Darlington Railway. She is one of the original engines in the Queen Street Museum. Another Queen Street original is G.N.R. 'Single' No. 1, which was removed from the museum in 1938, overhauled, and steamed as part of a campaign to publicize the Flying Scotsman. Later in that year, before returning to the museum, she was chartered by the Railway Correspondence and Travel Society to haul the first-ever rail tour. London, Brighton and South Coast Railway *Gladstone* of 1882 is a further Queen Street veteran. Bought in 1927 by the Stephenson Locomotive Society, she was restored to her original livery before being presented to the museum.

Many people consider that the South Eastern and Chatham Railway D class engines were the most handsome ever built, both in form and

L. & N.W.R. No. 790, the magnificent 2-4-0 Hardwicke, *was built in 1892, and took part in the Railway Race to the North in 1895, covering the Crewe–Carlisle section at an average 70 m.p.h.* Hardwicke *was withdrawn in 1932, and went to the Clapham Museum, and remains a part of the National Collection, so is now at York. She is seen here being prepared for the 'Rail 150'.*

livery. The Museum is fortunate to possess the last survivor, No. 737, beautifully restored to her original condition; also from the south is Southern Railway rebuilt Merchant Navy class, No. 35029, *Ellerman Lines*; one of the most fascinating locomotives in the collection, she has been sectioned to show the interior construction; her wheels and motion are electri-cally driven to demonstrate how they work.

Rolling stock

Rolling stock exhibited includes replica Liver-pool and Manchester Railway coaches of 1834, Royal saloons and travelling Post Offices as well as representatives of more everyday coaches. Goods vehicles are represented on a smaller scale and there are two working sets of points that can be demonstrated, one manual and one electrical. The small relics sections cater for everything from buttons to station name boards and from signals to silverware.

The Derwent Valley Railway

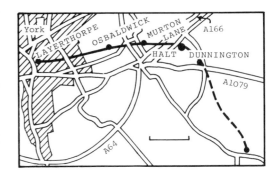

From time to time steam trains can be found running in York, on the privately owned Derwent Valley Railway.* Originally authorized by the Derwent Valley Light Railway Order of 1902, it was opened in July 1913, and ran from Layerthorpe in the City of York to join the Selby–Market Weighton branch of the N.E.R. at Cliff Common, sixteen miles away. York (Layerthorpe) Station is in Hallfield Road, York and is connected to B.R.'s Foss Island branch, by a spur from the York–Scarborough line. It has a large

Joem, *N.E.R. 0-6-0 tank (J72 class, built 1951) is now on the Derwent Valley Railway, a semi-rural line which leaves from York Layerthorpe Station, after a period with the K. & W.V.R. and the Yorkshire Dales.*

* Since this book was prepared, we have learnt that the passenger service has been withdrawn.

goods yard, with both ordinary and exchange sidings, which tapers into a single line heading east through Osbaldwick and Murton Lane, where it turns south to Dunnington. From here the railway followed the course of the river from which it takes its name, with stations at Elvington, Wheldrake, Collingworth, Thorganby and Skipwith.

At first an agreement was made with the N.E.R. to supply a locomotive and crew, but when this expired it was renewed for the hire of a locomotive only. After experiments with a Sentinel geared locomotive in 1925–6, the company reverted to hiring an engine from what was by then the L.N.E.R.; the practice continued into B.R. days, until 1961. By then suitable steam locomotives were no longer available, and a Drewry diesel shunting engine was supplied instead. This proving satisfactory, the railway purchased two similar machines from B.R. in 1969.

After World War I, the steady increase in bus services led to a decline in the number of railway passengers; apart from special excursions, all passenger trains ceased in 1926. Goods traffic continued to flourish however, as an enterprising management sought out new types of freight to replace those that died out. The closure of the line between Selby and Market Weighton in 1965 under the Beeching plan deprived the D.V.R. of its southern outlet. As a consequence, the southern part of the line, between Wheldrake and Cliff Common, was also closed in the same year. Elvington to Wheldrake was closed in 1968, followed by Dunnington to Elvington in 1973; this leaves only the four-and-a-half miles which survive today. Despite the reduction in the length of the line, the company continues to prosper. Shrewd management has led to the construction of a mechanical coal plant and an oil distribution centre at Layerthorpe, a concrete-making plant at Osbaldwick, and a grain-drying plant at Dunnington.

From time to time special passenger trains have run over the line. In September 1976, in co-operation with the National Railway Museum, a special test train was run, hauled by one of the Museum's working steam engines, L. & N.W.R. *Hardwicke*. The tests proved successful, and a few weeks later the same locomotive made three runs each way with a three-coach train, carrying in all some three hundred passengers.

A regular steam-hauled passenger service followed the acquisition of a small tank engine. This was *Joem*, built by British Railways in 1951 to a N.E.R. design of 1898. Her number is 69023, and she formerly worked on both Yorkshire Dales and Keighley Railways.

The North of England Open Air Museum, Beamish

Beamish Hall in County Durham is the home of the North of England Open Air Museum. 'Beamish', as the museum is usually known, was established in 1970 by a joint agreement of most of the larger local authorities of the North-East as 'an open air museum for the purpose of studying, collecting, preserving and exhibiting buildings, machinery, objects and information illustrating the development of industry and the way of life in the North of England'. Local Government re-organization in 1974 made it necessary for a revised agreement to be drawn up and signed on behalf of the four new County Councils of the North East; Northumberland, Tyne and Wear, Durham and Cleveland.

The site extends over two hundred acres of woodland and rolling countryside and is being transformed into several areas, each one covering some aspect of the former way of life in the North East. The Home Farm, part of the original estate, acquired a steam engine to drive its machinery in 1870. The chimney and engine house survived and a stationary steam engine built in Middlesbrough in 1852 has been obtained to power it so that the threshing machine, chaff-cutter and sawbench can work once more.

A typical North-Eastern colliery is being constructed, complete with a vertical winding engine built in 1855 and originally installed at Beamish Colliery. Steam for the engine is supplied by two Lancashire boilers brought from Shotton. A 'coffee-pot' vertical-boilered locomotive built in 1871 shunts wooden 'chald-ron' wagons from Seaham Harbour, and nearby can be found Beamish's *pièce de résistance*, *Locomotion*. This is a full-size working replica of George Stephenson's famous engine of 1825 which worked on the world's first steam-hauled passenger railway, the Stockton and Darlington. The replica was built as a training exercise by apprentices from all over the area for the Railway's 150th anniversary celebrations in 1975. (The original *Locomotion*, together with *Derwent*, a later engine from the S. & D.R., can be found at North Road Station Railway Museum in Darlington. See page 202.)

Wagons from the colliery will be rope-hauled up an incline to a coal staith by means of the Warden Law engine from Hetton Colliery. From here connection is made with a rebuilt section of the N.E.R. leading to a typical country station. This is Rowley station, opened in 1867, on the Stanhope and Tyne Railway, west of Consett. It

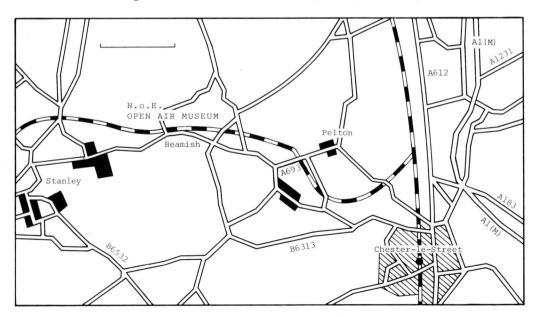

Rowley Station, reconstructed at Beamish after being moved from near Newcastle, where it was built in 1867, is the centrepiece of a complete N.E.R. scene, with N.E.R. 0-6-0 No. 876 (built 1889) the selected loco.

has been dismantled stone by stone and rebuilt at Beamish. A yard, complete with a small loco shed, signal box, goods shed, coal drops and weighbridge, completes this part. Route mileage is about one mile, but actual track mileage is nearly twice that. Six steam locomotives are in store or in process of being restored for use on the line. The principal one, already on the line, is N.E.R. C class 0-6-0 goods engine, No. 876 (B.R. No. 65033 of class J21) whilst the oldest is the Hetton Colliery locomotive built by George Stephenson in 1822. Five N.E.R. coaches are being rebuilt for use on the railway, together with a representative collection of goods rolling stock, including a snow plough.

A half-mile electric tramway provides a passenger service during the summer, and the largest item in the collection, a 100-ton steam excavator, is occasionally steamed. Hundreds of other items, both large and small, all add up to give a fascinating glimpse into a past era.

Those requiring refreshments are adequately catered for by the 'Simpkins Tea Room' and there is the added attraction of the 'Bobby Shafto' pub during the summer season.

Beamish is still in the development stage. Many exhibits have yet to be installed or restored to working order, and many more will be added to the collection as time goes on. Working exhibits, such as *Locomotion*, the steam excavator, a steam hammer, and so on, are demonstrated from time to time and details of these and other events, which include Horse Driving Trials, Reliability Trials and Commercial Vehicle Trials, can be obtained from the Museum.

Also at Beamish is the replica of Locomotion *also seen in the colour plates. This shows the wagons used for passenger-carrying; the mine area is behind.*

The Bowes Railway

The Bowes Railway is a former colliery railway, laid down to carry coal from the Northumberland pits to the rivers of the North-East for shipment by coast to London and the South-East. It is often forgotten that in mining districts large networks were owned not by the main-line companies, but by the collieries themselves. This line was originally, until 1932, called the Pontop and Jarrow Railway. The oldest section was designed by George Stephenson, and ran from Mount Moor Colliery via Springwell to Jarrow itself. At its fullest extent the railway was fifteen miles long. During its history it has served as many as thirteen separate collieries. It was linked to a section of the Pelaw Main Railway in 1955, thereby including a further three mines within its orbit. Pelaw is also a stop of the former N.E.R. line between Newcastle Central and South Shields. Jarrow Station is further to the east on the south bank of the River Tyne.

The railway had seven rope-worked inclines, and three locomotive-operated sections. It was not merely concerned with the shipment of coals, and for a time ran a passenger service. However, closures in the 1970s prompted conservationists and preservationists to look into the question of rescuing parts of this industrial railway. By 1974 only the section from Monkton to Jarrow was still in use, under the National Coal Board. With the closure of the line between Kibblesworth and Springwell Bank Foot, the Improvement Committee of the Tyne and Wear County Council considered a restoration project. In March 1976 the County Council completed the purchase of the length of track from Black Fell Bank Head (near the former Mount Moor Colliery) to Springwell Bank Head, a distance of $1\frac{1}{4}$ miles, together with the lineside buildings, winding engines, and forty-one wooden wagons. The whole is now being restored to full working order, except for the Black Fell engine. This will mean that trains of wagons may be hauled by ropes along the inclines to the east and west of Blackham's Hill.

The scheme is organized by the Tyne and Wear Industrial Monuments Trust, and supported by the County Council. This trust, which has much wider responsibility for industrial concerns, has set up the Bowes Railway Project Committee, to organize work on the site. Much work has been completed by volunteers, while further assistance has been provided by job creation schemes and youths on probation. The public may visit the railway, but they must first report to the site supervisor at Springwell.

In addition to the wooden colliery wagons, the railway trust has a locomotive coal wagon, a reel wagon and a Kibblesworth Drift bogie wagon. There are two saddle tank locomotives, both 0-6-0s. There is a Bagnall, No. 6, built in 1944, and a Hunslet named *Diana*, completed in 1943. Both Jarrow and Heworth (for Pelaw) are on the British Rail suburban line from Newcastle Central to South Shields. This route is now being thoroughly modernized and converted to electric traction, and will form a southern branch of the new Metro service, serving the whole of Tyneside. When it is opened there will be trains from Monument in the centre of the City.

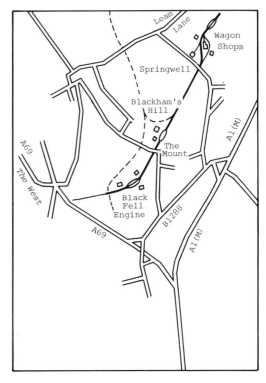

The Tanfield Railway

Tanfield Railway is being built on a 3-mile section of the former Tanfield Wagonway. This was the most famous of Tyneside's early wooden railways, opened as early as 1725. It was an advanced engineering enterprise, a worthy forerunner of the nineteenth century's steam railways. Amongst its original features were the Causey Arch, the world's first railway bridge, and the Causey Embankment, 100 feet high and still in use today on the rebuilt Tanfield Railway. The new line is being laid on a section of the old wagonway between Sunniside and East Tanfield, last used in 1962.

The essential industrial character of the wagonway is to be preserved, but of course the new line will be passenger-carrying. Locos have been selected from private manufacturers who had an established connection with the North-East. Coaches are both vintage and of comparatively modern designs, with a number of rebuilds from various sources. All are four- or

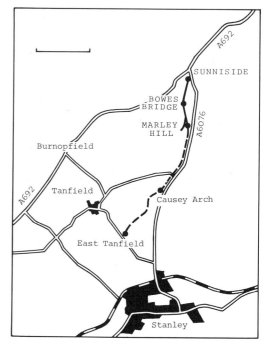

Sir Cecil A. Cochrane is a 0-4-0 saddle tank used. Built in 1948, it here trails a 4-wheeled balcony saloon.

Irwell, *built in 1937 to an 1870's design, is another typical Tyneside loco used on the Tanfield Railway.*

six-wheelers and constructed from wood.

Naturally with an industrial railway, most of the locomotives are saddle tanks. It is simplest to categorize them by maker. There are three Hawthorn Leslies, two 0-4-0STs, *Cyclops* built in 1907, and No. 2, built in 1911, and one 0-6-0ST named *Stagshaw*, completed in 1923. The most numerous engines are those manufactured by Stephenson and Hawthorn. There are seven from this stable, though three are in store elsewhere. One of these, *Sir Cecil A. Cochrane*, a 0-4-0ST, built in 1948, has recently been used to haul the steam service open to the public. They too are a mixture of 0-4-0STs and 0-6-0STs. There are two Andrew Barclay locomotives: *Horden*, built in 1906, a 0-6-0ST, and No. 32, a 0-4-0ST completed in 1920. There are a couple of Hudswell Clarkes, including the 1937-built 0-4-0ST *Irwell* (a fine industrial name this;

Brindley's first canal from Manchester to Worsley, crossed this river by an impressive aqueduct). A Black Hawthorn, *Holwell*, No. 3, which is the oldest of them all having been built in 1873, completes the locomotive stock.

The railway has an impressive collection of vintage rolling stock. There is a former Great Northern six-wheeled five-compartment coach, No. 2, which dates from around 1890. Their North Eastern four-wheeled compartment coach is in a state of disrepair and awaits rebuilding. There are two carriages, Nos. 1 and 4, which were built for the Tanfield Railway by its members, both four-wheeled saloons. The first was completed in 1976, the second the following year. There is also a Darlington-built saloon called 'Glass Carriage', dating from around 1880.

There are a number of wagons. These include an N.E.R. 20-ton wagon, formerly No. 39988, and a 10-ton hopper wagon from the old Pontop and Jarrow Railway. To assist with maintenance and lifting, there is *Joshua*, a 10-ton steam crane, built by Joshua Wilson.

Darlington North Road Museum

It is fitting that a terminus on one of Britain's first steam railways (the Middleton Railway was the first to use steam locomotives successfully for commercial purposes, in 1812) should have become the site for a local railway museum. On 27 September 1825 the first train was run from Shildon, via Darlington to Stockton. It was a mixture of mineral wagons, filled with either people or coals, together with the Company's carriage, aptly named *Experiment*. The line had been laid under the direction of George Stephenson with the assistance of his son Robert. Though this inaugural service proved to be immensely popular, the Directors did not institute a passenger service till 1833, and the railway remained a freight-only concern, although some passengers were horse-drawn.

The first steam engine to run along the line, on the opening ceremony, was *Locomotion No. 1*. Designed and constructed under the supervision of Robert Stephenson (though not with close attention), *Locomotion* continued to work on the railway till 1846, and sporadically after that. The company then sold the engine in 1850 for scrap when technology's advance had made it obsolete. Fortunately *Locomotion* was rescued from the breakers' yard, and sent to work as a pumping engine at Lucy Pit, Crook. The North Eastern Railway, which had absorbed the Stockton and Darlington, reclaimed the engine in 1857, realizing its historical importance. It was restored ready to be placed on display. They exhibited *Locomotion*, together with No. 25, *Derwent* (a 0-6-0 built in 1845), in their new Darlington Station. They were both placed on stands alongside the buffer stops in the central concourse, as mementoes of the

The fine structure of Darlington North Road station, now a museum.

Inside Darlington North Road is Derwent, *a 0-6-0 built in 1845. The original of* Locomotion *is also there.*

Company's history. In 1925 the L.N.E.R. decided to hold a centenary celebration to commemorate the opening of the Stockton and Darlington. *Locomotion* was taken from display to take part in the parade of steam engines. However, the company cheated. It appeared to watchers that *Locomotion* was steaming as she raced along with smoke billowing from her chimney. In fact an electric motor had been fitted in the tender, and cotton waste soaked in oil was burning in the firebox.

With the opening of this new museum in the former Darlington North Road Station, both *Derwent* and *Locomotion* have been moved from their old home in Darlington Bank Top. In addition, the museum houses two other N.E.R. locomotives, both vintage engines. There is the 0-6-0 No. 1275, built in 1874, and the 2-4-0, No.

1463, built in 1885. *Derwent* was withdrawn from service in around 1865, having worked on the S. & D. for twenty years. After working on colliery lines, No. 25 was presented to the N.E.R. in 1895 and was then placed on display alongside *Locomotion*.

Darlington North Road Station, situated on the line west to Shildon, has been rebuilt several times. It is a simple building, but distinguished for the unusual roof structure. The two bays were supported by a row of iron columns erected down the middle between the tracks. It lay in an exceptionally delapidated state for a number of years while funds were being raised for its restoration and conversion into a museum. Certainly the Shildon railway parade, organized to commemorate the 150th anniversary of the S. & D., helped to highlight its condition. Darlington Bank Top Station is on the main East Coast line between York and Newcastle, and there are local services from each, as well as express trains from King's Cross.

The Lincolnshire Coast Light Railway

North-east Lincolnshire possesses what at first sight is a vintage narrow-gauge railway. However, although the locomotives, rolling stock and track are indeed of vintage origin, the railway itself dates back to only 1960. The Lincolnshire Coast Light Railway Company Limited was formed by a group of railway enthusiasts in April of that year; by the end of August it had laid and opened a half-mile line from North Sea Lane, Humberston to Humberston Beach. Six years later the line was relaid on a new alignment, and was extended for a further half-mile to South Sea Lane, near to the centre of the Humberston Fitties Holiday Camp.

South Sea Lane on the Lincolnshire Coast Light Railway. This is rarely operated by steam. Here, diesel No. 4 with an Ashover Railway coach.

The original track came from the Nocton Estate Light Railway, an agricultural line near Lincoln, which in turn had obtained it from a World War I dump at Arras in France; it is of 60cm (approximately two-foot) gauge. Most of the extension track came from the Penrhyn Railway in Wales. Gradients are non-existent, and the railway's diminutive motive power copes quite easily with the one-coach trains. There are two steam locomotives, an 0-6-0 saddle tank built in 1903 called *Jurassic*, formerly owned by the Rugby Portland Cement Company, and an even older 0-4-0 saddle tank, *Elin*, dating back to 1899. Passengers are catered for by three bogie coaches, two from the Ashover Light Railway and one from the Sand Hutton Railway near York. A handful of diesel locomotives and an assortment of wagons completes the railway's rolling stock.

Traffic consists mainly of holiday-makers, and consequently the railway runs only from Whitsun until the end of October. Diesel haulage is used during the week with steam normally taking over at the weekends.

VIII
Scotland

Museums and Preservation in Scotland

Interest in old locomotives and other 'bits and pieces' linked with railways has been strong in Scotland at least since the 1850s when Alexander Allan, Locomotive Superintendent of the Scottish Central Railway, had one of the primitive Dundee and Newtyle Railway's 0-2-4 locomotives, *The Earl of Airlie*, restored and photographed before it was scrapped.

The first locomotive to be preserved in Scotland, however, came from over the border. This, the oldest steam locomotive in existence, is the *Wylam Dilly*, William Hedley's first locomotive, built for colliery service at Wylam near Newcastle in 1813. She was in operation till about 1867, when she was purchased by Hedley's descendants who presented her to the Royal Scottish Museum in Edinburgh in 1882 where she still is. All conventional railway locomotives can trace their descent from this, the first practical locomotive to run with smooth wheels on smooth rails. Her locomotive neighbours in the Royal Scottish Museum are some superb working models of British and foreign locomotives, made in the museum workshops, but the Museum also owns a narrow 2 ft 6 in. gauge electric locomotive from the Winchburgh Oil Works, West Lothian, which is at present in store. The Museum has also lent its largest locomotive to the Scottish Railway Preservation Society (see below).

The practical interest in the setting up of an industrial museum which found expression in the setting up of the Royal Scottish Museum, also found expression in the setting up of the Kelvingrove Museum in Glasgow, Scotland's great industrial city. Neither the original Kelvingrove House nor its magnificent successor was really suited to the display of heavy machinery, though a few full-size stationary steam engines were preserved for a time in the grounds. The opportunity to tackle something bigger came when Glasgow's tram service, once the envy of the world, came to an end in 1962. A horse tram had been set aside when the tramways had been electrified in 1901, and this

was joined by a selection of electric trams, restored to earlier forms of liveries in the paintshop of what had been the tramway workshops in Albert Drive. The popular success of this Transport Museum, which included a few horse drawn vehicles, some Scottish-built cars and a fine collection of bicycles, encouraged expansion, and it was indeed fortunate that the Museum was enabled to step in when British Railways policy on the preservation of steam engines in Scotland abruptly changed, and to take into care four locomotives which had been maintained in running order for the working of special trains. Two of these had been set aside by the London, Midland and Scottish Railway in the 1930s when the distinctive locomotives of the old Scottish railway companies were fast disappearing. Both are exceptional. Caledonian Railway No. 123 was built as that railway's exhibit at the Edinburgh International Exhibition of 1886. With her large single pair of driving wheels she was unusual on a Scottish line but she was very swift, and starred in the 1888 race to the North between the East Coast and West Coast routes. On the hilly Carlisle–Edinburgh section she managed to run the $100\frac{3}{4}$ miles in $102\frac{1}{2}$ minutes, for long a record. Thereafter she was used to haul special saloons, and ran ahead of the Royal Train as pilot engine to ensure the safety of the route. Ending her days on the level Perth–Dundee lines she was withdrawn in 1935 and restored to her original Caledonian blue livery. Her companion in the paint shop in the former Caledonian Railway's St Rollox workshops was Highland Railway 4-6-0 No. 103, the first locomotive of that wheel arrangement to run in Britain, and forerunner of a highly successful type that hauled all classes of trains on Britain's railways till the last days of steam.

When in 1957 the Great Western's *City of Truro* was brought out of York Railway Museum, and restored to working order, her public appearances were such a success that Mr James Ness, General Manager of the Scottish Region of B.R. put No. 123 through St Rollox Works, and she, very successfully, ran special trains over the next few years. Then in 1959 a Scottish Industries Exhibition was organized in Kelvin Hall, Glasgow, and Mr Ness, with an eye to publicity as well as sentiment, had No. 103

restored to working order. She was magnificently repainted in 'Stroudley's Improved Engine Green' (actually yellow), the colour remembered by her designer's daughter. Nos. 123 and 103 were joined by Great North of Scotland Railway 4-4-0 No. 49 *Gordon Highlander*, which had been withdrawn two years earlier, and North British Railway 4-4-0 No. 256, *Glen Douglas*, withdrawn from traffic for restoration. These four locomotives, together with *City of Truro*, imported for the occasion from Swindon, ran a series of special trains from Scottish towns and cities to Glasgow for the Exhibition. These ran to Kelvin Hill Station on the old underground Glasgow Central line, and proved extremely popular with the public and with enthusiasts. For the next seven years the quartet worked enthusiasts' specials all over Scotland, No. 103 having a special triumph in 1965, the centenary year of the Highland Railway, when she ran under her own steam to Inverness, and then worked a series of public special trains from Inverness to Nairn (the oldest section of the Highland Railway). There was strong public pressure to keep her in Inverness but back she came to the Lowlands to be moved with her sisters into the Transport Museum at Glasgow in 1966. The four locomotives preserved there were joined by two others. Caledonian Railway No. 828 is a 0-6-0 heavy goods engine built in 1899. She was withdrawn in 1963, and bought by the Scottish Locomotive Preservation Fund, formed by a Glasgow-based group of railway enthusiasts, chiefly members of the Stephenson Locomotive Society. No. 828 was restored to exhibition condition, though not working order, in Cowlairs Works, Glasgow, before she was moved into the Museum.

Glasgow and South Western Railway No. 9 was very much the 'poor relation' at first. Withdrawn in 1934 and sold to a colliery in North Wales, she survived to become the only Glasgow and South Western Locomotive. She was presented to the Museum by the National Coal Board in 1965. Dirty black, with a homemade chimney and patched tanks, she looked a sorry sight when first moved into the Museum. Her thorough 'facelift' included a wooden chimney made in a shipyard, and 'cosmetic' treatment of her tanks. Restoration was completed with a coat of G. & S.W.R. green, making her one of the most attractive exhibits in the Museum. Later this quintet of main-line locomotives was joined by an industrial shunting engine. This is a fireless locomotive, charged with steam from a stationary boiler, latterly used at the Dalmarnock, Glasgow, Power Station of the South of Scotland Electricity Board. She was installed in 1969.

Complementing the full-sized exhibits is a 4mm scale model of Carlisle Citadel station, operated at weekends; some fine models of Scottish built locomotives; a collection of early rails showing the evolution of the railway; and a remarkable collection of railway relics. Even the Museum Tea Room is dominated by railways with fine paintings of two early viaducts, collections of locomotive works plates, and gauge 1 model locomotives and rolling stock, and a carpet with representations of No. 123 and *Glen Douglas*.

The Scottish Railway Preservation Society

The realization that the eleventh hour was at hand, and that all too soon locomotives and other relics of the old Scottish railways would disappear, was certainly behind the raising of a fund to purchase C.R. No. 828 (see above) by a group which at first had had much more grandiose schemes to preserve a representative selection of Scottish locomotives. It was also behind the formation of the Railway Preservation Society in England. This also had grand aims which included the setting up of branches all over Britain. It arranged a public meeting in Edinburgh in November 1961. Those present decided not to form a branch of the R.P.S., but to found instead the Scottish Railway Preservation Society in co-operation with its progenitor. The aims were straightforward: 'to acquire relics of the railways of Scotland, to restore them to original condition wherever possible, and to display them to the public either in use on a line or in a static display.' Though the Society has no line of its own, its other aims have been abundantly achieved.

The curious, slightly comic, but real rivalry between Scotland's capital and its chief manufacturing centre be-devilled the early history of railway preservation in Scotland. The S.R.P.S. and the S.L.P.F. went their separate ways, and for a time it seemed that the Glasgow group might dominate. The sparks in the S.R.P.S.'s aims 'to acquire relics and to display them in use', however, were slowly fanned into a flame. With remarkable faith the still-new Society leased in 1964 an old transhipment shed in Springfield Goods Yard, Falkirk, as the large relics museum, and Murrayfield Station, Edinburgh (now demolished) as a small relics museum. The good-natured tolerance and support of British Rail was, in retrospect, obvious in their taking on trust an untried group of enthusiasts. The 300 ft-long transhipment shed had been built for the collection and sorting of iron castings for onward shipment for the many foundries in and near Falkirk. It had some years previously been badly damaged by fire. When the Society took it over it was partly roofless, and the wooden platform running the length of the building was largely a charred mass. With axe, saw, and sweat the rubbish was cleared and the first large relics made their appearance. These were: an ex-Great-North-of-Scotland ballast wagon of 1880, a primitive but interesting vehicle; and Caledonian Railway 0-4-4T, No. 419. She had been withdrawn in 1962 as B.R. No. 55189, and was one of a numerous class used for suburban and branch-line traffic all over the Caledonian and later L.M.S. system in Scotland. She was purchased by the S.R.P.S. with the help of a generous loan from an English member, Mr W. E. C. Watkinson, who also paid for her restoration at Cowlairs Works. It was the need to house No. 419 which really forced the S.R.P.S. to take on Falkirk, and it was the preservation of No. 419 which made many enthusiasts accept the S.R.P.S. as a genuine preservation society. A night glimpse of 419 at Eastfield locomotive shed gleaming darkly in her rich Prussian blue was the author's real introduction to the S.R.P.S., the beginning of a love-hate relationship that has lasted for more than a dozen years.

Another locomotive which came the way of the Society was *Ellesmere*. This tiny machine was built in 1861 by Hawthorn's of Leith, founded by the better-known Newcastle firm of R. & W. Hawthorn to build locomotives for Scottish Railways. Overtaken in the manufacture of main-line locomotives in the 1850s by other firms, the concern turned to the building of small industrial locomotives, mainly of the 'well tank' type which have the tanks for water between the frames. *Ellesmere* is one of these. As

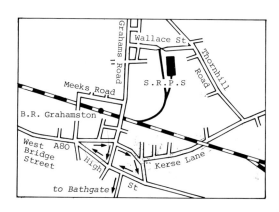

Caledonian Railway No. 123, a 4-2-2 built in 1886, is loaded at Govan Goods Yard for its final journey to the Glasgow Transport Museum.

her name suggests she was built for service in Lancashire, and when she was withdrawn in 1957, a group of enthusiasts secured her for preservation. It seemed sensible to preserve her in Edinburgh, and so she was brought up to Dalry Road Locomotive Shed. She languished there, and in various other storing places, until presented to the S.R.P.S. in 1963. Even then she did not finally reach Falkirk until 1966. As there

was no apparent possibility of restoring her to working order, and in view of her historical interest (she is the oldest surviving Scottish-built locomotive) the Royal Scottish Museum has acquired her from the Society for eventual display in Edinburgh.

Before *Ellesmere* reached Falkirk the collection there had begun to grow. A Caledonian Railway goods brake van was bought from the N.C.B. by two members, and arrived in September 1965. It was soon joined by a much more exotic vehicle, the only Royal Coach owned by a Scottish Railway Company. It was

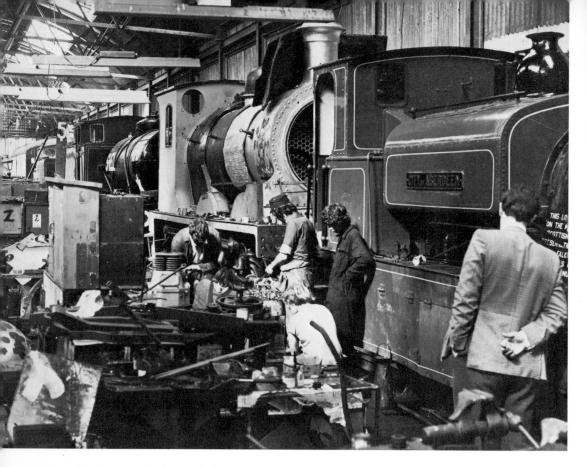

Inside the Falkirk depot of the S.R.P.S. near Grahamston Station, work proceeds on Maude, *North British 0-6-0 No. 673, built in 1891. On the right is* City of Aberdeen, *a 0-4-0 saddle tank used on street tramways which linked Aberdeen gas works with railway yards. Behind* Maude *are a Shell/BP tank wagon dating from 1897; the Barclay 0-6-0 No. 20, largest of the locos saved from the Wemyss Coal Company's private railway;* Caledonian Railway 0-4-4 No. 419 (1891).

built as a First Class Saloon in 1898, and was used by King Edward VII, Queen Alexandra, and the Prince of Wales (later George V), on a number of occasions between 1902 and 1910. The L.N.E.R. transferred the vehicle to the Engineers' Department in 1924, and an end-observation window was inserted. This most attractive vehicle, with a beautifully panelled interior, a kitchen compartment, and a tiny guard's compartment, was in a scrap yard when the Society decided to try to save it. Unfortunately, the agreement between B.R. and the scrap dealer did not allow resale to the Society.

For a time the situation looked black, but Sir Malcolm Barclay Harvey, historian of the G.N.S.R. used his influence to secure the release of the saloon, and generous donations by members and others paid for it. It has now been professionally repainted in its original red-and-cream livery.

The Society has, since its formation, been represented at many exhibitions all over Scotland. Its first excursion north of the Highland line was to Inverness for the Highland Railway Centenary Celebrations in 1965. A feature of the festivities was an auction of railway relics at which the Society secured some small items. Mr W. E. C. Watkinson bought the largest relic, a six-wheeled H.R. coach which had been converted for departmental use, for the Society. It was then completely restored externally, and partially renovated inside at Lochgorm Works, Inverness. Meticulous attention to detail was a feature of the work done at Lochgorm, genuine H.R. fittings being used wherever possible. One source of door handles and interior parts was a H.R. coach converted to a Scout Hut in a

Maude restored. She simmers gently in Falkirk yard in 1978.

Glasgow suburb. Mr Watkinson also bought a very early (c. 1870) four-wheeled coach which had been used as a bothy by platelayers at Inchlea Crossing on the H.R. main line. On removal to Falkirk it was found to be in remarkably good condition. After some years in store there, the coach was moved to Mr Watkinson's home in Worcestershire where he has been working to restore it for display on the Strathspey Railway.

With this little group of vehicles, a rusty iron shed, and no proper public access, the Society held its first open day at Falkirk late in 1965. B.R. kindly hauled the stock out of the shed on the Friday, and positioned it nicely for photography. Unfortunately it rained for most of the day, damping the spirits of those hardy enthusiasts and others who turned up. However towards evening the sun came out to shine on members trying to push the vehicles back into the shed. Unfortunately, although most of the

stock was returned, one of the locomotives could not be persuaded to move, despite the use of pinchbars and crowbars. With darkness, the attempt was abandoned and B.R.'s diesel shunter had to give the necessary push on Monday morning.

With its first public display, the Society began to win the confidence of industrialists and members of the public. The Carron Iron Company, in 1966, gave the S.R.P.S. one of its dumb-buffered wagons, the last in service in Scotland.

It had always been the Society's intention to acquire a North British Railway locomotive. The first choice was a 0-6-2T (L.N.E.R. N15) of a type used for shunting, banking and short-distance goods trains, but this had little appeal; accordingly attention shifted to a J36 (a 0-6-0 tender locomotive). This most successful class of engine was built between 1888 and 1900, and fifty were sent to France during World War I. On their return the N.B.R. named them after battles and generals. By 1963 the only named member of the class still running was *Maude*, B.R. No. 65243, and in the following year an appeal was launched for money to buy her. By the end of 1965 the fund stood at £36 but a concentrated appeal brought the total to £800 by July 1966, when the locomotive was withdrawn. A world shortage of copper forced the scrap price of the locomotive up and up, always ahead of the Society's fund raising. Finally negotiations were entrusted to Captain Peter Manisty, Chairman of the Association of Railway Preservation Societies. Captain Manisty arranged a 'package deal' for three locomotives wanted by members of the A.R.P.S. *Maude's* price was £1250, and a determined last-minute appeal raised enough money to secure her, and she was moved to Falkirk in January 1967. The locomotive had been run into the ground, and although some initial restoration work was taken in hand, it became apparent that a thorough overhaul, together with replacement of the tender tank was essential. From 1976 on, a determined effort was made, and *Maude* was re-steamed in 1978.

Later in 1967 the first of a steady stream of Scottish standard-gauge industrial locomotives made its way to Falkirk. This was the 'Fairfield Tram', an electric locomotive used beteeen 1940 and 1966 to move raw materials from the Govan goods yard to the Fairfield ship-building yard along Govan Road. Originally this was a tram route, and when the trams were replaced by trolley buses in 1958 the single collector was replaced by trolley poles. The locomotive was offered first to the Glasgow Museum of Transport, who declined it, but suggested that the S.R.P.S. might take it. It was moved to Falkirk by road, and is being restored by a group of tram-minded members. Fitted with batteries, it can and does operate on open days.

Other locomotives which appeared at Falkirk in 1967 were a Peckett 0-4-0 saddle tank presented by Colville's Ltd to the Locomotive Club of Great Britain (which found a temporary resting place at Falkirk before being moved to the Club's depot at Sittingbourne), and the Society's first diesel locomotive, a standard Ruston and Hornsby DS88 four-wheeled shunter presented by J. and A. Weir, papermakers of Kilbagie, Clackmannanshire.

The diesel brought life to Falkirk and ended the Society's forced reliance on B.R.'s good nature for movement of stock. Late in 1967, however, the Society received word of an even better present - its first steam locomotive in working order. No. 13 had, for some years, been the oldest working locomotive in Scotland, and preliminary approaches had been made to her owners, the N.C.B., about her acquisition. Built in Glasgow as *Kelton Fell* for an iron-ore railway in Cumberland, she had nevertheless spent most of her life in Scotland. On her withdrawal, the N.C.B., through Mr W. Rowell, Area Director, and Mr J. D. Blelloch, Chief Engineer of the Scottish North Area, presented her to the Society. The Presentation was made at Gartshore 9/11 Colliery in February 1968.

No. 13 was soon steamed by S.R.P.S. members, but disaster soon struck when a crank pin broke. Replacement was no easy matter. She had to be jacked up and her wheels dropped, the pin pressed out, and a new pin made and pressed in. While the locomotive was wheel-less the opportunity was taken to carry out a complete overhaul and repaint, and when No. 13 emerged from the shed resplendent again as *Kelton Fell*, she was the first of the Society's steam locomotives to be completely restored. A renaming ceremony was performed in March 1976 by Mr Blelloch, now Chief Engineer of the N.C.B.

No. 13 was soon joined by another N.C.B. locomotive, No. 1. Built as *Lord Roberts* in 1902 for the Coltness Iron Company, this engine is a large 0-6-0 tank used for heavy ironworks shunting. Used at Bedlay Colliery between 1955 and 1968, No. 1 broke a crosshead and was withdrawn from service. Another approach to the N.C.B. was successful, and No. 1 came to Falkirk late in 1968. There she lay until 1976, when work started on her overhaul.

The efforts to acquire locomotives, and *Maude* in particular, had diverted attention from the rapidly vanishing stock of older types of coaches and wagons on B.R. and in private ownership. When the B.R. preserved locomotives were moved into Glasgow Museum, there was no room for the two ex-C.R. coaches which had been restored to run behind No. 123. After being left in store for some time they were eventually offered for sale at £1000 each. At that price the S.R.P.S. was not interested, though the Bluebell Railway bought one of the pair. The

The S.R.P.S. specializes in goods vehicles and old coaches (which are used on Railtours). This selection of goods stock is hauled by Neilson 0-4-0 Kelton Fell, built in 1876 and donated to the Society by the National Coal Board in 1968. A G.N.S.R. ballast wagon is followed by a bulk grain van of the Leith General Warehousing Co., a dumb-buffered mineral wagon of the Carron Company (i.e. the buffers are not collapsible, but solid – in this case a wooden beam), and a Caledonian Railway 6-wheeled brake van.

A.R.P.S. again negotiated a package deal in which the S.R.P.S. secured the remaining coach for £500. Curiously enough, the Bluebell's coach came to the S.R.P.S. in 1974, though it had been sadly neglected and required extensive replacement of the metal sidepanels.

1968 was the year of the wagons. One of these came from Gartsherrie Ironworks, Coatbridge, with spares for No. 13, and remained at Falkirk.

The Scottish Tar Distillers Ltd gave a square tank wagon built as long ago as 1877, three more conventional tank wagons came from Shell and Briggs of Dundee, and two bulk grain hopper wagons were sold to the Society for a nominal sum by Robert Hutchison and Co., the Kirk-caldy maltsters. With a group of four wagons purchased from the Admiralty in 1969, and a further three acquired in 1971, these form one of the most comprehensive groups of wagons owned by any preservation society.

1969 was the year of the coaches. During the previous year the Society had become involved with the Highlands and Islands Development Board in discussions about operating the railway between Aviemore and Boat of Garten.

The prospect of being called on to run a railway stimulated interest in acquiring coaches of historic interest and also more modern examples which would be easier to keep in service. Two pre-grouping coaches were located at Bundeath Admiralty Armaments Depot, and as the internal train service there had ceased, they were obtained for a very modest sum. Structurally, both were in poor condition, and they had no vacuum brake gear, so they have had a low listing for restoration, though some work has been done on the smaller of the two, a G. & S.W.R. corridor coach.

The two modern coaches bought in 1969 were a compartment coach, of L.N.E.R. design though built to B.R.'s order in 1951, and a second-class 'open corridor' built by the L.M.S. in 1946. In the following year two more modern coaches of L.M.S. design were bought. By that time the Society had realized its aim of owning coaches from all the Scottish pre-grouping railways, with the exception of the N.B.R. N.B.R. coaches of a variety of types, in many locations, had been carefully examined by S.R.P.S. members, but none appeared satisfactory. However, a former invalid saloon, converted in 1957 to an engineers' saloon, was purchased in 1972. It has since been refitted with a corridor connection at one end, and has been repanelled and repainted in N.B.R. livery.

While the Society was buying these coaches, and increasing its wagon collection, more locomotives were arriving at Falkirk. Clydesmill No. 3, a typical Scottish industrial locomotive, was built by Andrew Barclay and Sons Ltd. of Kilmarnock in 1928 for the Clyde Valley Electric Power Company. She was given to the S.R.P.S. by the South of Scotland Electricity Board late in 1969. Arrangements were made to run her to Falkirk under her own steam, and on a cold January day in 1970 an epic voyage commenced. No. 3 had been in store for two years, and the first attempt to steam her had failed miserably. One of her axle boxes started heating, and at Whifflet two of the accompanying party were despatched to a nearby chemist's shop. At the next stop, Cumbernauld, the offending box was duly dosed with four large bottles of castor oil. It worked! No. 3 steamed happily into Falkirk, driven by a retired driver, Willie Bell. She arrived a trifle late, but was a sight for sore eyes.

In October of the same year, a much larger locomotive came to Falkirk Shed. She was No. 20 of the Wemyss Private Railway, and was one of a number of basically similar heavy 0-6-0 tanks used to transfer coal from mines originally owned by the Wemyss Coal Company to Methil Harbour for shipment or for transfer to B.R. The Private Railway's apparently assured future was cut short by a bad outbreak of fire in Michael Colliery, the most important pit on the line, in 1967. The line lingered on till 1970 though it had been little used during the intervening period.

In the late 1960s the west of Fife had been a stronghold of heavy industrial locomotives and with the prospect of the S.R.P.S. being able to operate a railway, there was inevitable talk of securing one. The Society itself was however fully committed and it was good to hear of the setting up of the Fife Industrial Locomotive Preservation Group - which aimed at preserving a Wemyss engine for service on a preserved line. The chosen engine was No. 20 because at the time of the Michael fire she was being re-boilered and overhauled. Thanks to the generosity of the Wemyss Estates, No. 20 was duly purchased together with a substantial quantity of spares including a complete set of wheels. Sadly No. 20's trip to Falkirk was not so successful as No. 3's had been. The engine ran hot, damaging her axle boxes and scoring her journals (the parts of the axle which rest in the box). The damage has been repaired sufficiently for No. 20 to be steamed, but she is not as strong as she was, and must be treated with care. The engine is now the property of the S.R.P.S.

The S.R.P.S. withdrew from negotiations with the Highlands and Islands Development Board and B.R. over the Strathspey line in 1971 (see above and further below). While the search for a more convenient alternative went on a policy of retrenchment was adopted at Falkirk. In 1972 the South Scotland Electricity Board kindly donated another Ruston DS88 Diesel shunter from Bonnybridge Power Station, while a third came from the North British Distillery, Edinburgh in 1974, and the North British Saloon made its appearance (see above). By 1973 the Society was actively considering another railway, the Alloa–Dollar branch, which had been retained for coal traffic from the Dollar Mine after passenger services had ceased. With rumours that the remaining locomotives at Woodham Brothers scrapyard at Barry were to be cut up, a group of S.R.P.S. clubbed together to form the Locomotive Owners Group (Scotland) Ltd (L.O.G.S.) to buy a B.R. suburban tank engine No. 80105. The purchase price of £4000 was raised surprisingly quickly, but the cost of removal from Barry to Falkirk (£1400 plus V.A.T.) seemed a stumbling block. At one stage the possibility of shipping the locomotive to Glasgow was investigated, but in the end it proved cheaper to use road transport, and No. 80105 came up the M6 and A80 in fine style, arriving at Larbert in October 1973.

The prospect of acquiring a railway put a premium on fund raising, and to house a sales stand an ex-L.N.E.R. pigeon van was purchased in 1973. This has done yeoman service. Two more diesels were added to the fleet in 1973–74. One was the third Ruston DS88, and the other was a Scottish-built 0-6-0 built by Andrew Barclay in Kilmarnock for the Admiralty in 1941. The most recent diesel is a 165 h.p. Ruston with electric transmission donated by the British Steel Corporation in 1975.

Prospect for the Alloa–Dollar line still seemed bright in 1974, when the Society opened negotiations with the Royal Scottish Museum about *Morayshire*. This locomotive had been bought in 1964 by an engineer, Ian N. Fraser, who had been a pupil of Sir Nigel Gresley. *Morayshire* was restored to her original L.N.E.R. green livery at Inverurie Works in Aberdeenshire in 1964. Mr Fraser then had the problem of finding somewhere to keep her. From 1965 to 1966 she rested in I.C.I.'s Ardeer factory where she was secure from vandals but exposed to a corrosive atmosphere. With no prospect of running the locomotive, Mr Fraser made an agreement with the Royal Scottish Museum that she should go on display there. Until then she was to be stored in an Admiralty Depot at Dalmeny, near the Forth Railway Bridge. She languished there for nine years, and with the postponement of museum development looked like staying there indefinitely. A group of S.R.P.S. volunteers with experience in locomotive restoration approached Mr Fraser, and then the Royal Scottish Museum with a view to restoring her to running order. The target date set for restoration was the Shildon 'Rail 150' cavalcade to celebrate the 150th anniversary of the opening of the Stockton and Darlington Railway. As *Morayshire* was built at Darlington Works, her appearance there would be most appropriate. A small squad worked on the locomotive from July 1974, but as August 1975 approached the effort was increased. There were a thousand and one tasks to be tackled, and on top of that No. 419, which was to accompany *Morayshire*, had to be overhauled and her tires re-profiled. At times it seemed that the work would never be completed to schedule. A major set-back occurred during the re-wheeling of No. 419 when one pair of wheels was inserted the wrong way round - a simple matter to put right in a well equipped workshop, but difficult in a dark and draughty shed with jacking and packing the only way of lifting the locomotive. However, all was well on the day, and the two locomotives with three restored coaches worthily represented Scotland and the S.R.P.S. at Shildon.

Unhappily the plans to secure the Alloa–Dollar line were hit by the recession and cutback in Local Authority expenditure, and the Society has had to fall back on Falkirk where work is actively in progress on the never-ending tasks of restoration and maintenance. The S.R.P.S. also runs rail tours all the year round. At least one each year uses some of the preserved coaches, which have travelled as far afield as Mallaig. The Society has also been represented at B.R. open days occasionally, by No. 419 in steam.

The depot at Falkirk is thus not a museum in the strict sense, but more a workshop where dedicated volunteers carry out considerable feats of engineering and restoration, albeit sometimes under rather primitive conditions. The ultimate aim is to open a branch line in Central Scotland operated by steam, and re-create the atmosphere of Scotland's distinctive railways. In the meantime, the public are welcome to view the stock preserved and undergoing restoration. There is usually no charge for admission, except on special open days, although of course support for the Society, by membership, is encouraged. There is a large shop selling railway material. Visitors always have a reasonable chance of seeing some movement, although it is usually only with a diesel shunter.

Lochty Private Railway

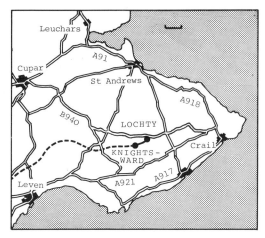

Since 1967 it has been possible to travel behind steam locomotives on summer Sunday afternoons on the Lochty Private Railway, a remarkable line owned by Mr John Cameron. He was one of many Scottish railway enthusiasts thrilled by the use of A4 streamlined Pacific locomotives on the three-hour Glasgow–Aberdeen express trains from 1961. *Union of South Africa*, No. 60009, was already familiar in Scotland, as for many years she had hauled Edinburgh–King's Cross expresses, and had been based at Haymarket Shed. When she was withdrawn from service in 1966, Mr Cameron bought her, originally for preservation in a museum. She bade a triumphant farewell to main-line operation in March 1967, when

Lochty station, off the B940 Cupar-Crail road in Fife, is the start of a 1¼-mile ride on the Lochty Private Railway.

piloted by a 'Black Five', and hauling a 700-ton 18-coach train, she achieved a record time of 87 minutes for the 89 miles from Perth to Aberdeen. Shortly afterwards she was removed by road to her new home at the Lochty. Mr Cameron had purchased a farm through which ran part of the route of the freight-only East Fife Central Railway, which terminated in a field at Lochty. He immediately saw the possibility of relaying part of the line for *Union of South*

L.P.R.: the loco is a Peckett 0-4-0 from the British Aluminium Company at nearby Burntisland. The 'nameplate' reads 'B.A. Co. Ltd.'.

Africa, and accordingly about half a mile of ex-colliery rail was laid by Mr Cameron and volunteer assistants, who form the Fife Railway Preservation Group.

One advantage of the railway being bordered by land owned by Mr Cameron is that no statutory authority was necessary for services.

In the summer of 1967 No. 60009 was steamed on her own, but in the following year one of the ex-L.N.E.R. 'beaver tail' observation cars built for the pre-war 'Coronation' Edinburgh–King's Cross high-speed service came to Lochty, and a public service was operated. Though Lochty is far from public transport, enough people found their way there to justify extension to a terminus at Knightsward, $1\frac{1}{4}$ miles from Lochty. No run-round facility exists at this terminal, so the train is gently backed to its starting point. *Union of South Africa* left Lochty in 1973 to 'return to steam' on B.R., but the summer service is still operated by one of the tiny Peckett 0-4-0ST engines from the British Aluminium Company's Works at Burntisland, an Austerity 0-6-0ST from the Wemyss Private Railway, and a Ruston Diesel Shunter from the North British Distillery, Edinburgh. No. 60009 runs occasional excursions, now based at Markinch, Fife.

The Strathspey Railway

The Strathspey Railway is undoubtedly the most ambitious railway preservation project in Scotland. It has about five miles of track between Aviemore and Boat of Garten and some track-bed beyond. The scheme had its inception in a schoolboy's letter to the S.R.P.S. in April 1967, suggesting that the Society acquire one of the two lines between Aviemore and Grantown-on-Spey, $12\frac{3}{4}$ and $14\frac{1}{2}$ miles long, to run a summer steam service initially, and eventually a winter service. The schoolboy was the son of a Highlands and Islands Development Board Official, and it was found the the H.I.D.B. was interested in developing a steam-hauled tourist railway on this route. Detailed investigation by the S.R.P.S. revealed that the aim of running to Grantown-on-Spey was impractical, and attention was concentrated on the Aviemore-Boat of Garten section of the line to Forres via Grantown. This had been built by the Inverness and Perth Junction Railway and opened in 1863, but had been abandoned for passenger traffic in 1965. The Aviemore–Boat of Garten section was

retained to give access to the G.N.S.R. line to Craigellachie till November 1968. This five-mile stretch is well suited to operation by a preservation group, as it is, despite its situation in the heart of the Highlands, almost level; there are no major engineering works. The S.R.P.S. had detailed discussions with the H.I.D.B. and B.R., but though the Board promised substantial help to the Society, the high price demanded by B.R. gave cause for concern. Delays in reaching agreement with B.R., concern about its ability to raise enough money to fulfil its side of the bargain, and the feeling that adequate voluntary help might not be forthcoming, led the S.R.P.S. to withdraw by resolution at its A.G.M. in 1971. The decision was, however, not unanimous, and a group of members made an independent approach to B.R. and H.I.D.B. to take over the project. The Strathspey Railway Company Ltd was registered, and reached agreement on price, £44,250, and grant. As a gesture of goodwill, the S.R.P.S. presented the new company with the distillery Pug *Dailuaine* and some wagons, which were at Aviemore and had been given by the Scottish Malt Distillers to the Society.

The Strathspey Company had acquired a very basic railway. The trackwork had been drastically simplified, and the locomotive shed at Aviemore, part of the property acquired, had

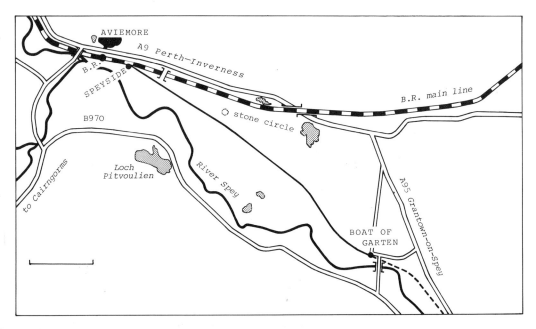

Boat of Garten station on the Strathspey Railway, impeccably restored. Ivatt 2MT No. 46464, built in 1950, heads a train in S.R. livery, purple lake and off-white.

not only been disconnected, but occupied by a scrap dealer and a joiner. Getting access to the shed at Aviemore has in fact been a serious problem for the Strathspey, and it was not until December 1976 that the first two roads in the shed were re-commissioned, though the re-laying of track to it had started late in 1972.

Stock

The first working locomotive arrived in 1972, a Simplex four-wheeled diesel from Aberdeen Gas Works, presented by the Scottish Gas Board, and this was followed by one of the 0-4-0STs from Granton Gas Works, Edinburgh, the first working steam locomotive at Boat of Garten. The S.R. named her *Forth*. To provide a focus for voluntary effort on the line, the Strathspey Railway Association was founded in April 1972, the relationship between the Association and the Company being modelled on the pioneer Welsh preserved lines.

Two of the Strathspey Railway's first Directors were Mr W. E. C. Watkinson and Mr Ian L. Fraser, both deeply committed to Railway Preservation. Mr Watkinson's generosity to the S.R.P.S. in its formative years has already been mentioned. When steam traction was finally abandoned by B.R. in 1968, he bought from them a Stanier 'Black Five' 4-6-0, B.R. No. 45025 (L.M.S. 5025), and during 1969 had her overhauled by the Hunslet Engine Co. in Leeds. (She was one of the first, built in 1934.) He intended her for the Aviemore–Boat line, and when the Strathspey Company was formed he promised that this locomotive would be available for work on the line. In the meantime she worked on the Keighley and Worth Valley Railway, where resplendent in L.M.S. black-lined livery, she attracted a good deal of attention. Eventually she became unfit for further work, and her move north was made via Kilmarnock where she was overhauled by Andrew Barclay and Sons Ltd. She reached Boat of Garten on 29 May 1975 after a ten-hour journey under her own steam. It was No. 5025 which marked the re-opening of the shed at Aviemore on 14 December 1976, by breaking a tape stretched across one of the tracks. The other main-line locomotive on the line is Mr Fraser's Ivatt 2-6-0 No. 46464, built at Crewe in 1950. She spent most of her life working round Arbroath, Mr Fraser's home; where she was known as 'The Carmylie Pilot' because she worked the light railway to the Carmylie Quarries. When she was withdrawn, Mr Fraser bought her from B.R. He offered her to the Dundee Corporation Museum, but unfortunately they could not accommodate her in their Museum and she was too large for any of their stores. She was therefore put under cover in a closely fitting wooden case in a warehouse at Dundee harbour, where she stayed till March 1975 when she too made her way to Boat of Garten. The Company bought a sister engine, No. 46512, from Woodham's scrapyard at Barry, in 1973, and she was moved to Bewdley on the Severn Valley Railway for preparation there before the journey north. Work has yet to finish, although it is progressing.

The other locomotives at Aviemore are all industrials. A third Barclay 0-4-0ST came in 1973 from the South of Scotland Electricity Board at Renfrew. The Company named her *Clyde*, and she hauled the first steam train on the railway, a Directors' and Shareholders' Special on 6 April 1974. She was also an attraction at the steam days held during 1974–5. A 0-6-0T has also been secured from the Wemyss Private Railway. The most recent acquisitions are three Austerity 0-6-0STs from English collieries. There are also two four-wheeled diesels from the Inveresk Paper Company's mill at Inverkeithing; they are *Inverkeith*, a Hudswell Clarke of 1939, and *Inveresk*, a diesel-electric by Ruston.

The rolling stock on the S.R. has been acquired with a view to economical operation, and is mainly of B.R. standard design. There are, however, coaches of L.M.S. and Great North of Scotland origin. A notable item is a buffet car 'Glenfiddich', once used on the Edinburgh–Glasgow multiple-unit diesel service, and presented to the Company by William Grant and Sons Ltd, distillers of Glenfiddich.

A journey down the line
An entirely new station has been built at Aviemore near the site of the engine shed, Aviemore Speyside. The increased traffic on the

B.R. line which has followed from the opening of the Aviemore Centre, means that the original Aviemore station could not provide facilities for the Strathspey Railway without interfering with B.R. services. The new station has a correct 'period atmosphere' because it is being, constructed with material from the disused station at Dalnaspidal, on the main Perth–Inverness line some twenty-five miles south of Aviemore.

Leaving Aviemore, the line runs past Spey Lodge, a railwaymen's holiday home, and out along the heather-clad valley (or 'strath') of the River Spey. Near the lineside are the remains of a stone circle built *c.* 1500 B.C. by the Beaker people – a reminder of more than three thousand years of habitation of the area. The railway then runs through the widening Strath, with the foothills of the Cairngorms to the south and east, and the Monadhliaths to the west of the line. There is no road near the line, only a track leading to a settlement which dates from mediaeval times, Kinchurdy farm, some three miles out of Aviemore. In the open country, wildlife may be seen, particularly deer, hares, and red squirrels.

Unlike many other sections of the Highland Railway, there are no steep gradients on the line, only a slight rise from each terminus to near the half-way point, at the bridge over the track to Kinchurdy. The railway is then only 800 feet above sea level, yet within ten miles are four of the five highest mountains in Britain. After the half-way point, the line descends gently to Boat of Garten, originally the junction for the G.N.S.R.'s Speyside branch, and therefore larger than it might have been. The buildings date largely from the 1860s, and a museum there contains photographs of the line in the past and a model of the station in the 1950s. There are two typical Highland Railway signal boxes. The footbridge is of the original (standard H.R.) design, but the actual structure was moved, like Aviemore Speyside station, from Dalnaspidal.

The Society already owns the track-bed from Boat of Garten onwards for about $4\frac{1}{2}$ miles to Broomhill. Regular passenger services from Aviemore Speyside to Boat of Garten started in 1979 (at weekends from May to September, with mid-week services in 'high season'). After seven years of hard work and sometimes of uncertainty, the Railway's future seems secure.

Gazetteer

Compiled by Roger Crombleholme

The following pages list all 60 railways described in the main text, and list and briefly describe 68 other sites of interest. These further entries are chiefly minor steam-powered railways offering rides, but some museums and centres of railway preservation, or even single engines of interest, are included. The choice is of necessity selective, but is intended to show the wide range of the steam preservation movement.

Each entry has
Name of Railway or Museum
Brief description
Address
O.S.REF. TO NATIONAL GRID
TELEPHONE
Access, including rail and bus services where possible.

Details

Opening times
Facilities

Symbols used for facilities are:

P parking
S shop selling railway items
R refreshments
M museum of railway items
pa picnic area
T timetable for railway appears in British Rail volume
A timetable is in *ABC Guide*
t railway issues its own timetable as leaflet

Each entry is numbered. Italic numbers (e.g. *26*, used for sites not in the main text) refer to the endpaper map. The numbers run roughly north-south and west-east within each area. Sites with main-text entries have bold numbers (e.g. **168**), which are page references as well as being on the map.

National Grid References
Every Ordnance Survey map is overprinted with a grid. In this *Guide*, references are given to four-figure accuracy. The two letters of the reference designate a hundred-kilometre square, the key to which is given on every map. The number then consists of a two-figure 'easting' and a two-figure 'northing', which together specify a one-kilometre square. Eastings come first. Counting starts from 00, not 11, within each lettered square, and runs across (left to right, west to east), and then upwards.

A.R.P.S. Brochure
The gazetteer refers to 'A.R.P.S. listings': these are given in a summary brochure updated each year. It is available from The Association of Railway Preservation Societies (Steam Train Guide), Sheringham Station, Norfolk NR26 8RA. Please send a stamped addressed envelope.

Whilst we have taken every care in compiling this gazetteer, we cannot be held responsible for any inaccuracies — apart from anything else, the details may change. For exact running times, etc., see the A.R.P.S. list or contact the railways directly.

I The South-West

1 **Lappa Valley Railway**
Passenger-carrying 15 in. gauge steam-operated light railway.
St Newlyn East, Cornwall.
O.S. REF. SW 8356
TEL. Mitchell 317

The railway offers a 1-mile ride along the track-bed of the former G.W.R. Newquay–Chacewater line, commencing from Benny Mill, about one mile north-east of St Newlyn East and running to East Wheal Rose Mine.

Operated daily throughout the holiday season.

P   S   R   pa

2 **China Clay Industry Museum**
A museum of locomotives, rolling stock and historical machinery associated with the Cornish china clay industry.
Wheal Martyn, Trenance Valley, St Austell, Cornwall.
O.S.REF. SX 0054

Amongst the locomotives on display are the 4 ft 6 in. gauge Peckett 0–4–0ST *Lee Moor* No. 1 and the standard gauge Bagnall 0–4–0ST *Judy*.

P   S

3 **Forest Railroad Park**
Passenger-carrying 7¼ in. gauge steam-operated railway.
Dobwalls, Liskeard, Cornwall.
O.S. REF. SX 2165
Nearest B.R. station: Liskeard.

The railway offers a 1-mile ride over perhaps the most arduous 7¼ in. gauge line in this country. It has severe gradients, high embankments, deep cuttings and six tunnels. Operation of the railway follows North American practice and features impressive steam locomotives modelled on Union Pacific and Denver & Rio Grande prototypes.

Operates at Easter, then Wednesdays and Sundays to Spring Bank Holiday, then daily until October.

P   R   pa

12 **Dart Valley Railway**
Buckfastleigh, Devon.
O.S. REF. SX 7466
TEL. Buckfastleigh 2338
On the old A38 Exeter–Plymouth Road.

Operated daily Easter week and mid-May to mid-September; weekends only April and early May.

P   S   R   T   A   t

4 **British Rail, Newton Abbot**
Static steam locomotive exhibit (broad gauge).
Newton Abbot station, Devon.

O.S. REF. SX 8671

South Devon Railway 0–4–0VBWT No. 151 *Tiny* is on display on the platform at Newton Abbot, and is the sole surviving engine from the G.W.R. broad-gauge era which came to an end in 1892.

18 **Torbay and Dartmouth Railway**
Queen's Park Station, Torbay Road, Paignton, Devon.
O.S. REF. SX 8860
TEL. Torbay 555872

Operates daily Easter week and mid-May to October; weekends April and May.

S   R   T   A   t

23 **West Somerset Railway**
The Railway Station, Minehead, Somerset.
O.S. REF. SS 9846
TEL. Minehead 4996

Operates all year. Daily diesel service (not Sundays); steam services in summer.

P   S   R   M   t

5 **Tiverton Museum**
Static steam locomotive exhibit.
Tiverton, Devon.
O.S. REF. SS 9612
Near centre of town, on St Andrew Street (near Bethel Assembly of God, which is signposted).

G.W.R. 0–4–2T No. 1442 is on display. Other small exhibits include a large model of a G.W.R. broad-gauge 4–4–0T *Lalla Rookh*, built c. 1870.

28 **Bicton Woodland Railway**
Bicton Gardens, East Budleigh, Budleigh Salterton, Devon.
O.S. REF. SY 0786
TEL. Budleigh Salterton 2820
On A376 Newton Poppleford–Budleigh Salterton road, slightly north of St Mary's Church. Nearest B.R. station: Exmouth. On bus route 40, Exmouth–Sidmouth.

Operated daily during holiday season.

P   S   R   M

6 **Beer Heights Light Railway**
Passenger-carrying 7¼ in. gauge steam-operated railway.
Peco Ltd., Beer, Devon.
O.S. REF. SY 2389

Locomotives are modelled on well-known narrow-gauge prototypes such as the Welsh Quarry Hunslet 0–4–0ST.

Operates on weekdays and Saturday mornings May to Sept. Half-mile ride offering scenic views across bay.

P   A   Peco Model Land

7 Seaton and District Electric Tramway

Passenger-carrying 2 ft 9 in. gauge electric tramway.
Seaton, Devon.
O.S. REF. SY 2590
Nearest B.R. station: Axminster. Thence by bus.

The tramway operates along the track-bed of the former L. & S.W.R. Seaton branch for 2½ miles as far as Colyton. A half-hour service of trams operates at peak periods, thoughout the holiday season.

P   S

8 Bristol Docks Railway

Passenger-carrying, steam-operated railway.
Bristol Industrial Museum, 'M' Shed, Bristol City Docks.
O.S. REF. ST 5872
Nearest B.R. station: Bristol Temple Meads.

A half-mile ride in a G.W.R. 'Toad' brake van between the Bristol Industrial Museum and the Great Western Dry Dock where Brunel's famous ship, the s.s. *Great Britain* is on display. Trains are hauled by the Peckett 0–6–0ST *Henbury*. The Museum houses machinery and vehicles associated with Bristol's industrial past.

The railway operates at intervals throughout the summer season in conjunction with the Industrial Museum.

The Seaton Tramway. On the right of the picture, passengers board No. 8 before it leaves Seaton for Colyton.

9 Bristol Suburban Railway

Preservation centre featuring steam open days.
Bitton Station, Bristol, Avon.
O.S. REF. ST 6770
Bitton station is on the A431 near Willsbridge.

The Bristol Surburban Railway Society has relaid all the track within station limits at Bitton on this former M.R. line, and offers steam-hauled rides on open days. Stock includes L.M.S. class 5 No. 45379 as well as examples of industrial tank locos from the three Bristol manufacturers, Peckett, Avonside and Fox Walker.

Open days at intervals throughout year, principally on public holidays.

P   S   M

10 Oakhill Manor Miniature Railway

Passenger-carrying 10¼ in. gauge steam-operated railway.
Oakhill Manor, near Shepton Mallet, Somerset.
O.S. REF. ST 6447
About 4 miles north of Shepton on the A367.

1½-mile ride through the grounds of Oakhill Manor. This railway is being extended to give a total run of 2½ miles through woodland glades and deep cuttings. Trains are hauled by a Bassett-Lowke L.M.S. 'Royal Scot' 4–6–0. Oakhill Manor Museum houses one of the finest collection of models in the country.

Operational each afternoon between April and October.

P   R   M   pa

32 East Somerset Railway

Cranmore Railway Station, Cranmore, Somerset.
O.S. REF. ST 6642
TEL. Cranmore 417
Three miles east of Shepton Mallet on A361 Frome road. Bus: 'Crown Tours' Shepton–Frome service.

Open daily except Christmas Day. Steaming Sundays and Bank Holidays, mid-March to end Oct.

P   S   R

11 Longleat Light Railway

Passenger-carrying 15 in. gauge light railway.
Longleat Park, near Warminster, Wilts.
O.S. REF. ST 8043
TEL. Maiden Bradley 579
Longleat is permanently signposted.

The railway offers a 1-mile ride through the grounds of the Marquis of Bath's Estate at Longleat. Stock includes the Curwen 0–6–2T *Dougal* built in 1970.

P   S   R   pa   amusements   wildlife

12 Great Western Railway Museum

Static steam locomotive exhibits.
Emlyn Square, Swindon, Wiltshire.
O.S. REF. SU 1484
TEL. Swindon 26161 ext. 562
Nearest B.R. station: Swindon.

On display are five G.W.R. locomotives, including *City of Truro* and a replica of the broad-gauge engine *North Star*.

223

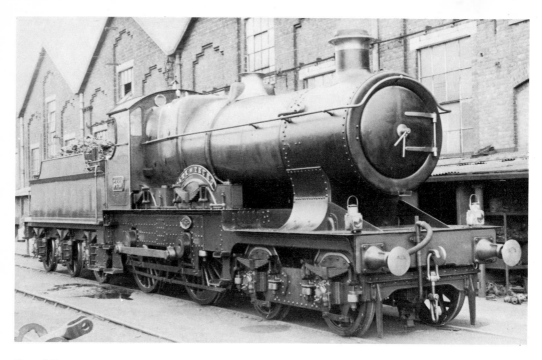

City of Truro, *G.W.R. 4-4-0 No. 3440, was built in 1903, and in 1904 was first British loco to exceed 100 m.p.h. It is now appropriately, at the Great Western Railway Museum in Emlyn Square, Swindon.*

There are also smaller railway items and records of G.W.R. interest.

Museum open Monday to Saturday and Sunday afternoons throughout the year. Closed Christmas Day, Boxing Day, New Year's Day and Good Friday.

P nearby

33 Great Western Society
Didcot, Oxfordshire.
O.S. REF. SU 5290
Access through Didcot B.R. station.

Steamings on many Sundays, April to Oct., and Bank Holidays, 11 a.m. to 5 p.m. For specific dates, see A.R.P.S. listings.

P S R

II London and the Home Counties

13 **Christchurch Miniature Railway**
Passenger-carrying 10 in. gauge steam-operated railway.
The Quay, Christchurch, Hants.
O.S. REF. SZ 1892
Nearest B.R. station: Christchurch.

Quarter-mile ride on seafront line, arranged in an irregular oval. The line is notable for its streamlined L.M.S.-style 'Pacific' built by Alfred Dove in 1948.

The railway operates at Easter, then each weekend to Spring Bank Holiday. Thereafter daily until dusk throughout the summer season until mid-October.

P

52 Mid-Hants Railway (The Watercress Line)
Alresford Station, Hampshire.

O.S. REF. SU 5832
On the A31 Guildford–Winchester road.

Open Saturday afternoons, Sundays and Bank Holidays, mid-March to mid-Oct.

P S R T t

14 **Hollycombe Woodland Railway**
Passenger-carrying 2 ft gauge and standard-gauge steam-operated railways and steam fairground.
Hollycombe House, near Liphook, Hampshire.
O.S. REF SU 8529
Nearest B.R. station: Liphook.

The 2 ft gauge line offers a half-mile ride through the grounds of Hollycombe House. The railway runs up to a quarry, where there is a vantage point with extensive views

No. 1 of the Hollycombe Woodland Railway, the 2 ft gauge Caledonia, *prepares to depart. When the mists clear, there are superb views over the South Downs from the upper end of the line.*

of the South Downs. At the quarry, connection is made with the 300-yard standard-gauge line, and demonstrations are given by steam-powered stone-handling and crushing machinery. There is also an extensive woodland garden, and a fairground with steam rides dating back to the turn of the century. Narrow-gauge stock comprises the Barclay 0–4–0WT *Caledonia* and the Hunslet 0–4–0ST *Jerry M*, together with coaches from the former Ramsgate Tunnel Railway. The standard-gauge line is powered by the Aveling Porter 0–4–0TG *Sir Vincent*.

Open Saturdays, Sundays and Bank Holidays, Easter to October.

P   R

55   Isle of Wight Railway
Havenstreet Station, near Ryde, I.O.W.
O.S. REF. SZ 5589
TEL. Wooton Bridge 882204
Turn left off A3054 Ryde–Newport road, or take bus 3 from Ryde or Newport.

Operates Sundays, early May to late September; Thursdays, July to mid-Aug., then daily to end August.

P   S   R

15   Hayling Billy
Static steam locomotive exhibit.
Hayling Billy public house, Hayling Island, Hampshire.

O.S. REF. SZ 7299
Nearest B.R. station, Havant, then bus.
L.B. & S.C.R. Stroudley 'Terrier' 0–6–0T No. 46 *Newington* is used as a pub sign. Like most Terriers, *Newington* led an eventful life, passing through the hands of the L. & S.W.R., the Freshwater, Yarmouth & Newport Railway, the S.R. and British Railways, before being purchased by Brickwoods the brewers in 1966.

Locomotive on display at all times; pub open during licensing hours.

16   Littlehampton Miniature Railway
Passenger-carrying 12¼ in. gauge steam-operated railway.
Mewsbrook Park, Littlehampton, Sussex.
O.S. REF TQ 0301
On eastern fringe of town. Nearest B.R. station: Littlehampton.

Half-mile ride through Mewsbrook Park. The locomotives are a pair of 4–6–4 tender locomotives constructed from parts manufactured by Bullock for two 10¼ in. gauge tank engines.

The railway operates at Easter, then at weekends until Spring Bank Holiday after which operation is daily until mid-Sept.

17   Great Cockrow Railway
Passenger-carrying 7¼ in. gauge steam-operated railway.
Hardwick Lane, Lyne, near Chertsey, Surrey.
O.S. REF. TQ 0266
One-mile ride, starting and finishing at Hardwick Central station. As many as six trains can operate simultaneously on this fully-signalled railway, which features a double-track

main line with interlinked single-track loops. The resident locomotive stock amounts to more than a dozen models of 'Big Four' prototypes, mainly of the 2–6–0 and 4–6–0 types. The railway is open on Sunday afternoons from Spring Bank Holiday until the end of September.

P

18   Science Museum
Static steam locomotives and other historic transport exhibits.
Exhibition Road, South Kensington, London S.W.7.
O.S. REF. TQ 2679

Amongst the many historic locomotives on view are *Puffing Billy*, *Rocket*, *Sanspareil*, and G.W.R. No. 4073 *Caerphilly Castle*.

Open daily (Sunday, afternoon only) throughout the year (not Christmas, New Year). Admission free.

19   London Transport Museum
Static steam locomotives and other historic transport exhibits.
Covent Garden, London W.C.2
O.S. REF. TQ 3182
Nearest Underground station: Covent Garden

The L.T. collection spans nearly 150 years of transport in the London area. Amongst the locomotives exhibited are the Metropolitan Rly 4–4–0T No. 23 and the Wotton Tramway 0–4–0TG built by Aveling Porter in 1872. The museum also houses London buses, trolleybuses and trams, posters, signs, tickets and other exhibits.

Open daily throughout the year (not Christmas, Boxing Day).

20   Brockham Museum
Museum of narrow-gauge locomotives and rolling stock.
Brockham Pits, near Dorking, Surrey.
O.S. REF. TQ 1951
Entrance is along unmarked track on north side of A25 Dorking–Reigate road, 160 yards west of Barley Mow pub.

The museum trustees are in the process of negotiating the precise terms for opening the museum to the public. When this happens, Brockham will be a working museum of narrow-gauge railways in their natural setting. The Brockham collection has 5 steam and 11 non-steam locomotives of various gauges, 39 pieces of rolling stock, and several hundred small exhibits.

Open third Sunday in each month, April to Sept., 11.30 a.m. to 5.30 p.m.

P   S

38   Bluebell Railway
Sheffield Park, Sussex.
O.S. REF. TQ 4023
TEL. Newick 2370
On A275 East Grinstead to Lewes road.

Open Sundays Jan., Feb., Dec.; Saturdays and Sundays Mar., Apr. and Nov.; Bank Holidays, Wednesdays, Saturdays and Sundays in May and October; daily June to September.

P   S   R   T   A   t

21   Volks Railway
Passenger-carrying 2 ft 8½ in. gauge electric railway.
Aquarium, Seafront, Brighton, Sussex.
O.S. REF. TQ 3103
TEL. Brighton 29801.
Operated by Brighton Council, Royal York Buildings, Brighton BN1 1NP.
Nearest B.R. station: Brighton. Any bus service to Palace Pier, Aquarium, or Old Steine.

The railway offers a breezy 1¼-mile ride along Brighton seafront from Aquarium to Black Rock. Volks Railway was the first electric railway in Great Britain, opened in 1883.

Trains run approximately every five minutes daily from April to September.

45   Romney, Hythe and Dymchurch Railway
New Romney, Kent.
O.S. REF. TR 0724
TEL. New Romney 2353
Near A259 Hythe to New Romney road.

Operates daily Easter to end Sept.; also Saturdays and Sundays in Mar., Oct. and Nov.

P   S   R   T   A   t

22   Birchley Railway
Passenger-carrying 10¼ in. gauge steam-operated railway.
Birchley House, Biddenden, Ashford, Kent.
O.S. REF. TQ 8437
TEL. Biddenden 291413
Nearest stations: Headcorn B.R. or Tenterden Town K. & E.S.R.

The railway will ultimately offer a ¾-mile run over a figure-of-eight track. Trains are operated over part of the layout whilst construction work is in progress. The line is notable for its working model of a Stroudley 'Terrier' No. 84 *Crowborough*.

Regular operation of the railway has not yet commenced though operating days are held from time to time. Visitors are asked to telephone beforehand to check whether trains are running.

48   Kent and East Sussex Railway
Tenterden Station, Kent.
O.S. REF. TQ 8833
TEL. Tenterden 2943

Operates weekends and Bank Holidays Easter to end Oct.; daily end July to early Sept.; Sundays to end of year.

P   S   R   T   A   t

58   Sittingbourne and Kemsley Light Railway
Sittingbourne, Kent
O.S. REF. TQ 9064
TEL. Sittingbourne 24899
Access is from Milton Road.

Operates every weekend from Easter to mid-Oct.; selected days throughout year (see A.R.P.S. listings).

P   S   R   t

III East Anglia

74 Nene Valley Railway
Wansford Station, Cambridgeshire.
O.S. REF. TL 0997
TEL. Stamford 782021
Just off A1, one mile south of junction with A47.

Open Sundays and Bank Holidays Easter to mid-Oct.,
Saturdays April to mid-Sept.; some trains run Wednesdays
and Thursdays in July and Aug., but telephone for details.

P S R t

23 The Cushing Steam Collection
*A unique collection of steam traction engines and fairground
organs, also incorporating a passenger-carrying 1 ft 10¾ in.
gauge steam-operated railway.*
Laurel Farm, Thursford, Norfolk.
O.S. REF. TF 9834
Off A148 Fakenham–Cromer road.

Three-quarter mile ride from behind the steam organ
museum through Norfolk farmland. Motive power on the
railway is provided by the Hunslet Quarry 0-4-0ST *Cackler*.

Operates at weekends, May to Sept. inclusive.

P

69 North Norfolk Railway
Sheringham Station, Sheringham, Norfolk.
O.S. REF. TG 1543
TEL. Sheringham 822045

Open mid-March to early Oct.; passenger service: Saturdays
and Sundays late May to early Oct.; Bank Holidays; also
additional days, for details of which see A.R.P.S. listings.

P S R M A t

24 Barton House Railway
*Passenger-carrying 3½ in. gauge steam-operated railway and
museum of full-size railway equipment (much from the M. &
G.N.).*
Barton House, Hartwell Road, The Avenue, Wroxham,
Norfolk
O.S. REF. TG 3017
TEL. Wroxham 2470
Nearest B.R. station: Wroxham.

80-yard ride round oval of raised track on 'sit-astride'
rolling stock.

Operates third Sunday afternoon of each month, April to
Oct., plus Easter Monday.

P nearby R

62 Bressingham Steam Museum and Gardens
Bressingham Hall, Diss, Norfolk.
O.S. REF. TM 0880
TEL. Diss 88386

Open Sundays May to mid-Sept.; Thursdays late May to
early Sept.; Wednesdays during Aug.; from 1.30 p.m.

P S R

25 Audley End Miniature Railway
Passenger-carrying 10¼ in. gauge steam-operated railway.
Audley End House, near Saffron Walden, Essex.
O.S. REF. TL 5336
Nearest B.R. station: Audley End.

One-mile ride through the grounds of Audley End House
through attractive woodlands, crossing the River Cam twice.
The line features three steam locomotives, two 'Atlantics'
and a 'Pacific', to the designs of David Curwen.

Operates when Audley End House is open to the public, i.e.
weekends and Bank Holiday afternoons during May to
September and Sundays during October.

P R pa

84 Colne Valley Railway
Castle Hedingham Station, near Halstead, Essex.
O.S. REF. TL 7736
TEL. Hedingham 61174.
On the A604, ½ mile north of Castle Hedingham. Nearest B.R.
station: Braintree.

See A.R.P.S. Listings for operating times.

80 Stour Valley Railway Preservation Society
Chappel and Wakes Colne Station, Essex.
O.S. REF. TL 8928
TEL. Earls Colne 2903
Off A604 Colchester–Haverhill road.

Steamings on selected days from Easter to October. See
A.R.P.S. listings.

P S R

IV The Midlands

26 Crewe and Nantwich Borough Council
Static locomotive exhibit permanently on display.
Crewe town centre shopping precinct, Crewe, Cheshire.
The famous L. & N.W.R. 2-2-2 No. 173 *Cornwall* has been
preserved in honour of the long association with the former
L. & N.W.R. locomotive works, and the place of Crewe in
railway history.

At Butterley Station, the Midland Railway Centre, L.M.S. class 3F 0-6-0 tank No. 16440, with passenger stock.

27   Churnet Valley Steam Railway Museum
Preservation centre featuring steam open days.
Cheddleton Station near Leek, Staffordshire.
O.S. REF. SJ 9852
Nearest B.R. station: Stoke-on-Trent. P.M.T. or Berrisford buses operate to Cheddleton from Leek and Hanley.

Short train rides available either steam- or diesel-hauled. The museum represents the first phase of the scheme to re-open a passenger railway in the Churnet Valley. The station buildings have been converted into a museum reflecting the original North Staffordshire Railway Company, 'Owd Knotty'. Preserved rolling stock includes L.M.S. 4F class 0-6-0 No. 4422.

Museum open daily April to Sept.; Sundays only Oct. to March. Operates Sundays and Bank Holidays.

P   S   R

104   Foxfield Light Railway
Dilhorne, near Cheadle, Staffordshire.
O.S. REF. SJ 9744
TEL. Uttoxeter 4669
Turn left off A50 Stoke–Uttoxeter road at Blythe Bridge.

Open every Sunday, April to Sept., and Bank Holidays.

P   S   R

28   Midland Railway Centre
Preservation centre featuring steam open days.
Butterley station, near Ripley, Derbyshire.
O.S. REF. SK 4052
On A61 road, 1½ miles north of Ripley.

The Midland Railway Trust Ltd has created a major steam preservation centre devoted to the Midland Railway and its successors. Butterley station is situated on the former Midland Ambergate–Pye Bridge line and is being painstakingly reconstructed to authentic M.R. designs. Pride of the collection is the superbly elegant Midland 'Single' No. 673, but also present are L.M.S. Pacific No. 6203 *Princess Margaret Rose*, M.R. Kirtley 2–4–0 No. 158A, and no less than four L.M.S. 'Jinty' 0–6–0Ts.

Steam open days at intervals, as advertised. Centre open at other times.

P (limited)   **R**

29   Lound Hall Mining Museum
Static steam locomotive exhibits.
Lound Hall, Bevercotes, near East Retford, Nottinghamshire. Enquires to: Industrial Relations Officer, N.C.B., Edwinstowe, Mansfield, Notts.
O.S. REF. SK7073

Two 0–6–0ST locomotives are on display together with examples of coal mining machinery.

Open first Sunday afternoon each month throughout the year.

30   Thoresby Hall Miniature Railway
Passenger-carrying 10¼ in. gauge steam-operated railway.
Thoresby Park, Ollerton, Newark, Nottinghamshire.
O.S. REF. SK 6371

750-yard ride alongside the River Medan and the smaller of the two lakes in the park, which is in the centre of Sherwood Forest. The railway is notable for its streamlined L.N.E.R. A4 Pacific No. 4498 *Sir Nigel Gresley*.

Operates Sunday afternoons and Bank Holidays, Easter to Sept.

106 Chasewater Light Railway
Chasewater Pleasure Park, near Brownhills, Staffordshire.
O.S. REF. SK 0307
TEL. 021-523 8516
Entrance is in Pools Road, off the A5 Cannock–Tamworth road near junction with A452.

Steamings second and fourth Sundays in each month April to Sept., and Bank Holiday Sundays and Mondays.

P   S   R   M

31 **Bass Museum**
Static steam locomotive exhibit in museum devoted to the history of brewing in Burton-upon-Trent.
Horninglow Street, Burton-upon-Trent, Staffordshire.
O.S. REF. SK 2423
TEL. Burton 45301 (office hours); Burton 45707 (all other times)
The Museum is at the entrance to Bass's brewery, housed in what was formerly the company joiners' shop and its surrounding buildings.

On display is Bass 0–4–0ST No. 9, built by Neilson Reid in 1901, and the directors' coach built in 1889. Much emphasis is given in the exhibition to Burton's Victorian railway boom.

S   R

103 Shackerstone and Bosworth Railway
Shackerstone Station, near Market Bosworth, Leicestershire.
O.S. REF. SK 3706
Turn right at Twycross on A444 Nuneaton–Burton road, then take unclassified road through Congerstone.

Open weekends and Bank Holiday Mondays, Easter to end Oct.

P   S   R   M

110 Cadeby Light Railway
Cadeby Rectory, near Market Bosworth, Leicestershire.
O.S. REF. SK 4202
TEL. Market Bosworth 290462
On the A447, one mile south of Market Bosworth.

Open second Saturday in each month.

P   S   R   M

32 **Leicester Corporation Museum**
Static steam and internal combustion loco exhibits
Abbey Lane Pumping Station, Corporation Road, Leicester.
O.S. REF. SK 5806
TEL. Leicester 61330.
Bus 54 from Charles St (shows 88 returning).

The principal exhibits are three standard-gauge industrial tank locomotives by Stephenson, Brush and Barclay; the last is a 'fireless' thermal-storage loco.

Open daily throughout the year.

P   S

94 Great Central Railway (Main Line Steam Trust)
Great Central Road, Loughborough, Leicestershire.
O.S. REF. SK 5419
TEL. Loughborough 216433

Open weekends and Bank Holidays from mid-March.

P   S   R   A   T   t

33 **Stapleford Miniature Railway**
Passenger-carrying 10¼ in. gauge steam-operated railway.
Stapleford Park, Melton Mowbray, Leicestershire.
O.S. REF. SK 8118

One-mile ride through the grounds of Stapleford Park, the house of Lord and Lady Gretton. The S.M.R. is one of the finest miniature railways in the country, having three stations, a tunnel, a fully automatic level crossing, and colour-light signalling. Boat trains operate to Lakeside Station where passengers can join scale models of ocean liners for a voyage on the lake.

The railway operates when the house and grounds are open to visitors: Easter Sunday and Monday, Spring Bank Holiday Monday and Tuesday and Late Summer Holiday Monday. Also every Sunday, Wednesday and Thursday afternoon from May to September.

P   S   R   pa

34 **Hilton Valley Railway***
Passenger-carrying 7¼ in. gauge steam-operated railway.
Hilton, near Bridgnorth, Shropshire.
O.S. REF. SO 7795
Alongside main Wolverhampton–Bridgnorth road.

One-mile ride through wooded pastures alongside rippling trout streams. The railway, like the Great Cockrow Railway, features intensive operation on proper main line principles using colour-light signalling interlocked with the train 'staff' system. The railway has a resident stock of nine locomotives, and these may be supplemented by visiting locos from time to time.

Operates summer Sundays and Bank Holidays.

P   R   pa

* This railway has now moved to Weston Park, Shropshire.

88 Severn Valley Railway
Bewdley, Worcestershire
O.S. REF. SO 7975
TEL. Bewdley 403816

Open weekends early March to late Oct.; also many Tuesdays, Wednesdays and Thursdays in summer, and daily mid-July to early Sept. See A.R.P.S. listings for details.

P   S   R   A   T   t

35 **Birmingham Museum of Science and Industry**
Static steam locomotive exhibits
Newhall Street, Birmingham 3
O.S. REF. SP 0687
Nearest B.R. station: Birmingham New Street.
The locomotives on display include three narrow-gauge

tank engines, dwarfed by the L.M.S. Pacific No. 46235 *City of Birmingham*, which is capable of being moved by an external power unit along a short length of track.
Open Monday to Saturday throughout the year.

P (nearby) S R

101 Birmingham Railway Museum (Tyseley)
Warwick Road, Tyseley, Birmingham 11
O.S. REF. SP 1084
TEL. 021-707 4696

Open for static display every Sunday from 2 p.m.; also open days to be announced.

36 Echills Wood Railway
Passenger-carrying 7¼ in. gauge steam-operated railway.
Echills Wood, Stoneleigh, Warwickshire.
O.S. REF. SP 3372
Echills Wood is adjacent to the Royal Agricultural Society's showground at Stoneleigh.

Half-mile ride around Echills Wood, with looplines to and from the main station at Harvesters. The usual locomotive stock amounts to more than a dozen models of a wide variety of prototypes, ranging from B.R. 4–6–2 *Duke of Gloucester* to Welsh quarry 0–4–0STs.

Operates only in conjunction with events at the Showground; closed (and stock removed) at other times. Usual times: the four days of the Royal Show, and three of the Town and Country Festival in August.

P R at Showground

37 Northamptonshire Ironstone Railway Trust
Collection of steam and internal combustion locos, rolling stock, and machinery associated with the ironstone quarrying industry.
Hunsbury Hill, Northampton.
O.S. REF. SP 7458
Nearest B.R. station: Northampton.

The Trust has formed the nucleus of a collection of ironstone relics in order to preserve something of the country's heritage. The site is the trackbed of the former ironstone tramway serving Hunsbury furnaces, which lies within the bounds of the proposed Hunsbury Hill Park. The collection to date comprises a dozen assorted locomotives of three different gauges.

Open to visitors at weekends, May to September inclusive.

100 'Steam in Hereford'
Bulmers Cider Factory, Whitecross Road, Hereford.
O.S. REF. SO 5040
TEL. Hereford 6182
Site is half a mile from City centre on A438 Brecon road.

Open for static display Saturdays and Sundays late March or early April to late Sept. Steamings last Sunday in each month, plus some extra days. See A.R.P.S. listings.

P S (on steam days) R

107 Dean Forest Railway Society
Norchard Steam Centre, New Mills, Lydney, Gloucestershire.
O.S. REF. SO 6205
TEL. Lydney 3423
Museum is at Parkend; journeys begin at Norchard. Norchard is 1½ miles, Parkend 3½ miles along B4234 road from Lydney (off A48). Nearest B.R. station: Lydney. Bus 40 from Lydney.

Open almost every Sunday afternoon, and Saturday afternoons from May to October. For steaming days, see A.R.P.S. listings.

P S R M pa

108 Dowty Railway Preservation Society
Northway Lane, Ashchurch, near Tewkesbury, Gloucestershire.
O.S. REF. SO 9233
Take A438 from Tewkesbury, turn left at Northway Lane, ¼ mile after crossing the M5 motorway (Exit 9). Nearest B.R. station: Cheltenham Lansdown.

Open every Sunday for static display. For steaming days, see advertising.

P S

38 Winchcombe Railway Museum
Static displays of railway signalling, lineside features, loco nameplates and small historical items.
23 Gloucester Street, Winchcombe, Gloucestershire.
O.S. REF. SP 0228
TEL. Winchcombe 602257
Nearest B.R. station: Cheltenham Lansdown.

The museum specializes not in locomotives and rolling stock, but in signalling equipment, lineside fixtures, horse-drawn road vehicles, tickets and all kinds of paperwork, lamps, and even a couple of railway gas-meters. There are indoor and outdoor displays in pleasant garden surroundings.

Open Easter, Spring and Summer Bank Holidays (Sunday and Monday), plus selected Sundays as advertised in June, July, August and September. Admission free.

P (in street)

39 Blenheim Palace Miniature Railway
Passenger-carrying 15 in. gauge steam-operated railway.
Blenheim Palace, Woodstock, Oxfordshire.
O.S. REF. SP 4416
TEL. Woodstock 811805
Blenheim is permanently signposted on all major surrounding roads.

The railway offers a ½-mile ride through the grounds of Blenheim Palace. Stock includes the Guest Pacific, No. 5751 *Sir Winston Churchill*.

Operates daily, Easter to end Oct.

P S R pa Blenheim Palace

109 Quainton Railway Society
Quainton Road Station, near Aylesbury, Buckinghamshire.

O.S. REF. SP 7318
TEL. Chesham 4845
Turn off A41 Aylesbury–Bicester road at Waddesdon (signposted).

Open selected days including Bank Holidays. See A.R.P.S. listings.

P S R M

112 Leighton Buzzard Narrow-Gauge Railway
Pages Park Station, Billington Road, Leighton Buzzard, Bedfordshire.
O.S. REF. SP 9224
TEL. Leighton Buzzard 3888
Billington Road is ½ mile from Leighton on A4146.

Open Sundays late March to mid-Sept.; also Bank Holidays.

P S R

114 Whipsnade and Umfolozi Railway
Whipsnade Zoo, Dunstable, Bedfordshire.

O.S. REF. TL 0017
TEL. Whipsnade 872995 (Zoo: 872171)

Open daily except Christmas Day; operates from Easter to end Sept. daily; also winter weekends and school holidays.

P M

40 Knebworth West Park and Winter Green Railway
Passenger-carrying 2 ft gauge steam-operated railway
Knebworth House, near Stevenage, Hertfordshire.
O.S. REF. TL 2220
TEL. Stevenage 812661
Knebworth is permanently signposted on all major surrounding roads. Nearest B.R. station: Knebworth.

The railway offers a 1¼-mile ride through the grounds of Knebworth House. Resident locomotive stock comprises six steam locos plus internal combustion motive power.

Operates daily from Easter to end Sept. Steam operation on weekends and Bank Holidays, plus one weekday during school holidays. Otherwise diesel.

P S R pa

V Wales

41 Penrhyn Castle Museum
Static steam locomotive exhibits.
Llandegai, near Bangor, Gwynedd.
O.S. REF. SH 6072
TEL. Bangor 3084
Nearest B.R. station: Bangor. Buses from Bangor and Llandudno.

Doyen of the collection of standard- and narrow-gauge locomotives on display is the Padarn Railway 0-4-0 *Fire Queen* built in 1848. Several makes and designs of industrial locomotives are on view, with particular emphasis on engines and rolling stock from the 1 ft 11½ in. gauge Penrhyn Railway.

Open daily, April to Oct.

P R Penrhyn Castle (National Trust)

136 Snowdon Mountain Railway
Llanberis, Gwynedd.
O.S. REF. SH 5859
TEL. Llanberis 223
On A4086 Caernarfon–Betws-y-Coed road.

Open Easter to early Oct.

P S R A T t

141 Llanberis Lake Railway
Padarn Park (Gilfachddu), Llanberis, Gwynedd.
O.S. REF. SH 5860
TEL. Llanberis 549
Turn off A4086 Caernarfon–Betwys-y-Coed road opposite Snowdon Mountain Railway entrance.

Open daily end May to early Oct.

P S R A T t

42 Welsh Highland Railway
2 ft. gauge passenger-carrying railway under construction.
Porthmadog (WHR) Station, Porthmadog, Gwynedd.
O.S. REF. SH 5639
Adjacent to B.R. Porthmadog station.

The Welsh Highland Light Railway Company have established their depot near the site of the old W.H.R. Portmadoc New Station. Track has been relaid and a growing collection of narrow-gauge locomotives concentrated on the site. It is hoped to offer passenger facilities over a short run whilst track is being extended over the old W.H.R. route to Beddgelert and Snowdonia.

117 Festiniog Railway
Porthmadog, Gwynedd.
O.S. REF. SH 6038
TEL. Porthmadog 2384

Weekend service to mid-March, then daily mid-March to end November, then weekend service. See A.R.P.S. listings for specific dates.

P S R A T t

43 Gloddfa Ganol/Festiniog Mountain Tourist Centre
Collection of narrow-gauge steam and internal-combustion locos and rolling stock housed at former slate mine now converted into a mountain centre.
Blaenau Ffestiniog, Gwynedd.
O.S. REF. SH 6946
Situated on the A470 Blaenau Ffestiniog–Betws-y-Coed road.

The collection of rolling stock belongs to Narrow Gauge

Enterprises Ltd and is still being added to. Ultimately, it will comprise over *seventy* locomotives from thirty different manufacturers on a variety of gauges.

Open daily from Easter to October.

P S R Slate Industry Museum
Land Rover tours children's play area

44 Llechwedd Slate Caverns/Ceudwll Llechwedd
Passenger-carrying 2 ft gauge electrically operated railway running partially underground through the Llechwedd Slate mines.
Blaenau Ffestiniog, Gwynedd.
O.S. REF. SH 6946
TEL. Bl. Ffest. 306.
Nearest B.R. station: Blaenau Ffestiniog. Bus R34.

Half-mile ride through the slate caverns, including a demonstration of mining techniques during a stop in a vast man-made slate chamber.

Mine open and tramway operates daily from March to November, and at weekends December to February.

P S R

45 Conwy Valley Railway Museum
Static locomotive and rolling stock exhibits.
Old Goods Yard, Betws-y-Coed, Gwynedd.
O.S. REF. SH 7956
Adjacent to B.R. Betws-y-Coed station.

The displays cover the whole railway scene with special reference to standard- and narrow-gauge lines in North Wales. The smaller exhibits are in a purpose-built museum, whilst the collection of standard-gauge vehicles is arranged round the site.

Open daily throughout summer.

144 Rheilfford Llyn Tegid (Bala Lake Railway)
Llanuwchllyn Station, Gwynedd
O.S. REF. SH 8830
TEL. Llanuwchllyn 666
Turn off A494 five miles south-west of Bala (signposted) onto B4403. Station is half a mile through village. Bus D93–D99 (Crosville).

Open daily Easter week and mid-April to end Sept.; weekends to mid-Oct.

P S R pa t

146 Llangollen Railway Society
Llangollen Station, Clwyd.
O.S. REF. SJ 2142
Llangollen is on A5. Nearest B.R. station: Ruabon. Buses D1, D93, D94 (Crosville).

Open daily. Special events on some Bank Holidays and during International Eisteddfod. See A.R.P.S. listings.

S R

139 Fairbourne Railway
Fairbourne, Gwynedd.
O.S. REF. SH 6112

TEL. Fairbourne 362
Off A493 coast road from Dolgellau to Tywyn. Nearest B.R. station: Fairbourne.

Open Sundays Easter to end May, plus Bank Holidays; then daily to end Oct.

P S R t

46 Narrow Gauge Railway Museum
Static collection of narrow-gauge steam locomotives, rolling stock, equipment and small exhibits.
Wharf Station, Tywyn, Gwynedd.
O.S. REF. SH 5800
TEL. Tywyn 710472
The museum adjoins the platform at Tywyn Wharf Station on the Talyllyn Railway. Nearest B.R. station: Tywyn. Buses 26, 28, 30.

The museum can justifiably claim to house the most comprehensive collection of exhibits from narrow-gauge railways in the British Isles. Slate quarry railways predominate, but there are locomotives from a brewery, a gas works, and other industries. The museum has considerable educational value.

Open daily from Easter to Oct.; out-of-season, on request.

R

123 Talyllyn Railway
Wharf Station, Tywyn, Gwynedd.
O.S. REF. SH 5900
TEL. Tywyn 710472
Open daily end March to end Sept.; then to end Oct., not Mondays or Fridays.

P S R M (see 46) A T t

47 Corris Railway Museum
Static display of small exhibits connected with the Corris Railway.
Corris station, Corris, near Machynlleth, Gwynedd.
O.S. REF. SH 7507
200 yards from the A487, five miles north of Machynlleth.

Track is being reinstated on a short length of the old Corris Railway track-bed adjacent to the museum and a replica of an 1898 bogie coach is being built.

The museum is open on Bank Holiday weekends and Tuesday to Friday during July and August.

P S

132 Welshpool and Llanfair Light Railway
Llanfair Caereinion, Powys.
O.S. REF. SJ 1006
TEL. Llanfair Caereinion 441
Four miles west of Welshpool on A458.

Open weekends April to late May, and mid-Sept. to mid-Oct.; daily late May to early Sept.

P S R T t

128   Vale of Rheidol Railway
Aberystwyth, Dyfed.
O.S. REF. SN 5881
TEL. Aberystwyth 612377

Open late March to early Oct.

P   S (at Devil's Bridge)   **R**   **T**   t

149   Gwili Railway
Bronwydd Arms Station, Dyfed.
O.S. REF. SN 4025

Two miles north of Carmarthen on A484 Newcastle Emlyn road. Buses (not Sundays) from B.R. Carmarthen.

Open weekends and Bank Holidays as advertised. See A.R.P.S. listings.

P   S   R

48   Caerphilly Railway Society
Collection of standard-gauge steam locomotives housed at the former Rhymney Railway locomotive works.
Harold Wilson Industrial Estate, Van Road, Caerphilly, Mid Glamorgan.
O.S. REF. ST 1686

The most notable locomotive in the collection is Taff Vale Railway No. 28, the only Welsh-built standard-gauge locomotive to be preserved.

Open days as advertised in the railway press.

P

49   Brecon Mountain Railway
2 ft gauge passenger-carrying railway under construction.
Ponsticill station site, Powys.
O.S. REF. SO 0612
Formerly B.R. Pontsticill Junction on the old Brecon–Merthyr line.

Locomotives and rolling stock have been gathered at Pontsticill as construction of this entirely new narrow-gauge railway proceeds. When complete, the line will give passengers an unrivalled eight-mile ride through the spectacular scenery of the Brecon Beacons. Amongst the impressive collection of narrow-gauge steam locomotives that will operate the line is a Baldwin Pacific imported from South Africa. It is reported that the line may open over a short distance in 1980.

50   The Railway Club of Wales/Y Clwb Rheil Cymru
Collection of standard-gauge industrial locomotives housed adjacent to the Swansea Industrial and Maritime Museum.
South Dock Railway, Victoria Road, Swansea, West Glamorgan.
O.S. REF. SS 6592

The club owns a Barclay and a Sentinel steam locomotive and a Ruston Hornsby diesel, whilst next door at the Museum can be seen a Barclay fireless loco and a section of Swansea and Mumbles Railway electric car No. 7.

Operates most summer Sundays. Enthusiasts' days as advertised, when steam locomotives are in operation; diesel service at other times.

VI Lancashire and the North-West

168   Isle of Man Railway
Douglas, Isle of Man.
O.S. REF. SC 3775
TEL. Douglas 4646

Open Sundays to Fridays mid-May to end September.

P   S   R

51   Manx Electric Railway
Passenger-carrying 3 ft gauge electric railway.
Derby Castle station, Douglas, Isle of Man.
O.S. REF. SC 3977
TEL. Douglas 4549
Adjacent to the northern terminus of the Douglas Horse Tramway. Nearest station: Douglas I.M.R.

18-mile ride from Douglas to Ramsey along the east coast of the Isle of Man. At Laxey, the M.E.R. connects with the Snaefell Mountain Railway, another electrically-worked line which climbs almost five miles and 2000 ft to the top of Snaefell. The M.E.R. is unique within the British Isles, being a genuine electrically worked light railway dating from 1893. It runs through magnificent scenery, and no visitor should miss the opportunity of a ride on one of its trains. Approx single journey time 75 minutes.

P at Laxey Station.

152   Ravenglass and Eskdale Railway
Ravenglass, Cumbria.
O.S. REF. SD 0896
TEL. Ravenglass 226
Off A595 Barrow–Whitehaven road. Nearest B.R. station: Ravenglass.

Open Easter to end Oct.; limited winter service.

P   S   R   A   T   t

157   Lakeside and Haverthwaite Railway
Haverthwaite Station, near Newby Bridge, Cumbria.
O.S. REF. SD 3484
TEL. Newby Bridge 594
On A590 Barrow road. Railway connects with Sealink Windermere steamers to Bowness and Ambleside, and with lake cruisers.

Open daily, mid-May to end Oct.

P   S   R   A   T   t

160   Steamtown Railway Museum
Warton Road, Carnforth, Lancashire.
O.S. REF. SD 4970
TEL. Carnforth 2625 and 4220

Lytham Motive Power Museum is a centre for industrial locos. North British Locomotive Co. 0-4-0 saddle tank Gartsherrie No. 20 was built in 1908, and worked at Baird's at Gartsherie, near Glasgow. The L.M.P.M. collection includes smaller railway items, some of which are visible in the background, and also displays cars and aircraft exhibits.

Take Exit 35 from M6, or take A6 from Lancaster or Kendal. Adjoins Carnforth B.R.
Open daily except Christmas Day. Steamings: Sundays March to Oct.; Saturdays May to Sept.; daily mid-July to end Aug.

P   S   R   model railway

52   Lytham Motive Power Museum

Static steam locomotive exhibits; also 1 ft 10¾ in. gauge Lytham Creek Railway which runs through Museum grounds and is steam-operated on Sundays.
Dock Road, Lytham Lancashire.
O.S. REF. SD 3827
TEL. Lytham 7971.
Nearest B.R. station: Lytham. Bus No. 11A.

Lytham Motive Power Museum is the home of an attractive collection of industrial steam locomotives, all restored to superb exhibition finish. The collection also includes a Pullman coach, vintage cars, a traction engine and steam roller, gas lamps and aircraft exhibits. The Lytham Creek Railway offers a ¾-mile ride from the Museum, offering panoramic views of the Ribble Estuary from the Pennines to the Fylde coast. The line's steam motive power is provided by the Hunslet 0-4-0ST *Jonathan*.

Museum open daily from mid-May to mid-October, except Mondays and Fridays.

P model railway

166   Steamport Southport

Derby Road, Southport, Lancashire
O.S. REF. SD 3416
TEL. Southport 30693

Open every weekend afternoon, Easter, and daily from end May to mid-Sept.

53   Liverpool Transport Museum

Static collection of steam locomotives and rolling stock associated with Liverpool's railway history.
Merseyside County Museums, Land Transport Gallery, William Brown Street, Liverpool 3.
O.S. REF. SJ 3490
TEL. 051-207 0001
Buses Nos. 12 and 24.

Pride of the collection is the Liverpool and Manchester Railway 0-4-2 *Lion* which took the title role in the film *The Titfield Thunderbolt*.

Open daily throughout the year. Admission free. Closed Christmas Day, Boxing Day, Good Friday.

54   Bury Transport Museum

Preservation centre featuring steam open days.
Castlecroft Road, Bury, Lancashire.
O.S. REF. SD 8010
TEL. 061-764 7790.

The Museum, which is the headquarters of the East Lancashire Railway Preservation Society, houses a collection of industrial steam locomotives, rolling stock, a steam roller, fire engines, buses, and various other road vehicles.

Open Saturdays and Sundays throughout the year; also Easter Monday, Spring and Late Summer Bank Holidays. Engine in steam last Sunday of the month, March to Sept.

P   S   R*   model railway*   (*steam days only)

170   Dinting Railway Centre
Dinting Lane, Glossop, Derbyshire.
O.S. REF. SK 0294
TEL. Glossop 5596

One mile from Glossop on A57 Manchester road. Adjoins Dinting B.R. Buses 236/7, 125, or 394.
Steaming Sundays early March to end Oct., and Bank Holidays.

P   S   R   pa

VII   Yorkshire and the North-East

---

55   Newcastle-upon-Tyne Museum of Science and Engineering
Static steam locomotive exhibit.
Tyne & Wear County Museums and Art Galleries Service.
Exhibition Park, Great North Road, Newcastle-upon-Tyne.
O.S. REF. NZ 2465
TEL. Newcastle 815129
Nearest B.R. station: Newcastle.

The locomotive is the Killingworth Colliery 0–4–0 *Billy*, built in 1826.

The Museum is open daily throughout the year. Admission free.

199   Bowes Railway (Tyne and Wear Industrial Monuments Trust)
Springwell, near Gateshead, Tyne and Wear.
O.S. REF. NZ 2858
TEL. Washington 461847
On B1288 Wrekenton–Washington road. Buses 188 and 189. Also at Blackham's Hill, signposted from Wrekenton.

Open weekends from 10.30 a.m. Operates on selected days throughout year: see A.R.P.S. listings.

P   R   M

56   Lake Shore Railroad
Passenger-carrying 9½ in. gauge steam-operated railway.
Boating Lake Park, South Shields, Tyne and Wear.
O.S. REF. NZ 3767

The railway offers a ⅓-mile ride round the boating lake in the park. It is operated by an American style 4–4–2 No. 3440 *Mountaineer*.

Operates daily during July and August.

200   Tanfield Railway
Marley Hill Engine Shed, Marley Hill, Tyne and Wear.
O.S. REF. NZ 2057
One mile south of Sunniside, off A6076 Sunniside–Stanley road. Buses 701–4 connect from Marlborough Crescent, Newcastle. Alight at Andrews House.

Marley Hill shed is open every Sunday throughout year. Trains operate on Sundays from Easter to end Sept.; also

Easter, Spring and Summer Bank Holiday Mondays. Half-hourly service during afternoons.

P   S

196   North of England Open Air Museum
Beamish Hall, Stanley, County Durham.
O.S. REF. NZ 2154
TEL. Stanley 33580
Off A 693 Chester-le-Street–Stanley road.

Open daily except Mondays, from Easter to end Sept.; also Mondays and Bank Holidays in July and Aug. From 10 a.m.

P   S   R   M

57   Monkwearmouth Station Museum
Static rolling stock exhibits housed at the restored Monkwearmouth station.
Monkwearmouth station, North Bridge Street, Sunderland.
O.S. REF. NZ 3959
TEL. Sunderland 77075

Preserved and restored railway goods vehicles are on display in the sidings adjoining the station.

Open daily throughout the year. Admission free.

58   Whorlton Lido Railway
Passenger-carrying 15 in. gauge steam-operated railway.
Whorlton Lido, near Greta Bridge, Barnard Castle, County Durham.
O.S. REF. NZ 1014
Approx. a ½-mile from the A66.

The railway offers a half-mile ride through attractive woodland scenery with deep cuttings and a 33-yard tunnel. The railway is notable for its Bassett-Lowke 4–4–2 *King George* built in 1912.

Operates from Easter until the end of September every weekend. The line is also in operation on most days during the school holiday periods, subject to demand and weather conditions.

P   pa

202   Darlington North Road Museum
Static steam locomotive exhibits
North Road station, Station Road, Darlington, Co. Durham.
O.S. REF. NZ 2916
TEL. Darlington 60532
Half a mile from town centre on A167 Durham road.

By far the oldest exhibits in the Museum, which was formerly the terminus of the Stockton and Darlington Railway, are, fittingly, *Locomotion* (built 1825) and *Derwent* (built 1845). Other locomotives, mainly of N.E.R. origin, are on loan from the National Railway Museum, York.

Open Monday to Saturday throughout the year and Sunday afternoons in summer.

P   S

59   Preston Park Museum
Static steam locomotive exhibit
Cleveland County Council, Preston Park and Museum, Yarm Road, Eaglescliffe, Stockton, Cleveland.
O.S. REF. NZ 4315
Nearest B.R. station: Eaglescliffe. Buses 10 and 10A from Stockton.

The locomotive is a Head Wrightson vertical-boilered 0–4–0T, built in 1870. Also exhibited are bicycles, motorcycles, cars, carriages and commercial vehicles.

The Museum is open Monday to Saturday throughout the year. Admission free.

P

172   North Yorkshire Moors Railway
Trust Office, Pickering Station, North Yorkshire.
O.S. REF. NZ 8204
TEL. Pickering 72508
B.R. connections at Grosmont Junction.

Open most days to end Oct.

P   S   M   A   T   t

60   Newby Hall Railway
Passenger-carrying 10¼ in. gauge steam-operated railway.
Newby Hall, Skelton-on-Ure, Ripon, North Yorkshire.
O.S. REF. SE 3468

The railway offers ½-mile ride along the wooded banks of one of the most secluded stretches of the River Ure. Trains are hauled by a Battison L.M.S. 'Royal Scot' 4–6–0.

Open Wednesdays, Thursdays, Saturdays, Sundays and Bank Holidays from Easter Saturday to second Sunday in October.

P   R

188   Yorkshire Dales Railway
Embsay Station, Embsay, Skipton, West Yorkshire.
O.S. REF. SE 0053
TEL. Skipton 4727
Nearest B.R. station: Skipton. Buses (Ribble): Skipton–Embsay service.

Open weekends and Bank Holidays throughout the year.

P   S   R
9½ in. gauge passenger-carrying railway alongside approach

181   Keighley and Worth Valley Railway
Haworth Station, Keighley, West Yorkshire.
O.S. REF. SE 0337
TEL. Haworth 43629
Trains leave from Keighley station, which still has B.R. trains running to it.

Open daily in July and Aug., weekends and Bank Holiday Mondays and Tuesdays March to Oct.; winter weekend service rest of year.

P   S (at Haworth)   R   A   T   t

61   Eccleshill Industrial Museum
Static steam locomotives and road transport exhibits.
Bradford Metropolitan Corporation, Moorside Mill, Eccleshill, Bradford, West Yorkshire.
O.S. REF. SE 1835
TEL. Bradford 638068
The locomotive on display is the 1922 Hudswell-Clarke 0–4–0ST *Nellie*. Other items of interest include a Smith Rodley steam crane, a Sentinel steam wagon and a Bradford tram and trolleybus.

P (nearby)   R

190   Middleton Railway
Tunstall Road, Leeds 11, West Yorkshire.
O.S. REF. SE 3030
Access from M1: Exit 45. Turn right at Tunstall Road, right at roundabout. Tunstall Road platform is then on right. On bus routes 74 and 76 from Leeds City Station.

Open weekends and Bank Holidays, 2 p.m. to 5 p.m.

P   S   R

192   National Railway Museum, York
Leeman Road, York, North Yorkshire.
O.S. REF. SE 5951
TEL. York 21261
Short walk from York B.R. Station.

Open weekdays from 10 a.m., Sundays from 2.30 p.m. Closed New Year's Day, Good Friday, Christmas Eve, Christmas Day and Boxing Day. Admission free.

P   S   R   M

194   Derwent Valley Railway
Layerthorpe Station, York, North Yorkshire.
O.S. REF. SE 6152
TEL. York 58981
Half a mile from City centre in Hall Field Road off Layerthorpe Road.

Train leaves Layerthorpe daily at 2.30 p.m., except Saturdays, May to mid-Sept.

P   S   R   A   t
Since this book was prepared, we have learnt that the passenger service has been withdrawn.

204   Lincolnshire Coast Light Railway
North Sea Lane, Humberston, Grimsby, Humberside.
O.S. REF. TA 3305
Nearest B.R. station: Cleethorpes or Grimsby; on bus routes 12, 12X or 3C.

Open Whitsun to end Oct. Steam at weekends, otherwise diesel.

VIII Scotland

218 Strathspey Railway
Boat of Garten Station, Highland Region, Scotland.
O.S. REF. NH 9419
Off A9. Take A95 Grantown road, then first right to Boat of Garten (signposted). Bus: Highland Aviemore–Grantown service. Aviemore (Speyside) Station is off A951 to Cairngorm. Nearest B.R. station: Aviemore (underpass access).

Operates Saturdays and Sundays, mid-May to end Sept.; also Tuesdays, Wednesdays, Thursdays, July and August.

P S

62 Glasgow Museum of Transport
Static steam locomotive exhibits as well as tramcars, buses, cars, motorcycles and horse-drawn vehicles.
25 Albert Drive, Glasgow 41.
O.S. REF. NS 5863
TEL. 041-423 8000
Nearest B.R. station: Pollokshields East. Nearest underground station: Bridge Street. Buses 5, 7, 7A, 12, 14, 21, 23, 38, 38A, 39, 43, 44, 45, 45A, 48, 48A, 57, 59.

The Museum houses a comprehensive collection of transport relics, predominantly of Scottish manufacture or use, or associated with the City of Glasgow. All the principal pre-grouping Scottish Railways are represented by a locomotive, these including the historic Caledonian 'Single' No. 123, the Highland Railway 'Jones Goods' 4–6–0 No. 103, and the Great North of Scotland 4–4–0 *Gordon Highlander*.

Museum open Mondays to Saturdays and Sunday afternoons throughout the year. Closed Christmas, New Year's Day. Admission free.

P nearby S R

208 Scottish Railway Preservation Society*
Wallace Street, Falkirk, Central Region, Scotland.
O.S. REF. NS 8980
TEL. Falkirk 20790
Half a mile north of town centre along Grahams Road. Near Grahamston B.R.

Open most weekends. Steaming on selected days: see A.R.P.S. listings.

P S R
* Since going to press, the Society has moved to Bo'ness.

63 Royal Scottish Museum
Static steam and electric locomotives on display.
Chambers Street, Edinburgh 1.
O.S. REF. NT 2573
TEL. 031-225 7534
Chambers Street is a right-hand turn half a mile south from Waverley Bridge. Nearest B.R. station: Edinburgh Waverley. Buses: 1, 3, 5, 7, 8, 14, 23, 27, 31, 33, 39, 41, 42, 45. Doyen of the locomotives on display is William Hedley's *Wylam Dilly*, built 1813.

Open weekdays and Sunday afternoons throughout year.

P in street S R (Monday to Saturday)

216 Lochty Private Railway
Lochty, Fife, Scotland
O.S. REF. NO 5208
TEL. St Monans 210
On B940 Cupar–Crail road, six miles from Crail.

Open Sundays mid-June to early Sept., 2 p.m. to 5 p.m.

P S

Appendix : Ireland

64 The North-west of Ireland Railway Society*

Passenger-carrying 3 ft gauge steam railway under construction.
Londonderry (Victoria Road) Station, Northern Ireland.
TEL. Londonderry 44776

Details may be obtained from K. Thompson, 64 Prenen Park, Londonderry, Northern Ireland. The Society was formed to restore part of the former County Donegal Railways System extending from Victoria Road Station alongside the River Foyle. When open, the Foyle Valley Railway will extend some 1½ miles to Riverside Park. Meanwhile, two former C.D.R.J.C. locomotives, *Drumboe* and *Columbkille*, diesel railcars, and some rolling stock have been saved and are undergoing restoration.

Public open days are held at intervals when rides are given in one of the railcars over a short length of track.

P   S

65 Shane's Castle Light Railway

Passenger-carrying 3 ft gauge steam-operated railway.
Shane's Castle, Antrim, Northern Ireland.
TEL. Antrim 2216

The Shane's Castle Light Railway is currently the only narrow-gauge steam-operated railway in regular use anywhere in Ireland. The railway runs from the terminus on the edge of Antrim through a largely wooded setting to the ruins of Old Shane's Castle, a distance of 1½ miles. The area is also a nature reserve, which is jointly managed with the R.S.P.B.

Operates Sundays, April, September and the first half of October; Easter weekends; Wednesdays, Saturdays, Sundays and Bank Holidays, June to August. Runs throughout local July holiday fortnight.

P   S   R

66 Railway Preservation Society of Ireland

A collection of operational 5 ft 3 in. gauge steam locomotives and rolling stock which is used on advertised excursion trains in Eire and Northern Ireland.
Whitehead Excursion Station, Co. Antrim.
Nearest station : Whitehead N.I.R.

Regular advertised open days are held at Whitehead, when several locomotives can be seen in steam, and short steam-hauled rides are given within depot limits. The forte of the R.P.S.I. is its steam railtours, several of which are run each year. The principal two-day tour over C.I.E. tracks each year involves the use of two locomotives, and provides photographic run-pasts, train-splitting, and lineside buses to make sure participants get maximum enjoyment. R.P.S.I. tours are advertised in the railway Press. Additionally, details are available from R.P.S.I. Secretary, Robin Morton, 2 Cranmore Park, Belfast 9. The Society's regular performers on railtours are Great Northern 4–4–0 No. 171, *Slieve Gullion*; Great Southern and Western 0–6–0 No. 186, and L.M.S. (N.C.C.) 2–6–4T No. 4.

Open at Whitehead Sundays in July and Aug. For tours, see A.R.P.S. listings or contact Secretary.

P   S   R (at Whitehead)

67 Belfast Transport Museum

Static locomotive, rolling stock and tramway exhibits.
Witham Street, Newtownards Road, Belfast 4.
TEL. Belfast 51519
Nearest station : Belfast N.I.R.

Belfast Transport Museum is the largest collection of historical transport exhibits in Ireland. It houses part of the Ulster Folk Museum collection, and contains over one hundred vehicles, also models, equipment and records. The largest locomotive in the collection is the Great Southern Railway 4–6–0 No. 800 *Maeve*. The Irish sub-standard gauge of 3 ft is well represented by steam and diesel locomotives and petrol railcars from the County Donegal Railways, and locos and rolling stock from the Cavan & Leitrim, the Clogher Valley Railway, and the Portstewart Tramway.

Open weekdays (not Sundays) throughout year.

68 Irish Steam Preservation Society

Passenger-carrying 3 ft gauge steam-operated railway.
Stradbally Hall, Stradbally, Co. Laois, Eire.
TEL. Stradbally 25163

Stradbally is 8 miles from Athy, Co. Kildare, and 6 miles from Portlaoise, Co. Laois, the nearest C.I.E. railway stations. It is also served by certain C.I.E. buses on the Dublin–Kilkenny route.

The railway offers a ⅓-mile ride through the grounds of Stradbally Hall. In addition, the Society has a steam Museum in the town of Stradbally which is opened on request at any time, by prior appointment.

The railway operates in conjunction with the National Traction Engine Rally held in the grounds of Stradbally Hall at the beginning of August each year, and on other occasions as advertised. Intending visitors should contact the Society's Secretary, Mrs Olive Condell, Main Street, Stradbally, Co. Laois. (Tel. Stradbally 25163) for appointments to visit the museum, and for details of operating dates for the railway.

---

* As we go to press, we hear the Society has lost its Londonderry site. All stock has been transferred to Shane's Castle.

Index

Numbers in roman refer to the pages of the gazetteer; numbers in **bold** refer to the main text; numbers in *italic*, in brackets, are entry numbers in the gazetteer. Bold and italic numbers also refer to the endpaper map.

Steam
Railways
of
Great Britain
and
Ireland

56
57
55 199 200 196
216
63
208
218
62
66
65
64